Also by Tim Cahill

A WOLVERINE IS EATING MY LEG

JAGUARS RIPPED MY FLESH

BURIED DREAMS

ROAD FEVER

Pecked to Death by Ducks

PECKED TO DEATH BY DUCKS

▲

Tim Cahill

RANDOM HOUSE　NEW YORK

The articles in this work were originally published in different form in *The Discovery
Channel Magazine, GEO, Islands Magazine, National Geographic, Outside, Rolling
Stone*, the *San Francisco Examiner*, and *Travel Holiday*.

Library of Congress Cataloging-in-Publication Data
Cahill, Tim.
Pecked to death by ducks/Tim Cahill.
p.   cm.
ISBN 0-679-40735-9
1. Adventure stories, American.   I. Title.
PS3553.A365P4   1992
814′.54 — dc20   92-53635

Manufactured in the United States of America
2   4   6   8   9   7   5   3
First Edition

Book design by Lilly Langotsky

For Linnea Larson

Contents

The Natural World

Other People's Lives

Risk

Introduction

▲

There are no ducks in this book, except, I think, a fleeting mention in the Bali story. It's worth noting, however, that my Balinese friend Nyoman Wirata is pleased to refer to me as "Sanghyang Bebec." This, loosely translated, means "God-entranced duck." Or, more to Nyoman's point, "funny duck."

Ducks, I think, are funny on the face of it. Leda might be raped by a swan. We can sort of handle that. But a duck? Raped by a duck? Get outta here. You can't have a noble myth about someone being raped by a duck. People would laugh.

In Bali I was examining ceremonies in which men and women, overcome with religious zeal, fell into trances and acted like various animals: horses, monkeys, pigs. These people were said to be "sanghyang." A man who becomes entranced and stomps like a horse is called "sanghyang djaran."

I had noticed that there were domestic ducks all over Bali. Children brought them back from a day of feeding in the rice paddies: You'd see a lovely child with a white flag in her hand leading a row of waddling self-important ducks over the levee just at sunset.

Why, I asked Nyoman, is it that I never see someone fall into a trance and become *bebec,* a duck? Nyoman said he really didn't know. It just wasn't done. Nobody knew how to act like a duck.

I explained that in my country, there was a semireligious figure —very famous—named Donald, who was a duck. Every child in the United States can talk like Donald.

"Show me," Nyoman said.

And so I squawked and croaked like Donald Duck to show Nyoman Wirata how a man might become *sanghyang bebec.* This, apparently, was the funniest thing that ever happened in Bali. Everywhere we went—and we went all over the island— Nyoman begged me to do *sanghyang bebec.*

"Do angry *bebec,*" Nyoman begged, and I'd throw one of Donald's hysterical fits. Nyoman's stomach hurt from laughing.

But that's about it for ducks in this book. There are one or two stories that needed to be told for reasons that will become apparent. Most of the pieces collected here, however, are about travel, or about people I've met traveling. The last few stories are about the business of risk.

I've said this before, but it bears repeating: I believe all these stories exist in the realm of certain shared dreams. I think there was a time when all of us saw the world in terms of exotic travel and thrilling adventure. We want to be Tarzan or Huckleberry Finn, Richard Halliburton, Clyde Beatty, even Marlin Perkins. We want to be Dian Fossey or Jane Goodall or Amelia Earhart. Somewhere along the line—usually on the first day of the first real job—we find that those dreams have gone dormant. Since they were the dreams of our youth, we try to discard them entirely, in the interest of maturity.

But it doesn't happen. Dreams are indestructible. They seethe and roil beneath the surface. There is a vague sense of discontent, and different people deal with it in different ways. Scorn is popular. Mention that trip down the Amazon you've been thinking about, the cabin you want to build in the woods, and someone is sure to call you a horse's ass. Other people have a way of making our dreams seem small. The urge to realize any early dream is labeled with names that suggest psychic aberration: the big chill, a midlife crisis, a second childhood.

What I have been doing for the last fifteen years is chronicling, in various magazines, that urge in all of us. I have the sense that, in my foolishness, others find inspiration. If this clown can do it, I imagine a reader thinking, so can I. There is some small and distant nobility here: For the past fifteen years I have been in the business of giving people back their dreams.

Not that it pays to take it all that seriously. The titles of two of my previous books, both chronicles of adventure and travel, should have been a hint: *Jaguars Ripped My Flesh; A Wolverine Is Eating My Leg*. There were no jaguars in the former and no wolverines in the latter.

Not long ago, as I was finishing up work on this book, a group of friends ambushed me at a dinner party. What was I going to call this third compilation? There were many suggestions: *Sparrows Pecked My Spleen; Nematodes Invaded My Intestinal Tract; Gerbils Ate My Undershorts*. This sort of thing went on all through dinner. There were sexual innuendos involving rhinos and elephants, moray eels and orangutans.

I pleaded with my friends to stop. "I feel," I said, "like I'm being pecked to death by ducks."

The phrase hung in the air.

Pecked to death by ducks?

"Are there any ducks at all in the book?" someone asked.

"Of course not."

"Then," my friends agreed, "it's perfect."

"*Sanghyang,*" I said.

TIM CAHILL
MONTANA
AUGUST 15, 1992

THE UNNATURAL WORLD

▲

Kuwait Is Burning: A Postcard from the Apocalypse

▲

During the occupation of Kuwait, Iraqi soldiers often defecated in the finest rooms of the finest houses they could find. It was a gesture of hatred and ignorance and contempt. Then, in retreat, the Iraqis literally set Kuwait on fire. There was no strategic significance to this, no military advantage for the retreating Iraqi troops. Blowing the oil wells—nearly all the oil wells in the country—was the environmental equivalent of crapping on the carpet.

Because fierce desert winds would carry smoke and soot at least five hundred miles in any direction, Iraqi children would breathe carcinogens along with the children of Saudi Arabia and Kuwait. Iraqi farmers would likely suffer acid rain. These Iraqi troops, under Saddam Hussein, had done something that no other animal on earth does: They had fouled their own nest.

The conflagration in Kuwait—the country is still aflame as you read this [July 1991]—is madness made visible, madness with possible global consequences.

I had spent the Fourth of July and the two following weeks

dashing around the burning oil fields of Kuwait in company with photographer Peter Menzel, attempting to assess the extent of the madness. But this day, toward the end of our stay, was set aside for a long, leisurely drive. The madness, we felt, had soiled us just as surely as the soot and the purple petroleum rain that fell from the drifting black clouds. This rain created lakes of oil that covered acres of desert, and when these lakes caught fire, the smoke was thick and blinding, so that directions to various wells had to be quite specific as to roadside landmarks: "Turn left at the third dead camel."

I particularly wanted to forget the three dead Iraqi soldiers I had had every reason not to bury. They were still out there in the desert, near the Saudi border. The wind covered them with sand. And then, after a time, it uncovered them.

So: Why not spend the day in pursuit of recreational diversion? Peter and I would climb Mount Kuwait. Go to the beach. See the emir's gardens. Maybe even take in a drive-in movie. Think about things a bit.

Mount Kuwait sits in an area of newly formed oil lakes, south of the oil town of Al-Ahmadi, past the distinctive Longhorn fire, and a few miles off the Burgan road. Because we envisioned a long day, and because the summer temperatures in the desert often exceeded 120 degrees Fahrenheit, it was a good idea to start early.

At three-thirty in the morning the air felt cool, about 85 degrees, and the streets of Kuwait City were empty. The traffic lights worked, but there was no traffic. It was a great place to run red lights, which I count as a fine recreational activity.

A gentle breeze from the north had swept the sky clear of smoke. The city center might have been Miami, except that businesses and homes were abandoned, windows were broken, and the major hotels all showed evidence of recent fires. There were streaks of soot on most of the buildings. In March the city had been covered over in a thick shroud of smoke, and when the spring rains came, they fell black and soiled all they touched.

By July the fires in the oil fields south of the city had been beaten back dozens of miles. More than two hundred fires had been "killed," and the best estimates had another five hundred still burning. Fire fighters were working from the north with the prevailing winds at their backs, and Kuwait City was seldom inundated by smoke. Some days were whiskey brown; others were bright and blue and hot.

The outskirts of the city looked like Phoenix, where futuristic divided and elevated highways ran over single-story poured-concrete houses. We exited the freeway and plowed down a two-lane blacktop toward the oil fields. There was a mound of sand and a sign in English that said, ROAD CLOSED. As journalists, we assumed the sign did not apply to us.

Levees of sand kept ponds and lakes of oil from consuming the road. The oil lakes seemed to glow, silver-red, with the light from the fires on the southern horizon. After a few miles the shimmering in the distance separated itself into individual fires: great plumes of flame that dotted the flat desert landscape. The shapes of the plumes themselves had become familiar landmarks. Some looked a bit like Christmas trees; some geysered up every thirty seconds; some lay close to the ground and seemed to burn horizontally. Not far past Al-Ahmadi, the most distinctive of the fires howled out of control. Two plumes shot out along the ground— one to the west, one to the east—and each turned up at the end. The fire fighters, most of them Americans from Texas, called this one the Longhorn fire.

It was close to the road, and the western plume was directed at passing vehicles like a pyromaniac's wet dream. Here the moonless night was bright as day, only the light was red, flickering, hellish. A twenty-mile-an-hour wind carried inky billows of smoke to the south, but along this road and others in the oil fields the winds sometimes sent impenetrable clouds of gritty soot rolling over passing vehicles.

Not far from here, on April 24, a small Japanese sedan had swerved off the oil-slicked road and into a burning oil lake, killing two British journalists. The driver had apparently been disoriented by the smoke and falling soot. Two other vehicles, a pumping truck and a tanker, had apparently followed the tracks of the sedan into the flames. At least one fire-fighting crew had passed by the three vehicles without raising an alarm: Burned-out cars in burning oil lakes are a common sight around Al-Ahmadi. Those who finally recovered the bodies had seemed unaffected when they described the horror, but they mentioned it a lot, especially to journalists who assumed written warnings didn't apply to them.

The sun finally rose, a sickly orange color that I could look directly into without squinting, and in the near distance a rocky butte about three hundred feet high, the highest piece of ground in all the oil fields, appeared. It took, by my watch, a little over two minutes to stroll to the top of this bump that oil workers had long ago named Mount Kuwait. It was supposed to be a joke, the name, like calling a bald-headed guy Curly.

The whole world smelled like a diesel engine. There were fires burning in all directions, more than thirty at a count, and they thundered belligerently. The lake below was burning in streaks and ribbons, with the flames hanging low over a mirrorlike surface that was unaffected by the wind. The ground was black, the sky was black, the drifting clouds were black, and only the fires lived on the land.

What I was seeing, it seemed to me, was the internal-combustion engine made external.

The country of Kuwait sits atop a vast reservoir of oil, 94 billion barrels of known reserves. This reservoir is two miles deep in places, and the oil is under tremendous pressure. Drop a pipe deep enough into the ground and oil erupts to a height of thirty, fifty, seventy, one hundred feet. Wells are capped with valve assemblies, the oil is transferred to gathering centers, then piped to sea terminals for export. It is used in internal-combustion engines around the world.

Iraqi troops had wired nearby wells to a single detonator. These wires still lay across the black sands. The explosions—dynamite directed downward by sandbags—had blown the caps off the wells and ignited the gushing oil.

Kuwait, on this day in July, would lose about $100 million worth of oil. That was the generally agreed-upon figure, though the effects of the fires on the people and on the environment had yet to be coherently assessed. Toxic metals, released by combustion, will surely contaminate the desert soil and the sheep and goats and camels that graze there. Many of these food-borne metals might then cause brain damage and cardiovascular disorders in humans.

Meanwhile, a month earlier, a National Science Foundation team, flying over the burning oil fields, had said that environmental damage was a "concern" and not a crisis. Environmental Protection Agency experts measured pollutants common to American cities—the results of internal combustion—and decided, mostly from planes flying twenty thousand feet over the smoking hell below, that the air quality was not deadly. Further, the flights proved that while plumes rose thousands of feet, the fires weren't propelling the heavy smoke high enough into the atmosphere to cause worldwide climatic change.

Still, in April, about 5 million barrels of oil a day had gone up in flame. Black rain had fallen in Saudi Arabia and Iran; black snow had fallen on the ski slopes of Kashmir, more than fifteen hundred miles to the east. And no one had yet measured pollutants peculiar to this crisis: a class of carcinogens called polyaromatic hydrocarbons generated out of partially burned oil. As I stood on the summit of Mount Kuwait, my own assessment was bleak. The desert, here in the oil fields, was both dead and deadly. It was a sure vision of the environmental apocalypse.

By the time we scrambled down Mount Kuwait, the sun was higher in the sky. A purple petroleum rain had fallen while we'd been climbing, and the evidence could be seen as pinpricks on the windshield. Peter fired up the Land Cruiser, but it was hard to hear the internal-combustion engine over the roar of the surrounding external combustion. I thought about those unburied Iraqi soldiers out near the Saudi border; one of them had been decapitated. In the gathering heat the oil on the windshield now turned a streaky red, so that it looked like dried blood.

On the way to the emir's gardens, deep in the southern oil fields, we saw a brown Land Rover, coated in black, gummy sand, parked by the side of the road. American fire fighters drove Ford and Chevy pickups, Kuwaiti oil executives drove Mercedes. The Land Rover, we knew, had to belong to our friends in Royal Ordnance, a subsidiary of British Aerospace. Composed mostly of former British military explosive experts, RO had won the contract to dispose of explosives in this area of the fields.

When Iraqi troops blew the wells, they sometimes salted the surrounding area with antipersonnel mines to sabotage the fire-fighting effort. But what RO was mostly finding were the universally feared Rockeyes that had been dropped by American pilots onto Iraqi positions. A Rockeye is a metal cylinder, maybe three feet long. When it is dropped it splits apart, releasing 247 six-inch-long rockets designed to explode on impact. The deadly submunitions look like fat lawn darts. All over, all across the black desert sands, there were Rockeye submunitions buried about three inches deep. Sometimes the pilot had dropped the Rockeyes too low to the ground; sometimes the submunitions had hit very soft sand. In any event RO estimated that between 30 and 50 percent of the submunitions were still live. They were black with oil and could be identified only by their three fins. Usually, there was a blackened Rockeye canister nearby.

Our RO friends had the dirtiest, meanest job in the fields. Whereas the fire fighters who followed them worked with the north wind at their backs, which meant that they often had blue sky overhead, the RO teams worked in heavy smoke in the midst of the fires, looking for explosives within a 150-foot radius of a burning well.

Three teams of ten apiece were now walking the hellish landscape. I could just make them out through the shifting clouds of soot that blotted out the desert sun. They were illuminated, in silhouette, by a nearby plume of fire some eighty feet high. They walked with their heads down, very slowly, looking like a precision-drill team composed of very depressed men. The Rockeyes were marked with red-and-white tape fluttering at the end of a metal stake driven into the sand.

Later that day another man would come through the field, stopping at each of the markers. He would dig a hole next to each of the Rockeyes, place a wad of plastic explosive in the hole, string a long wire, and detonate the deadly submunitions from a safe distance.

Now, however, Lance Malin was standing by the Land Rover, coordinating the three teams currently walking the sand. The process of locating and destroying live ammunition was called explosive ordnance disposal, or EOD, and I knew it amused Malin that American fire fighters were using the acronym as a verb: "Has this area been EODed?"

He was talking to a man wearing heavy leather gloves. There was a large spiny-tailed lizard, about two and a half feet long, dangling from the man's index finger. The RO men had found a lot of these lizards, known locally as dhoubs, stuck in the sand, too weak to free themselves. They took them back to their head-quarters in Al-Ahmadi and fed them bits of apple until they regained their strength and snapped at anything that moved. Fi-nally, the lizards took a ride in one of the Land Rovers and were released in the relatively pristine northern desert.

The RO men had no choice. They were British. They had to rescue the lizards.

Malin stowed this particular dhoub in the Land Rover and asked if I had been to the big mine field that RO was working near the Saudi border.

A couple of days ago, I said.

"The Iraqi corpses still there?"

We admitted that they were. Right where everyone had left them. Unburied. For five goddam months.

There was no one at the guard station that flanked the entrance to the emir's gardens, a weekend retreat for Kuwait's ruling fam-ily. It would have been cruel to station a man there. Fire-fighting teams had not yet reached the large walled compound—they were working far to the north—and the fires burning on all sides kept the area shrouded in heavy smoke no matter which way the wind was blowing. It was, at ten o'clock on a desert morning, dark as dusk, and the temperature under the smoke stood at 80 degrees. It was 105 in the sun.

We drove through a shallow pond of oil at the entrance and onto a circular driveway fronting a modest group of buildings. There was a children's play area nearby: teeter-totters and monkey bars coated in oil. On the ground were the oily remnants of a cow that had been slaughtered, presumably for food, by occupying Iraqi troops. There were other black cowlike shapes on the ground, interspersed with the corpses of several large birds, presumably from the compound's aviary. The largest and highest plume of flame I saw in Kuwait—I estimated its height at two hundred feet—boomed and thundered just beyond the north wall.

This fire was a smoker, and it had formed a lake that abutted the eight-foot-high wall. Where there were breaks in the blackened cinder blocks, tongues of oil seeped into a low-lying palm orchard. These small rivers were burning and running down irrigation ditches, where they lapped at the tree trunks.

My boots were caked with a black sandy muck so that I walked in a clumping, stiff-legged manner, like Frankenstein's monster. Visibility was limited to about fifteen feet, though I could see, through the falling soot, the large fire and half a dozen others leaping above the north wall. I moved toward them, careful to avoid stepping on the nubbly tracks of coke, a rocky, coal-like by-product of the burning oil. In some places the coke was several feet deep, but it was also possible that the coke could be mere scum over a burning stream below. Crack the coke, I thought, and the entire track could reignite.

Presently, I saw a man-size break in the wall and moved toward it through the swirling, granular darkness. The inferno beyond lit the break with a shifting, red-orange light, and I could feel the heat on my face like a bad sunburn. Everything that wasn't burning was black: the earth, the familiar shapes of the trees, the animal carcasses that littered the place. This was ground zero for the largest man-made environmental disaster in history. It was a perfect vision of hell.

I moved through the break in the wall and stopped. The next step would put me in the burning lake, which was throwing up the thickest, grainiest smoke I had yet encountered. It blinded me and made my eyes water. Despite the bandanna I wore over my nose and mouth, I found myself choking, and then I was coughing in fits that bent me over at the waist.

It was a sudden misery, and yet something that lives in my soul —some compelling, godawful urge—found this horror grotesquely enthralling. It is the same urge, I think, that drives us to observe the destructive effects of a hurricane or tornado, an avalanche or flood. We shudder deliciously in the face of incomprehensible forces, in the wake of events that insurance companies call "acts of God."

But this was an act of Man, which made it a palpable evil: madness made visible in flame.

I fled back into the black gardens, clumping over the burning trenches, coughing uncontrollably as tears streamed from my eyes.

On our way back north to the Al-Ahmadi drive-in we decided to stop and see how Safety Boss was doing on its fire. Safety Boss Ltd. is a fire-fighting crew out of Calgary, Canada. The other three outfits fighting the fires—Boots & Coots, Red Adair, and Wild Well—were all from around Houston. All were experienced pros, good teams that worked well together.

Safety Boss—I loved the name—hadn't been in the business nearly as long as the other companies, but the Calgary group thought its men worked safer, harder, and dirtier than anyone else. This was a matter of constant argument. Every fire fighter thought he worked safer, harder, and dirtier than anyone else.

Safety Boss had started on this new well yesterday and thought it would have it under control today. That was fast: I had watched some other fire fighters work two full weeks to extinguish a particularly nasty smoker.

The road here was a newly plowed lane—sandy white against the oily desert—built in part through an oil lake that was showing a bit of ripple under a freshening afternoon wind of about forty miles an hour. The wind had swept the area clear of smoke, and the sky was clear. We drove past burned- and bombed-out Iraqi tanks, armored personnel carriers, bunkers, and ammunition depots. Every half-mile or so we passed a Rockeye canister. Red-and-white RO marking tape waved on metal spikes, indicating that the field to the south hadn't been fully EODed.

It was pleasant to breathe fresh air again after the burning oasis we had just visited. In March the town of Al-Ahmadi had looked much like the emir's gardens, and doctors there had been treating a large number of respiratory complaints. Now, with the fires beaten back around the town, the air was still smoggy, but at least you could see through it.

One foreign industrial-health specialist at the hospital in Al-Ahmadi had shown me a chart indicating that sulfur-dioxide levels had dropped to the point where they were hardly measurable. A Kuwaiti chemist had argued with the man: The industrial-health specialist was measuring known pollutants, the by-products of internal combustion; how could he—how could anyone—know what toxic substances were being released by all the external combustion surrounding the town?

The chemist was one of the few Kuwaitis I met who seemed concerned about the level of toxins in the air. People in Al-Ahmadi, for instance, having undergone months of smoky dusk at noon, now lived under mostly blue skies. The air was breathable, it had no odor, and things could only get better. So they seemed to think. The chemist believed that it would be years before anyone knew for certain just how badly the Kuwaiti people had been poisoned.

Safety Boss was now just up the lane. We turned, as we had been instructed, at the third dead camel, which was a rounded, camellike lump of tar lying on its side and baking in the sun. Arranged to the north of a seventy-foot-high plume of flame were a few three-quarter-ton American pickups, a backhoe with an eighty-foot-long shovel, two water tankers, an eighteen-wheel pumping truck, a huge crane, and a bulldozer with a tin shed on top to protect the operator from the heat. There was also an eighteen-wheel mud truck, an indication that Safety Boss thought it would have the fire out momentarily. Mud trucks are called in just before a fire is killed.

The plume of flame billowed orange and black against the blue sky above and the smoke to the south. I had spent days staring at such plumes. They were transfixing. You couldn't be near them and not stare. They were hell's Lava Lites.

Two man-size backless tin sheds had been erected a hundred feet or so from the fire. Large hoses ran from tanks of water, through the pumping trucks, and up to the sheds, where they were mounted on tripods like heavy high-power rifles. There was a man in each shed, working the hose through a rectangular slit in the front of his enclosure.

A crew foreman gave me a hard hat and permission to walk up to the sheds. I had a scientific thermometer to measure the heat near the fire, but it was useless. At one o'clock in the afternoon it was already 122 degrees. The thermometer pegged at 125.

One of the men had his hose trained on the arm of a backhoe that was chopping away at what had been a seven-foot-high mound of coke at the base of the well. The coke accounted for the curious shapes of the fires, bending and twisting the flame as it accumulated. It was necessary to clear the wellhead of coke before it could be capped.

The concussive stress on the backhoe, combined with the heat, often resulted in broken shovels. This one was digging close to the wellhead, and one of the hoses was trained on its dinosaur head, keeping it cool.

The backhoe swung around and deposited another shovelful of steaming coke on the ground eighty feet from the well. Because this coke, even eighty feet away, could reignite the well once it was extinguished, the bulldozer quickly pushed a mound of sand over it.

The fellow manning the water monitor in the shed where I stood was spraying the fire. My completely useless thermometer said 125 degrees. It was hotter than that. There was no talking above the jet-engine howl of the fire, and though I wore earplugs, I could feel the sound reverberating in my chest. The ground literally shook under my feet.

The billowing plume of fire looked as fierce as any burn I had seen, but it had already been beaten. When the backhoe finished its work, one man trained a stream of water at the wellhead.

About fifteen minutes later the fire went out. But only at the well-head. The geyser of oil above it was still burning. And then both hoses started putting the fire out from the bottom of the geyser up.

When the plume had been killed to a height of perhaps twenty feet, it reignited from below. The hoses started again. It only took a few minutes for the fire to surrender at the wellhead. When the hoses had beaten it up to the twenty-foot level, one held steady, right there, at the point where the fire wanted to reignite. The other worked its way up the wavering plume, and when the fire was out to a height of thirty feet, the whole thing died, puff, like that, revealing a gusher of rusty black oil shooting seventy feet into the air.

In the relative silence I heard the *crump-crump-crump* of a controlled RO explosion to the south. A few hundred yards away, in the smoke, another drill team of depressed men was wheeling slowly around a nearby burning well.

The Safety Boss crew moved back behind its trucks. Only two men would work with the damaged wellhead. It was the most dangerous job for a fire fighter. The first order of business was to remove the wellhead. There were bolts to be loosened—bolts that had been fused by explosives and fire—but sparks from power tools could turn the gusher above into a massive fireball. The men used wrenches and hammers made of a special alloy that didn't spark, and they worked in a downpour of oil. The black pool they stood in was hot and burned their feet so that every few minutes they jumped away from the wellhead and let the men with hoses spray them down.

Half a dozen men hooked a series of hoses to the mud truck and ran the line toward the well. A new wellhead was lowered onto the gusher with a crane. Two men with ropes directed its fall, then bolted it into place. Oil erupted out of the new wellhead as before, but this assembly had a pipe projecting from its side.

The hose from the mud truck was screwed onto the side pipe. At a signal, the mud man began pumping a mixture of viscous bentonite and weighty barite into the well. This "mud" had been formulated to be much heavier than oil, and it was pumped into the well under extremely high pressure. The gusher dwindled to thirty feet, to twenty, to ten, and then it died, smothered in mud.

No one shouted, and no one shook hands. These men had been working since five in the morning. It was now past two in the afternoon, and they were ready to move out, to get on to the next well.

The only break the Safety Boss crew had had all day was a brief catered lunch. A few of the men had chosen to eat several hundred yards away, near a bombed-out Iraqi tank. There were always interesting things to be found in the tanks: live ammunition, helmets, uniforms, diaries, war plans, unit rosters, oil-smeared pictures of Saddam Hussein.

Near this tank, the crew had found a man-shaped lump of tar lying on its back with a black clawlike hand raised in death. Graves details had long ago buried all the dead they could find but hadn't been able to work their way through the choking smoke of the oil fields, over land that had yet to be EODed. The Safety Boss crews, which were working farther south than the other companies, were always finding bodies: the bodies of men who had fought for oil and died for oil and finally, horribly, been mummified in oil. The Safety Boss crew had buried this soldier on its lunch break. They had buried him where he fell and driven a stake into the ground to mark his final resting place. They always buried the dead they found.

A huge bomb crater graced the entrance to the Cinema Ahmadi Drive-in, which was baking in the heat under relatively blue skies. Surrounded by a high white cement fence and featuring an immense screen, it was perhaps the most luxurious and high-tech drive-in on earth. Every speaker post featured a thick hose ending in a device that looked like something that might be used to clean draperies but in fact provided air-conditioning for each car. Occupying Iraqi troops had ripped the gadgets off each and every post so that the place as a whole looked like an explosion in a vacuum-cleaner factory.

The theater was otherwise empty except for a few late-model American cars that had been stripped of their tires. The doors were open, and the windshields had been smashed. The wind, now gusting to fifty miles an hour, was the only sound inside the world's most luxurious drive-in theater.

In the refreshment stand, behind a broken window sporting an advertisement for Dr Pepper, I found a number of Iraqi helmets, uniforms, grenades, rifles, and ammunition clips. The troops had defecated in the projection room, which they had also thoroughly trashed. Dozens of reels of film had been methodically cut up into four-inch pieces. That would teach those Kuwaitis, all right: Rip out their air-conditioning, crap in their projection room, and cut up their film! Ha!

I held one of the film strips up to the light: A lovely Arab woman was comforting a sick old man. Other strips featured other lovely Arab women in family situations: cooking, eating, tending children.

These gentle family films hardly seemed appropriate for a post-apocalyptic drive-in. This was *Mad Max* territory, this was *Road Warrior* turf. Australian director George Miller's vision of postnuclear desolation—depraved individuals driving a disparate variety of vehicles powered by internal-combustion engines and battling each other for . . . well, for oil—seemed, in this place, less a B-movie triumph than a sagacious prophecy.

Scenes from just such a movie were being played out in the Burgan field every day. Caravans of odd vehicles moved slowly through the darkness at noon, their headlights pathetic against the swirling smoke. Sometimes they were illuminated by the flickering light of a nearby fire: a few pickups, an eighteen-wheel mud truck festooned with valves, a bulldozer with a metal enclosure, a huge backhoe . . . all these vehicles, most of them like nothing seen anywhere else on earth and all of them moving against a backdrop of fire, deeper into the blackness, into the smoke and soot and falling purple rain.

The postapocalyptic town of Dubiyah, forty-five minutes south of Kuwait City, was a fenced-off vacation community for midlevel Kuwaiti oil executives. Iraqi troops had thought to make a stand here, and the beaches were very obviously mined. I could see a

number of Italian-made mines about the size and shape of flat-tened baseballs littering the sand. They were designed to maim, to tear a man's leg off at the knee. It takes several men to care for one wounded soldier. The mines, which didn't kill, were there-fore militarily efficacious. A few weeks earlier, a Kuwaiti teen-ager, ignoring the posted signs, had strolled out onto the beach and lost a leg for no military reason whatsoever.

Now the town was deserted. The wind had swept the skies clear of smoke, but the sea itself, washing up onto the mined beaches in sluggish waves, was covered over with a faint rainbow sheen of petroleum. Dead fish rotted on the beach next to the mines.

Sometime in mid-January Saddam Hussein's troops had pur-posely spilled an estimated 6 million barrels of oil into the Gulf. The spill was actually a series of releases, with the main dumping on January 19 at Sea Island, a tanker-loading station not far from Dubiyah. Prevailing winds had carried the massive slick south, sparing Kuwait. Saudi Arabia took the brunt of the spill, and its beaches had become heavy mats of tar. The glaze of oil here, off Dubiyah, had come from the petroleum rains, from rivers of oil that had flowed from the fields to the sea.

Closer to where I stood, the beach that fronted the deadly sea was decorated with a double row of concertina wire, and behind the concertina wire was a trench reinforced with cement blocks that stretched for miles. There were houses three rows deep be-yond the trench. They were blocky cement buildings with faded lawn chairs and tattered umbrellas on concrete patios. Most of them were undamaged, except for those that fronted antiaircraft guns, which had been deployed about every half-mile along the beach. Each and every gun had been destroyed. Some were mere heaps of shredded metal. The houses behind the guns had taken some corollary damage. They were, in fact, piles of rubble. All the other homes were intact, undamaged but for a broken win-dow or a kicked-in door. And there was no one there, not a soul in this town that must have housed thousands of people. It felt as if the apocalypse had met the Twilight Zone at Kuwait's Last Resort.

I stepped through broken floor-to-ceiling windows and invaded any number of these houses. Dozens of them. Everywhere it was the same. At least one room was completely full of human excrement. Sometimes every room was packed with the stuff.

Peter and I, being journalists, felt compelled to quantify the mess. I don't know why, really, but that's what we did.

"I got thirty-four piles in here," Peter yelled.

"Seventeen in the kitchen," I shouted, "and twenty-four in the laundry room."

We examined the condition of the piles.

"These guys," I said, "weren't healthy."

And then it occurred to us that maybe the soldiers had been scared. Maybe they'd shit in these houses because they were afraid to go outside during the bombardment. Maybe the odor, at least here in Dubiyah, wasn't so much contempt as fear.

Someone had drawn on a wall in red Magic Marker. There was an idyllic scene of an Arab boat, a dhow, floating in a calm lagoon. Near that, on the same white wall, was another drawing in another hand: a man and a woman staring at one another with a large heart between them.

Iraqi soldiers, I knew, had been allowed to listen to only one radio station: twenty–twenty news straight from the mouth of Saddam Hussein himself. Those who disobeyed could be disciplined or killed. Kuwaitis who had talked with Iraqi soldiers before the bombardment said that the occupying troops had no idea that forces were massing on the Saudi border, for they weren't hearing that news on their single radio station. What they didn't know would kill them. And poison their world. They defecated in bathtubs and drew pictures of men and women in love on the wall.

I thought about the day we had driven to an oil field near the Saudi border. There the Iraqis had installed a mine field that stretched from horizon to horizon. They had marked it off with a pair of concertina-wire fences. Presumably only portions of the field were heavily salted with mines, and the fence had been built to give the advancing troops pause. On the Kuwait side was a deep pit, which was, I suppose, meant to contain oil that could be set afire.

The Allied troops had easily punched through the mine field, and there was a cleared road over the oil pit and through the fence. I could see rounded antitank mines, about the size and shape of home smoke alarms, scattered around beyond the fence. They were a beige color, hard to see in the sand until my eyes adjusted. Then I could see dozens of them.

There were three corpses in Iraqi uniforms alongside the road. Presumably they had lain there for at least five months. It was 118 degrees, the wind was blowing a low-level sandstorm, and the dead men were partially covered in sand.

Someone—the Saudis, I was told—had decapitated one corpse, and the head lay on the man's lap in an obscene position. The lower portion of the face was all grinning bone, but the upper portion of the head, protected by hair, was intact. The skin was desiccated, a mottled yellow. I have seen mummies in museums and in the field. This scene, these corpses, was five months old and already looked like ancient history.

Peter and I were alone, and we thought to bury the corpses, as was the custom. We had equipped our Land Cruiser with a shovel to dig ourselves out of the sand. Still, I didn't want to dig a grave in a mine field.

We discussed the possibility of putting the dead men in the back of our vehicle and driving to a place where we could dig. But the idea of having that desiccated, grinning head rolling around in the back was distressing.

"We could just leave them here," Peter said. "To illustrate the horror of war."

Which is what we told ourselves we were doing as we drove off into the desert, leaving three men unburied in contravention of Muslim and Christian custom. I felt mildly guilty about this and knew that I should feel very guilty about it, so I ended up feeling very guilty about feeling mildly guilty.

I was still thinking about those dead men as I stepped carefully through the chalets that fronted the oily beach.

"Oh, man," I heard myself shout as I moved into one of the grander chalets. It had a fine view of the mined beach and the dead fish and the glittering petroleum sheen that was the sea. And in one big room, in front of the broken picture window, were well over a hundred remnants of the men who had invaded this land. Souvenirs of ignorance, all in fear-splattered piles.

Outside, not far away, contaminants released by the howling fires were poisoning children; they were creating acid rains that would kill crops so that people could starve in the name of oil; they were spawning rivers of flame that ran to the sea and killed what lived there; they were throwing 3 percent of the world's carbon-dioxide emissions into the air, intensifying the greenhouse effect that would bake the earth in drought before an alternative to the internal-combustion engine could be found. It was the beginning of the end, the environmental apocalypse, and here I was, in the oblivion of the Last Resort, thinking about the unburied dead and counting crap.

The Throne of Terror

▲

Her name was Betty. She had blond curls in ringlets, and I loved her desperately, spiritually. We were both eleven years old. One Thursday in spring, when my heart felt ready to burst into bloom, Betty was absent, and I was bereft. Her absence was almost too much to bear. On Friday she brought a note to school. I had planned to walk her home that very night and declare my undying love. Given my commitment, it seemed only proper to sneak a peek at the note she had brought, a note the teacher had left open on her desk. It was from Betty's mother. In graceful, flowing script, it said: "Betty couldn't come to school yesterday because she had diarrhea."

My heart wilted inside my chest. Diarrhea? I didn't want to know about Betty's bowel problems. I didn't want to know Betty. Couldn't even talk to her at recess. Never carried her books home from school again. And she was aware that I had seen the note and knew her dark secret.

I think something of this sort has happened to all of us. Diarrhea is a universal ailment that convinces us we cannot possibly be any more than merely human. For this reason, people suffering bowel troubles don't generally mention it every fifteen minutes. If they have to miss a day or two of work, they don't like to specify the condition: "Some stomach trouble" is how I might put it. Around home, bad bowels are an embarrassment best kept hidden. They are a hammer to the crystal of love.

But, oh, develop the most minor irregularities on a camping trip, and everyone gets to hear about your symptoms. In nauseous detail. The more remote the campsite—the greater the perceived distance from home—the more clinical these descriptions become. This is Cahill's first law of bowel babble.

Recently, I spent a few weeks in a third-world country known for an ailment called Delhi Belly, though the same problem is called Montezuma's Revenge elsewhere and is known, generically, as traveler's diarrhea. Delhi Belly was rampant on this trip. It was an international party, and everyone, without exception, suffered some symptoms. We talked about those symptoms. Oh boy, did we talk about them. At breakfast. At lunch. At dinner. Every fifteen minutes an update.

I took Lomotil, an antidiarrhea agent prescribed by my doctor, but this drug, while it relieves the symptoms, is not a cure. Others took antibiotics, codeine, paregoric, or double-dosed their water with iodine. Nothing worked. Nothing ever seems to work for me. Not right away.

Once, in Guatemala, while fishing for tarpon in Lake Patexbatum, a small, shining body of water completely surrounded by a thick, nearly impenetrable jungle, I got one of my worst cases. Near the place of my suffering there were several Mayan ruins that archaeologists had just begun excavating. The lodge where I was staying had been built by and for these scientists. When they weren't working, it was rented out to fishermen to help defray expenses.

It seemed almost unbearably romantic, sitting on the veranda in the midst of a violent twilight thunderstorm. The clouds rolling in had been operatic, Wagnerian. The world was pure purple, punctuated now and again by neon-bright stroboscopic flashes of lightning. There were Mayan ruins, one thousand years old and older, out there in the jungle, covered over in grass and leaves. I was philosophic about the fragility of man's greatest achievements and, consequently, settled on the fine idea of having an alcoholic beverage. We had brought fresh meat to the lodge, and there was still a bit of dirty ice at the bottom of the cooler. I put a chunk in my glass of rum.

The first mild cramps struck some hours later. Albert, the ancient caretaker, directed me to the outhouse behind the lodge. He was Guyanese, Albert, and he spoke an elegant, lilting brand of Caribbean nineteenth-century English. He loved to talk but had neglected to tell me about the minor problem with the outhouse. When I screamed, as I suppose everyone does on the first visit to the place, Albert shouted, "They doan bite, mon."

The outhouse represented a serious error in judgment, an exercise in zoological ignorance. Rather than dig a latrine, the scientists had constructed the classic two-holer over a large, rocky abyss. A cave. They had overlooked a fact I would think to be somewhat important: *Bats* live in caves. And the bats hated what humans were doing to their home. They came belching up out of the unoccupied hole, they screeched their little sonar screeches, they rose up and gently brushed certain exposed portions of the anatomy. I thought of the place as the Throne of Terror.

And, over the course of the evening, I had ample reason to visit the Throne of Terror several times. The bats hated me, and I hated them.

The only person I know who was delighted to develop a life-threatening case of diarrhea is Dr. Conrad Aveling, a British biologist who specializes in wildlife conservation. Aveling was working in the Sudan when he was captured by terrorists, whose cause I will not dignify here. The terrorists didn't purify their water, and Aveling was ill for several weeks. Had he not been prepared—if he hadn't had rehydrating salts in his pack—he would have surely died from dehydration. As it was, he was merely comatose, and the terrorists decided, smart fellows that they were, that a dead hostage is worse than no hostage at all. Aveling was released.

Generally, however, doctors describe traveler's diarrhea as a relatively mild illness, by which they mean the victim suffers the miseries of hell for only a few days. There are descriptive terms for what doctors call peristaltic rush that I hope never to hear again. This last trip was the worst.

And so, home again, and with a view to obviating forever the campsite conversations regarding the health of one's bowels, I talked to Dr. John Spika, an epidemiologist in the Enteric Diseases Branch of the Centers for Disease Control in Atlanta. Traveler's diarrhea, he said, is generally mild, but if the victim continues to drink water containing the bacteria that caused the problem in the first place, dehydration could be a problem. "You could lose a lot of fluids," said Spika. He recommended the rehydration salt packets, which are available in many health-food stores. You add salts, he said, to a liter of water—"good water, of course."

Adding iodine solution to water is a good way to purify it, as is boiling it for twenty minutes. Dr. Spika said he would have to look into the filters in water purifiers, but my experience with them has been very good.

Dr. Spika recommends against taking antibiotics on a preventive basis, which "puts a lot of pressure on bacteria to develop resistance." Additionally, some antibiotics can "give rashes that are aggravated by the sun." In rare cases antibiotics can be fatal. As traveler's diarrhea is seldom life-threatening, Spika didn't like the idea of exposing large numbers of people to antibiotics on a "prophylactic" basis.

He did recommend carrying antibiotics for a quick cure, however. Bactrim and Septra are two of the most effective drugs, though both contain sulfa, to which some people are allergic. A doctor can recommend certain tetracycline-based antibiotics for the sulfa-allergic traveler.

So there it is: Purify the water you drink, carry rehydration salts, and take antibiotics at the first rumbling of a problem. The situation should not last for more than twenty-four hours, and Lomotil, if your doctor prescribes it, should control the symptoms during that period.

Do yourself a favor: Take this stuff with you on every camping trip. Take it with you on every trip outside the country. Do it so I will never again have to listen to three weeks of bowel babble. Do it for me. Do it for a pretty little girl named Betty.

Bolts of Blue Lightning

▲

Two members of the Church Universal and Triumphant were sitting in my living room discussing the bolts of blue lightning everyone in town had been talking about. They wanted to explain that the list of names that had been circulating around Livingston, Montana, was not a church "hit list." The fact that my name was on it should cause me no undue alarm, they said. The article about that list published in the local paper was distorted, they said, and the inclusion of church prayers, called decrees, was misleading. And while it was true that the prayers were accurately transcribed, they were easily misinterpreted by those unfamiliar with the church's teaching.

"Bolts of blue lightning in to the very cause and core of all opposition to the victory on this planetary body this day," one of the prayers went. "I demand the binding of all opposition to the victory. I demand the binding of all opposition to the victory. I demand the binding of all opposition to the victory now! Blue lightning bombs descend! (8x)." The prayer went on to demand "the binding of all criticism, condemnation, and judgment arrayed against me" and then: "I demand a bolt of blue lightning in through the cause and core of all criticism, condemnation, and judgment working through (insert name)!"

Since the names on the list were, in fact, compiled by the church—and because about two hundred local residents were on it—church members were out visiting these people. They meant no harm, they said. They were not praying against people whose names might be inserted in the decrees. They were praying for them.

The Church Universal and Triumphant, called CUT, is thought to have between 75,000 and 150,000 members worldwide. Several years ago, the church bought its first piece of land in Park County. In the summer of 1986, CUT sold its California property, a 215-acre site near Los Angeles, and plans were made to move all its operations to Montana. Ed Francis, vice president of CUT, said that the church would relocate its headquarters, its businesses, and educational operations to Park County. Only about four hundred employees would move to the county and join the several hundred CUT members already in residence. CUT leaders deny that the organization is a cult. If the church has to be characterized at all, members would prefer the term "new religion."

This new religious group has become the second-largest land-owner in my county. Aside from the twelve-thousand-acre Royal Teton Ranch that abuts Yellowstone Park, CUT also owns the thirteen-thousand-acre Lazy W Ranch, the thirty-three-hundred-acre O-T-O Ranch and a five-thousand-acre residential subdivision. Some residents have expressed concern that CUT may try to take over the county economically and politically, in the manner of that famous Rolls-Royce collector and Bhagwan, late of Antelope, Oregon. Others worry about CUT's plans for development on the environmentally sensitive land north of the world's first national park.

I had, in fact, been talking with *Outside* editors earlier in the day about CUT's plans to draw hot water from a 458-foot geothermal well near La Duke Hot Springs. Ominously, the La Duke well is just ten miles north of Mammoth Hot Springs, in Yellowstone Park. Mammoth is a series of five multicolored terraces flooded by steaming water released from various springs. The high terraces consist of sedimentary rocks formed as minerals precipitated out of the natural flow from boiling springs. The terraces are brilliant with the colors of various minerals and look, in total, like some great dirty rainbow of a cataract frozen in stone. The formation is considered to be one of the park's treasures.

Geologists have stated flatly that CUT's use of geothermal energy could affect the Yellowstone's geysers, and specifically, Mammoth Hot Springs. Dr. Irving Friedman, a research geochemist with the U.S. Geological Survey says that "when there has been geothermal development next to features such as geysers, it has severely affected them—dried them up in fact. Once you've disturbed them, there's no way to turn the water back on."

The church, for its part, contends its use of the geothermal energy it owns should have no effect at all on the geothermal features of Yellowstone Park. They insist that La Duke Hot Springs discharges as much as five hundred gallons per minute naturally, the amount of water the church intends to use. Unfortunately, the spring where the water is discharged is located inconveniently, across the Yellowstone River from CUT's proposed greenhouse, swimming pool, and buildings. Hence the need for a 458-foot-deep well to intercept the naturally occurring discharge.

A hydrological report, commissioned by the church, "supports what we've said all along," CUT vice president Ed Francis maintained in a press release. "The well was drilled only to access the La Duke Hot Springs aquifer, and our relatively minor use of the spring water will have no impact on Park resources." To its credit, the church released copies of this report to the media. Prepared by the consulting scientists and engineers of a firm called Hydrometrics out of Helena, Montana, the report stated that since the well is about ten miles from Mammoth and five hundred feet lower in elevation, "it is quite unlikely that hydraulic impacts from pumping could be transmitted to Yellowstone Park"; that the geologic structure makes it "highly improbable" that there is any connection with Mammoth; and that it is "highly unlikely that a discharge point such as the thermal well would have any impact on ground far upgradient . . ."

The terms "highly unlikely," "quite unlikely," "highly improbable"—and this from CUT's own commissioned report—were not as convincing to some as they were to the church. Paul Varney, Yellowstone Park's chief of research, said, "We would have hoped that they would have been a little more cautious." The Park Service, Varney said, does not have "hard evidence" to support a claim that La Duke and Mammoth Hot Springs are connected. It's all circumstantial. "There appears to be a common chemical signature," Varney said, and this indicates "a common aquifer." Varney wasn't so sure that ten miles of distance and five hundred feet of elevation made it "unlikely" that Mammoth and La Duke might be connected. There is evidence, for instance, that suggests that Mammoth and the Norris Geyser basin are connected by underground faults. Norris is twenty-five miles south of Mammoth and one thousand feet higher. Varney echoed Dr. Friedman's concerns. Experience in other parts of the world, he said, has shown that each time man has tampered with geothermal areas, the natural geothermal systems that existed before have been permanently destroyed.

In discussing the controversy with *Outside*'s editors, I said there really wasn't a column in it. "By the time a column would appear," I said, "CUT leaders will have come to their senses. They are not stupid people."

Two hours after I told *Outside* I didn't want to do a column about the geothermal controversy, a pair of church members arrived at my house to discuss the blue lightning bolts. Tim Connor I knew. A well-dressed young man of yuppie mien, Connor is CUT's business manager, though he sometimes deals with the press. The other man, Edwin, was a rangy fellow dressed like a rancher. I didn't catch his last name.

The CUT emissaries looked apprehensive, but soon enough we were sitting in the living room, talking and laughing. The list, Connor said, was not a hit list, and not a shit list. He delicately spelled out the word "s-h-i-t." The compilation of names was really "an informational fact sheet" distributed to church members. (One section of the original fact sheet was headed "Local Groups and Individuals—Negative attitudes and Malintent Expressed Against US." A malintent of my acquaintance believes he "made the list" simply because he told some church members he does not approve of mixing real estate and religion. The version of the informational fact sheet that had been circulating around town, Connor pointed out, had been typed from the original fact sheet by a persistent local critic of the church named Marie Mar. She had probably gotten the original from a dissident ex-member of CUT. It was Marie Mar who had attached the decrees to the list.

The blue-bolts-of-lightning decree had come from a book of church prayers. There were probably two hundred decrees in that book. If I looked very closely, I would see that these prayers, which are chanted so rapidly it is impossible for an outsider to understand the words, do not call for harm to fall on the person named. For instance, the decree titled "For the Electronic Presence of Saint Germain" contains the sentence "Roll it back and mow them down, roll it back and mow them down, roll it back and mow them down now those demons and discarnates." The decrees then, were calling destruction down on discorporal beings whose malintent might have caused people to speak ill of CUT. The decrees were prayers of love.

Connor explained to me that a person could be good and yet occasionally possessed by demons that other well-intentioned folks might want to mow down. "Jesus said, 'Get thee behind me Satan,'" Connor explained, "and yet he was talking to Saint Peter."

Edwin, meanwhile, had noticed the large Buddha on my mantelpiece and mentioned that the lord Buddha was one of CUT's ascended masters. The ascended masters—Buddha, Jesus, Saint Germain and Hercules and others—speak through church leader Elizabeth Clare Prophet, affectionately known in CUT as Ma Guru. Edwin was trying to establish some common theological ground and failing badly. It's true that I am a fan of the Buddha's teaching. I'm also a fan of Larry Bird's, and I can't sink two free throws in a row.

Tim Connor said he was concerned that people might get some wrong ideas from the article in the *Livingston* (Montana) *Enterprise*, written by Tom Shands. Connor pointed out a sentence that particularly bothered him. "The decree calls for two of CUT's ascended masters to expose those who lie about the church and to 'Roll it back and mow them down.' " Connor said, "See how he puts church critics in the same sentence with 'mow them down?' "

"I'm not a journalist," Connor said, "but I could tell you some things." He shook his head sadly. CUT feels it is often misunderstood by the media, and that reporters rely on information from dissidents who have left the church, like former CUT president Randall King, who told the *Los Angeles Herald Examiner* that "when I left the Church in 1980, we had a monthly budget of a quarter million dollars and most of it came from donations. We didn't mess around with a 10 per cent tithe. If a guy was worth 150 grand, we figured 100 grand was ours the first year." Former church member Raphael Dominguez, grandson of former Dominican Republic dictator Raphael Trujillo, told Los Angeles TV station KCBS that CUT's ascended masters, speaking through Elizabeth Clare Prophet, kept sending dictations to the effect that the Dominguez family should fork over a cool $750,000 to the church.

In a letter to *People* magazine, after it published a story the church deemed negative, CUT vice president Ed Francis explained how all this negative publicity comes about. Ex-members of CUT and "other churches have discovered a sure-fire scheme to make big money," he wrote. "The formula is simple: sue for damages claiming mind control and brain washing, then go to the media and generate negative and sensational publicity (a temptation the media can't resist), then either try to collect the money in settlement negotiations or convince a jury to assess damages by putting the unorthodoxy of the religion on trial."

Edwin, Connor, and I talked for a while about journalism and karma. I was given to understand that the law of karma, as interpreted by CUT, meant that people would get what was coming to them in the fullness of time and in the natural course of events. CUT did not take it on itself to punish its detractors or dissident ex-members. In fact, such actions would be against their religion.

I said I rather believed them on this point. Four years ago I spoke at a public "cult awareness" meeting. Citing ten years of experience reporting on cults in California, I said I had seen some good ones and some bad ones. On the downside, I had been beaten by cultists, seen culties take over whole towns, seen a friend nearly killed by one group, and walked through Jonestown, through the stench of death in that steaming South American jungle. I suggested back then that CUT open a dialogue with the community "so that mutual paranoia doesn't feed on itself."

I think that talk may have placed me on CUT's informational fact sheet. And yet, in the almost four years since then, I haven't suffered any harassment at all, and church members have always been pleasant to me. Evidence to date suggests CUT is not in the business of meting out physical punishment to its critics. And now, propelled by Tom Shands's article in the *Enterprise,* CUT members were out opening up a dialogue with the community. I said I thought this was a good and hopeful sign.

"We understand that we don't exist in a vacuum," Tim Connor agreed.

And then, since we had found some common ground, I asked Tim and Edwin about the geothermal well. "I just told *Outside* that a column on the controversy would be premature," I told Connor. "I figure using that well is such bad public relations that you guys will scrap the idea before May."

Edwin said, "You know, one reason why I joined this church is that we don't do things for public-relations reasons. We do what is right."

Tim Connor cited CUT's hydrology report. I said I found it ambivalent and quoted a geothermal researcher and former senior research scientist with the National Oceanic and Atmospheric Administration. Dr. John Rinehart has written that "Yellowstone National Park is the only area in the world where the natural beauty of geysers has been maintained."

In that context Edwin complained that there were people in the world "who don't want you to step on a blade of grass. How is a man supposed to make a living and feed his family?"

I argued that even the most infinitesimal chance of drying up Yellowstone's thermal features was a chance not worth taking.

Edwin said, "The Bible says man shall have dominion over the earth."

And that was that. Man shall have dominion over the earth. It's in the Bible. CUT intends to go ahead with its plans to pump water from its well, and I had a column to write about a church that understands it doesn't exist in a vacuum. They even have a mailing address: Elizabeth Clare Prophet, Box A, Corwin Springs, MT 59021.

Author's Note:
This story was written in May of 1987. In the following months, the Church Universal and Triumphant was bedeviled by allegations that it had been stockpiling guns in anticipation of a coming apocalypse. In order to ease tensions in the community, the church held an open house, where I had the opportunity to meet Ed Francis, who complained that he had received over ninety letters in response to the above article. Mr. Francis accused me of stirring up hatred for the church because of its unorthodox beliefs.

These guys, I realized, just didn't get it.

Elizabeth Clare Prophet, relying on astrology and advice from "ascended masters," was able to foresee a coming nuclear holocaust, and church members began building bomb shelters in May of 1989. On October 13 Ed Francis plead guilty to a charge of conspiring to buy guns illegally and began serving a jail sentence.

The church's main bomb shelter, designed to house 756 people, was buried, secretly, in a pristine mountain meadow hard by the border of the world's first national park. It was about the size of a large suburban high school. In mid-April of 1990 underground fuel tanks at this shelter began to rupture in the spring thaw. More than thirty-one thousand gallons of diesel fuel and gasoline polluted soils and groundwater only three miles from Yellowstone Park.

It was the first instance of armed pollution in the 1990s. Saddam Hussein bumped the stakes up to global levels about a year later.

The state of Montana charged that the church had established "a pattern of secrecy, deceit and intentional evasion" in dealing with state agencies.

Meanwhile, Montana congressman Pat Williams introduced a bill to ban geothermal development in the area surrounding Yellowstone Park. The bill passed the House on November 25, 1991. As of April 1992 the bill had yet to go to the Senate floor for final approval. Ed Francis—who had served his time in jail and was once again handling church affairs—announced that the church was investigating other ways to tap hot water from the naturally occurring outflow of La Duke Hot Springs.

Done properly, this is acceptable. Mr. Francis is to be applauded. It appears as if the well I wrote about in 1987 will never be tapped. It only took a federal law to stop it.

Since the oil spill two years ago, the church has been remarkably quiet and has, it seems, attempted to mend its relations with the local community. I have a number of acquaintances and friends who are members of the Church Universal and Triumphant. I wonder though: Do they still find my outrage over the oil spill and the geothermal well an instance of religious bigotry? Or—Jesus, I'm naive—maybe their religion is big enough to encompass the faith expressed in those ninety letters.

I suggest that we all keep an eye on them.

The Game of Living Things

▲

"I am David," the man said.

I noticed he wasn't wearing shoes. I noticed that right away because I had been asleep on the floor of an abandoned barroom in the middle of the town of Darwin, California. Darwin is the first taste of civilization due west of Death Valley, an old mining town on a downhill run into the scrap heap of history.

The bar had passed on some years ago. It was a ghost. The floor was unpainted and splintered. There were shards of broken glass scattered about. A shaft of harsh desert sunlight penetrated the eyeless window of the old bar. There were dust motes floating in the light that ended at the man's feet, which were big and splayed and callused.

Quite probably, I assured myself, this is a dream.

"Like David in the Bible," the voice above the feet proclaimed.

I sat up. It appeared that this was not a dream of dirty feet. The man was burly and broad-shouldered. His face was shadowed.

"David is a symbolic name," he explained. "David is God's warrior."

He squatted so that he could look directly into my face. The mottled light hit his eyes at an odd angle.

"David," he said fervently, "is God's executioner."

The desert is hateful.

There are those who can make you love it. Edward Abbey, Joseph Wood Krutch, even Zane Grey. But you love it from a chair.

In the desert, at high noon, there are no shadows, and the sun weighs on you with the weight of centuries. The land seems dead or dying, and the desert is like an aging movie star, under merciless light. Oh God, look at those dry washes, that eroded landscape.

Try walking through any major desert in the season of its fury, and you can learn to hate the land. It is not the heat, the great convection oven of desert valleys, that kills so much as the ground temperature. Like a sidewalk under the midsummer sun, the ground collects heat, radiates it. In Death Valley ground temperatures as high as 200 degrees have been recorded. Don't fall here. Don't faint. A few hours lying on unshaded ground can kill very easily. It can literally bake the brain inside the skull.

Even walking—slow, steady walking—can become painful. A burning plain is not kind to the feet and gives great and literal meaning to the word "tenderfoot."

Nick Nichols and I had started walking from Death Valley, in midsummer. My boots gave out the first day. They were light ankle-high canvas affairs, and the glue that held the thick Vibram soles to the body of boot had begun to melt. I took the boots off and doctored them a bit with some tape from the first-aid kit. This was a mistake. My feet had expanded a size or so in the heat, and I couldn't get the boots back on. After some time sitting on the burning ground under the burning sun, it seemed a good idea to keep walking, no matter what. I used my knife to cut several portholes in the canvas to make the boots somewhat wearable.

Originally, we had planned to sleep during the heat of the day, but our tents tended to concentrate the ground heat and baked us until we felt woozy and barely conscious. It was safer to walk.

So there we were, Nick and I, limping down the western flank of the Panamint Mountains under a cloudless sky at high noon. Nincompoops in the noonday sun. Little else seemed to live on the face of that burning rock and sand.

To pass the time, we began playing the Game of Living Things. We were moving due west, and Nick had the entire world to the south. The north belonged to me. One living creature was worth one point. I had seen a dull-gray sparrowlike bird in a stand of sage and was way ahead, one to nothing. We had argued fiercely about ants. For the purposes of the game—this was an hourlong debate—a man had to stop and count precisely one hundred ants to make one living thing. This was an uncomfortable process, hot and boring. For all practical purposes ants didn't count in the Game of Living Things.

Suddenly, a rabbit—more properly, I suppose, a hare— gray as the dull desert rock, burst out from under some sage between us. It broke northwest, nearly crossed my path, then cut south into Nick's world.

"My point," Nick said.

"That was my rabbit," I pointed out. I noticed that my teeth were tightly clenched. "I scared him up."

Half an hour later Nick said, "The rabbit ran south. It's my rabbit."

Half an hour after that I said, "He ran north first." The tape had come off of my right boot so that the rubber sole flopped annoyingly. My feet were being chafed badly by the holes in the boot, and I was walking in a sore-footed shuffle, rather like Charlie Chaplin as the Little Tramp except that I had to lift the right foot high above the ground to avoid getting burning pebbles in between the flopping sole and my foot. If I had that shuffling, hopping walk on videotape, I suspect I'd be able to see some small comedy there. As it was, the sun had baked me sour.

"So it's one to one," Nick said some time later. I could feel the muscles bunching up in my back and found it necessary to shuffle-hop a hundred paces north into my own world and out of easy conversational range. An hour later, I heard myself shout, *"JUST SHUT UP ABOUT THE DAMN RABBIT!"*

The desert is a lover.

At dusk, when the sun sets and the sky explodes into gaudy pastels, when shadows mirror the colors of the sky, when the breeze is a cooling purple caress, the desert is beautiful.

We were eating, Nick and I, laughing a bit about the Game of Living Things. Amazing what the desert does to you: It focuses wants and needs. At noon I had wanted no more than shade and water. It was absolutely all I could think about, and I knew then that if I had a cool place to sit and jug of water, I would be happy.

Now, with both water and the blessing of night, I felt certain new needs creep into the equation. Nice to have something better to eat than another chili mac. A soft drink would be nice. Well-chilled champagne: If I had that, I would be happy. A chair to sit on. A table with some proper utensils. A white linen tablecloth. A house with a pool. A certain woman . . .

Before our little stroll through the desert, I had read some books on desert survival and had come across something called *The Wisdom of the Desert* by Thomas Merton, an American Trappist monk. The book is a collection of the sayings of the Desert Fathers, men who had gone into the deserts of Egypt, Palestine, Arabia, and Persia to meditate: Christian hermits of the fourth century A.D. There was absolutely no desert lore in the sayings of the Desert Fathers: They were concerned entirely with an interior landscape.

"Abbot Pastor said, 'Get away from the man who argues every time he talks.' He also said, 'He who gets angry is no monk.' "

I began to see some of the desert peeking through the sayings I recalled. Nick and I were no monks, but we were good friends. Friends who had been about to come to blows over a rabbit a few hours before, in the season of our least want.

I prattled on a bit about the Desert Fathers, committing some fractured theology, I imagine. It seemed to me that the twenty-four-hour cycle of waxing and waning wants suggested a spiritual significance in the calculus of human need. Something. I was still trying to work it out.

We got into Darwin after dark, slept on the street near an abandoned gas station, and woke with the sun. There were people in the town—about forty of them, I learned later—and we moved into the old barroom for a little privacy. An hour later I was awakened by God's executioner.

Nick was sitting on the bar itself. "I met David on the street," he said. "David is a preacher."

David shook his head violently. He was not a preacher. He had strong beliefs; he didn't mind talking about them, but he wanted to be careful. "People around here say I preach too much," he explained.

There was the mechanical click of a camera shutter, and David literally jumped. He turned to face Nick, who was composing another shot. "Don't," he said. "I don't like pictures." He squatted again and stared into my face. "They took my picture in Colorado," he said. There seemed to be tears in his eyes. "The police." David was a stout, solidly built man—he walked around in the desert barefoot—and I felt the unmistakable presence of something powerful and out of control.

Nick did too. He said, "Well, I think I'll go walk around a bit."

"And they hit me with their sticks," David said. "For no reason. I wrote the president. I said that I was willing to renounce my citizenship. All I wanted was five thousand dollars and an airplane ticket somewhere else. Anywhere." David was trembling with some powerful emotion. "He never wrote back."

"Uh, Nick," I said, "maybe you should stay here. This is fascinating stuff."

"I want to shoot some pictures," he said. David turned and glared at him. "Outside," Nick added. I struggled to my feet, just in case I needed to protect myself. David, it seemed, was highly sensitive to what I had thought was a secret defensive posture. "Powerful emanations," he said, not at all taken aback.

"See you guys," the traitor, Nick, said lightly. And then he was gone: I considered his exit the Revenge of the Rabbit.

David had a triangular shard of glass in his hand. I stepped back. He held the glass to his eye and peered through it. "This is on the dollar bill," he said. "The all-seeing eye. In the pyramid." David's blue eye seemed to spin wildly behind the broken glass.

"God tells us not to forget our first love. Doesn't he?"

"Sure He does," I said, not at all sure.

"And what is our first love?"

I said I didn't know. David seemed to lose control of the muscles of his face. He dropped the glass and stared at his hands in wide-eyed wonder. He gurgled happily. I realized that David was showing me an infant.

"Our body is our first love," he said.

David discussed love, as he understood it, for three more hours.

Five miles outside of Darwin, in the purple breeze under a setting sun, Nick said, "You know, there are about fifteen artists that live in that town. Do good work, too."

After a time I said, "You left me alone with David."

"Well, people said he's all right, just a little intense."

"A little?"

In *The Wisdom of the Desert* Thomas Merton said of the Desert Fathers that "if we were to seek their like in Twentieth Century America, we would have to look in strange, out of the way places."

I wondered if the Desert Fathers, concerned with their own Game of Living Things, seemed just a tad mad to those who encountered them. In the distance we heard the nightly concert begin. The coyotes were yipping and baying, howling in the wilderness.

Marquesas Magic

▲

I was lying on my back on the black sand beach of Puamau Bay when the mayor's son came galloping up on one of the small, sturdy island horses. "Edmundo," he said, "is dead." The tragic news had just come over the village radio, which was in the mayor's house.

I had had dinner with Edmundo the night before in Atuona, which was only four hours away by boat. Over an island feast of river shrimp and raw fish marinated in coconut milk and lime, we had talked about these islands, the most remote on the face of earth. The Marquesas are 3,500 miles due west of Peru and about 740 miles northeast of Tahiti. They stand alone, out in the middle of the Pacific Ocean, and sometime around the time of Christ, men in great canoes had come out of the west, from Tonga, perhaps, or Samoa, and had settled this chain of verdant volcanic islands. It was the last of the islands settled by the people who became known as Polynesians.

Edmundo was a Chilean archeologist. He had spent twenty years studying the great stone heads on Easter Island, about twelve hundred miles to the southeast. He hadn't been in the Marquesas very long and didn't want to talk about his theories, but it was my impression that he expected to find some cultural correlation between those great staring heads on Easter Island and the ancient stone gods of the Marquesans. These gods, called *tikis,* can be found in dense groves of coconut and banyan trees, usually atop an overgrown stone terrace, a *me'ae,* like the one I saw on a hill rising out of the Taaoa valley, near Atuona. It was an impressive ceremonial place that lay just above a rich grove of mangoes, bananas, and coconuts. The terraces were two feet high, one rising above the other, and all were thirty-three feet across. The side walls of large, piled rocks were three to five feet high. The ground had once been tiled with stone so there was not much vegetation, and one had a sense of the place as it must have been.

Six terraces rose to two short ones that were both about ten inches high. Precisely in the middle of the eighth terrace was the tiki, a squatting, scowling god carved out of a single piece of nearly triangular basalt about five feet high. The face was three times the width of a man's shoulders, and the tiki was almost all face. The arms and legs were tiny, deformed; the eyes were huge, with no pupils; and the mouth was a single angry line. It seemed to have erupted out of the earth in rage and fury.

Three more terraces rose behind the tiki, and on the last of them there was a huge, gnarled banyan tree whose hanging branches had rooted and grown again so that the tree covered half an acre. The branches and leaves of the tree broke the early afternoon sun so that light fell on the tiki with a strange, gloomy, subaqueous glow.

In the time before the first Euro-Americans landed, the Marquesans who carved the tikis called themselves the Men. The coconut and breadfruit trees they had brought on the big canoes took root and grew in the volcanic soil of the islands; the pigs and goats prospered. Feasting was a way of life. The men sculpted wood, and they decorated their bodies with elaborate, swirling tattoos.

They lived in the drainage basins, along the rivers that fell from peaks three thousand and four thousand feet high. Each village had its sorcerer, and there was warfare between villages; there was human sacrifice and ritual cannibalism.

In 1595 Alvaro de Mendana landed on Hiva Oa and named the islands for the Marquesa de Mendoza. America occupied the islands briefly in 1813, but President Madison wasn't interested in such a remote colony. In 1842 France declared that the Marquesas were a part of its empire. Catholic missionaries from that country set about to eliminate what they saw as promiscuity and to destroy the old religion of the stone gods. In this they were aided by diseases brought on the big ships. Of an estimated fifty thousand Marquesans in the eighteenth century, only five thousand descendants survived in 1900.

Today there are about six thousand Marquesans on six inhabited islands. Nuku Hiva is the northern administrative center, and Hiva Oa the southern. The culture of the Men is no more, but relics of the past litter the drainage basins and stone gods squat in the gloom.

Edmundo had come to document the tikis. He would measure them and photograph them; he would preserve what he could, and in a way, the culture of the Men would live through Edmundo. Many Marquesans advise travelers to avoid the tikis: They speak of a malevolent power. There were at least twenty-five of them in the Puamau Valley. I was supposed to meet Edmundo there for a bit of exploration. And now he was dead.

I was, frankly, spooked. The air was heavy with the scent of mangoes and the sun was heavy on my back, but I found myself shivering in a gentle sea breeze. In the distance I could see the mayor's son galloping again along the beach in my direction. He pulled his horse to a halt beside me and shouted, "Edmundo is alive!"

As I pieced the story together, Edmundo hadn't been able to get to Puamau. He had a mild flu, and decided to put the trip off for a few days. He didn't want anyone to worry about him, so he'd called on the radio. In Marquesan, however, the word for sick is very similar to the one for dead. There had been some static on the radio. A mistake was made.

But now that Edmundo was alive, we would feast this night. There was pork for roasting, there was chicken and passion fruit, fish from the sea, bottles of wine from France.

* * *

In the Marquesas, hand gestures, body movements, and facial expressions often carry the weight of words, which are faulty in that they can sometimes kill living archeologists and bring them back to life in a matter of hours. Marquesans can talk to one another for minutes on end without even opening their mouths. Watch these two Marquesan fishermen coming into port in their boats, a pair of wheezing thirty-foot craft running diesel engines that routinely belch smoke. It is hot and the men waste no energy on conversation. They lift their chins to one another in greeting. One holds the position slightly longer. He is asking, "Did you catch any fish?"

The second man smiles. He spreads the fingers of both hands and brings them together in front of his chest. "I caught a lot of fish." The first man cocks his head again. "Any big ones?" The second stretches his right arm straight out to the side. With his left hand he mimes flicking a fly off his right wrist. "I caught one so big," this gesture says, "that my arm isn't long enough to encompass its length."

The two men regard one another gravely, then the successful fisherman cocks his head to ask, "How'd you do?" The first man replies with an abrupt masturbatory gesture. "Nothing," he means to say. "I was just wasting my time out there."

Marquesan gestures have little of the anger or contempt implicit in the hand gestures of certain other cultures (various southern European countries spring to mind). People who have studied the Marquesans believe these gestured conversations are simply a way of conserving energy in a hot land. I don't know about that: It seems to me that a brief *kahua* (hello) wouldn't wear a guy down any more than a nod of the head.

I like to think the tradition arises out of the physical beauty of the Marquesan people, that the simple grace of these gestures is the unspoken poetry of the islands.

The Marquesas have never attracted tourists, a fact that has attracted artists. Robert Louis Stevenson and Herman Melville both spent time on the northern island of Nuku Hiva. The Belgian-born songwriter Jacques Brel died on Hiva Oa. In 1900 the

French artist Paul Gauguin came to Atuona, on Hiva Oa, looking for inspiration in "unspoiled savagery." There was some tension between the artist and the local bishop regarding Gauguin's relations with various island women. Gauguin nailed obscene pictures to his door and called his place the House of Pleasure, using a word that, in French, has a sexual connotation. There were legal problems fueled by the bishop's rage. Gauguin died in 1903, and he is buried in a small graveyard above Atuona. His grave is neatly tended and much photographed. The bishop is buried there as well. You have to clear away the weeds to see his stone.

On the spot where the House of Pleasure stood, there is a new wood-and-concrete bungalow erected by the mayor of Atuona where tourists may stay. Commercial hotels are rare in the Marquesas. The islands are so remote, so little visited, that one simply seeks out the mayor of the village, who makes it his business to provide lodging, usually in his own house. The mayor of Atuona, a rich man by Marquesan standards, had built three bungalows for such travelers. I was staying in the bungalow built on the site of the House of Pleasure. Alone.

I stayed with the mayor and his wife in the village of Puamau. One day, not long after Edmundo's resurrection, I was walking back from the beach when I heard people laughing from some distance away. The mayor's wife and a dozen other women were sitting on the covered patio with the poured-cement floor that was such a luxury people gathered there nearly every afternoon. (Many Marquesans live in thatched-roofed huts with dirt floors.) The television set was on, as it is for two hours a day. The programs are beamed down to the villages by transmitters located on the high peaks of the islands. One French official told me that the government provides TV for the people because they love it. They love it so much that it is feared many might move to Tahiti just to watch *Dynasty*. But Tahiti is already crowded, employment is scarce, and the government figures it is cheaper to provide the Marquesans with TVs at home than with subsidized housing in Tahiti or Bora Bora. The mayor's TV was the village TV, and it had been provided by the government.

The women were watching *The Towering Inferno,* which had

been dubbed in French. Nobody was looking at the set, except when the building was shown in flame. Then the women were intent on the special effects, and no one spoke.

The love scenes, on the other hand, set everyone off at once, talking and laughing in a merry cadence. I came to understand that the women of Puamau thought Paul Newman's kisses were the funniest part of the movie.

The patio was open on three sides. An old man hobbled up to the women and said a few words. The mayor's wife said a single word in Marquesan and began laughing, as did the old man, and all the rest of the women. On the TV, someone started kissing someone else. It was all too much. The women laughed until tears formed in their eyes. First the quip about the elderly fellow with the bad legs and now all this hilarious kissing.

The next morning, at breakfast, I asked the mayor's wife what she had said to the old man. "Parachute," she told me. Just the thought of it got her giggling, and her husband had to tell me the story. About thirty years ago, he said, the man with the bad legs had been about sixty feet up a tree, shaking coconuts loose. He lost his grip and fell, but not before tearing off a palm frond, which he tried to use as a parachute. The man had broken both his legs. The mayor, his wife, and their three sons and two daughters were rocking back and forth with laughter. Now, the mayor said, hardly able to continue, whenever anyone saw the fellow limping along a path, they thought of the failed green parachute. It was a joke that had kept everyone in Puamau laughing for thirty years.

The French brought horses to the Marquesas, and like the goats and pigs and breadfruit trees, the horses multiplied beyond counting on the provident land. There are more horses in the Marquesas than anywhere else in the South Seas. Wild horses have to be cleared off airstrips before planes can land. Horses run free in the steep, sloping jungles, in the thick grasses on the plains at three thousand feet. They can be seen drinking from rivers, a waterfall in the background, orchid petals or plumerias on their backs where they brushed against the vegetation.

The horses—you can tell from the configuration of the heads—are a mix of Arabians, thoroughbreds, and the original Chilean horses brought by the French. They have adapted to the steep jungles of the Marquesas, bred themselves down, suffered some degree of island dwarfism. Smaller than American mustangs, they are strong climbers and eager runners.

The horses are so plentiful that Marquesans in need of transportation simply take a mare in heat out to the jungle. The strongest stallion to approach is roped and wrestled to the ground by hand. Marquesans ride the horses belly-deep through the surf to break them. It is not unusual to look out to sea and watch a horse lifted up and carried toward the beach by a large wave.

The thought of riding along the black volcanic sand beaches with the surf pounding in was wonderfully romantic, though the reality chafed a bit. Marquesans ride on hand-carved wooden saddles. Stirrups are bits of twisted wire tied to the saddle with old rope. The fact that there are stallions in the jungle or roped to trees along the trails makes riding another stallion an exciting process of rearing, chasing, biting. During these fights and near fights stirrups break, cinch straps snap, and the wooden saddle raises nasty sores on the rider. It is better to ride bareback.

One day I borrowed a horse and rode to the deserted beach at Taaoa, near Atuona. I rode bareback, like the people in Gauguin's paintings, and the mountains above caught the drifting South Pacific clouds that turned the high peaks slate-blue with distant rain. Gauguin had painted the mountains this blue—it had been a matter of much hilarity in Paris.

Later, I visited the basalt god that squatted on the stone terraces above Taaoa. There was something indelibly Marquesan about the idol. The people are professed Catholics on these islands, they watch TV, the children go to schools, yet few will consent to visit the tikis at night. The old gods still have some power. I wanted to talk about this power with Edmundo, the formerly dead archeologist, over dinner that night.

I placed a gold-colored Central Pacific franc at the feet of the tiki, as is the custom, and rode out of the shadowed forest until I could see the sun and sea at the end of the trail below. When I

judged I was far enough away, I shouted, "Edmundo is alive!"
The horse spooked, but I brought him under control and sat
looking back into the darkness. I felt like a child throwing rocks
at a haunted house. "Alive!" I shouted, and kicked the horse so
that we galloped into the light.

A Dismal Lack of Mutilations

▲

Two years I've been out here at the ranch on Poison Creek, and in that time—despite the fact that we are dealing with 750 fairly remote acres and a hundred head of cattle—terror has refused to reign. I'm talking about the dismal lack of cattle mutilations at Poison Creek: no bloodless carcasses with the genitals and other soft parts surgically removed. None of that.

I find the lack of mutilations curiously dispiriting, probably because I've put in quite a few hours collecting theories about who or what is responsible for the gory phenomenon. I even placed an ad in the *Los Angeles Times:* "Researcher needs information on cattle mutilations." The ad ran for a week. A rather surprising number of psychics wrote offering spiritual advice for material dollars. Many letters mentioned UFOs, and some people seemed to be in direct contact with the extraterrestrials piloting these crafts. Other writers suggested that the mutilations were expressions of an alien science, though one man envisioned simple sadists from outer space: "Mutilations occur with increasing frequency and soon THEY will tire of cattle. Human men will be next, and the first order of mutilation will be the MALE'S PHAL-LIC ORGAN OF REPRODUCTION!"

There were those writers who dismissed UFOs out of hand: Castrators from Outer Space indeed. The mutilations were clearly the work of some perverse cult of blood-drunk Satanists. To explain the usual lack of footprints around the tortured cattle, one writer suggested blood-drunk Satanists in helicopters.

Another letter proposed an intriguing conspiracy. Noting that several mutilations had occurred near a large military installation in Colorado, the writer suggested that agents of the U.S. government were skulking about the fields on moonless nights, scalpels in hand. Their job: horribly mutilate the cattle in brutal and inexplicable ways so as to cause terror in the souls of the local ranchers who would then sell their land to the military at cut-rate prices.

The most intricate explanation came from a certain F. Smith, of Colorado. In a striking booklet entitled *Cattle Mutilation: The Unspeakable Truth,* Smith works hard to demolish the arguments of conventional UFO theorists, of those who favor Satanists in choppers, and, most especially, of those scientists who see the mutilations as the work of such predators as foxes and flies.

Smith starts by setting the record straight on certain important cosmic matters. First of all, no planet can remain habitable forever, and this prevents the universe from "going to seed and becoming inbred." The time when humans must leave Earth is called Judgment Day. At that time we will join the great cosmic community of humans beyond the solar system. We refer to that community as "heaven."

It follows, then, that extraterrestrials are not merely aliens, but angels. These angels are pretty rough customers. Smith states that they are not "neutered individuals" or "chubby infants," but are, instead, the mighty soldiers of scripture, "ENEMY soldiers" whose duty is to prevent us from traveling beyond the solar system until the Day of Judgment, a day that is rapidly approaching. Smith sees evidence of the Apocalypse in the population explosion itself. "An explosion can be described as an extremely rapid release and degradation of energy. It booms, then busts . . .'' The bust, the Day of Judgment, will come when we can no longer reproduce.

Smith's enemy angels apparently consider earth a dull duty. They are getting restless and impatient down here, waiting for the moment when we all become sterile. These antsy angels are handcuffed by an immutable law of the cosmos that states that human beings, created in the likeness of God, may not be dissected for scientific purposes. Cattle, however, live in close proximity to man, and the angels know well that mutagenic agents, such as plutonium, migrate to the gonads in both cattle and man. If your prize bull's balls are full of plutonium, so are yours. The extraterrestrials, these warriors from heaven beyond the solar system, spend a lot of time mutilating cows and studying bovine genitals in order to figure out just how much longer they are going to have to wait until Judgment Day. And that is the Unspeakable Truth.

People like Smith, "mutologists," save their harshest comments for conventional scientists and men like Kenneth Rommel, a former FBI agent who headed up a fifty-thousand-dollar government study of the phenomenon. "If surgeons are doing it, they're doing it with their teeth," Rommel said at a news conference, and he backed up his contention with a series of color slides showing predators such as coyotes and wild dogs gnawing away at the soft parts of down cows. The precision-surgery effect, Rommel explained, is caused by shrinkage and desiccation of the tissues. Crows or magpies take the eye, flies mass in the resultant pulpy mess, sun and wind dry the tissue, which then shrinks away from the wound in a perfectly rounded circle. A coyote may start his meal with soft and accessible delicacies like the genitals. Every one of the twenty-four New Mexico mutilations Rommel investigated was caused by natural predators: coyotes, wild and domestic dogs, eagles, crows, vultures, and flies.

The predator theory—disappointing and anticlimactic as it is— seems the most convincing to me. Still—gory close-up photos notwithstanding—blowflies lack the pizzazz of enemy angels in UFOs, and this, I think, partially explains the persistence of convoluted theories about the mutilations. I mean, really, isn't it more fun like this:

The ship sits on an alfalfa field near the pond on Poison Creek. It is no saucer, but a quivering, jellylike cell, and it glows from within with a color out of space, a color out of time: a blue and strangely hypnotic incandescence in the long shadows at the end of a long Montana summer day.

The cattle scatter in panic. One yearling, slower than the rest, is seized from behind, and it bellows in lusty protest. The Mutilators gibber and click, then set up a gurgling dirge as laser scalpels flash into readiness. The genitals first, then the anus—oh so carefully now—and eyeballs and lips and tongue. The yearling's bellows rise in pitch, then subside into hopeless sheeplike bleats and end in a single, strangled, tongueless croak.

The tentacles of the Mutilators drip with certain fluids of delight, and the cell of the ship pulses with a deeper incandescence. The cattle are bunched in dumb horror in a corner of the fence line, and the Mutilators from Outer Space lurch toward them in cold reptilian glee.

Ah, but here come the boys, the cowboys, protectors of the cattle, human beings. They are bouncing over the field in an old Jeep, and they are clutching shotguns and gleaming hunting knives, fury spinning like fire in their eyes. The ship keens out a warning and pulses red, a burning red, like molten steel. The Mutilators cower in terror. Their tentacles are dry as parchment, and they recoil before the rough and thunderous rage of the boys. Now there is brutal carnage in the alfalfa field. The boys have fired all their shells, and they are hacking about with the razored hunting knives. Green reptilian blood erupts out of jagged wounds: cold green blood, thick as vomit. The boys are whirling, thrusting, piercing, ripping. It is like some sick, Martian samurai movie out there in the alfalfa field. . . .

Alas.

Cosmic Camping

▲

It was late summer, and the deerflies were fierce on the lower slopes of the Beartooth Range, so I broke camp and moved up to a small, sloping meadow under a high ridge. There were patches of snow where rock shadowed the ground, and the snow was clean and cold, so the deerflies, bloodsuckers born of excrement and carrion, avoided it. Judging by the signs, other large mammals—deer, elk, a black bear—had pretty much the same idea. It pleased me to realize that a primitive mechanism was at work here, that I was thinking like an animal and was at least as bright as the average elk.

Everything involved in camping—from picking the proper site to cooking on an open fire—serves to engage that sort of mindless exhilaration. At the time, during that Beartooth trip, I had just finished the outline for a long and complicated book. I knew I was done with it, but my mind didn't. It kept ragging at me to make little changes; it kept me up half the night adding anecdotes, switching chapters around, and generally speeding off in all directions at once toward no discernible goal. I couldn't work on anything else, or even begin the book, because the finished outline kept wanting to rearrange itself into another kaleidoscopic pattern. I felt like a gerbil on a treadmill.

And so I had arranged to spend several days in the mountains, alone, with no particular goal and nothing to do. No Walkman, no book. Just me and my journal.

The first day, as always, was the worst. I worried about the phone calls I was missing, about the work I had to do, about the book and the outline. I slept badly. By the second day, however, my body began to fall into the desultory rhythms of camp life, and it dragged my mind along with it, so that I was thinking, rather lazily, not about outlines or commitments, but about moving to a new site, on a windy ridge. The idea was that the wind would scatter the deerflies. Still, sitting there on the ridge, being battered by a ceaseless wind for a couple of days, didn't sound like all that much fun, either. Which is when I hit on the perfectly obvious idea of moving up above the flies the way the elk do.

It was a reasonably challenging climb. I set up my tent and lay back in the bright afternoon sun, thinking about how much fun it was not thinking. My mind was puttering about, cleaning up minor details it had recently ignored. Every once in a while, I made a little note in my journal.

If I had been sentenced to sit in my chair at home, to empty my mind and think about nothing and everything all at once, I couldn't have done it. The phone would ring, and someone would say, "You are twenty days overdue on your mortgage payment, and a late fee has been charged to your account." The doorbell would ring, and a pleasant, older woman would ask me if I knew that "Satan rules the world," and then she'd try to sell me a *Watchtower* magazine, which would explain everything.

Even without these interruptions, I'd have found several hours of emptiness oppressive. Who sits for three hours without picking up a book, listening to music, watching TV, drinking?

What happens in the woods is this: The mind is forced to deal with certain niggling but elemental details. Those things we take for granted—shelter, food, basic conveniences, comfort, brute survival—require all our attention and must be attended to. When a storm is blowing in and the tent isn't set up, worrying about mortgages and outlines is a luxury. Later, such concerns seem an imposition. Primitive necessity, it seems, can snap the thread of linear thinking. It can send us skittering from deerflies directly into the cosmos.

Or so I thought, lying on my back in the high-country wild-flowers. Directly above, the sky was a thin, shimmering blue, that bright, soaring blue you see high in the mountains, a blue that seems to rise forever. Staring into it, I had the sense of space beyond and a feeling that, if I really worked at it, squinted a little, I could see them up there, all those exploding stars and swirling nebulas dancing their mad galactic polka.

I was visualizing the shape of the galaxy—I have a lawn sprin-kler that throws out water in the same pinwheel pattern—but I had just returned from flying over and then into a full-blown hurricane with the air-force hurricane hunters, and I had a feel-ing. Photographs of that storm, taken from the GOES satellites, showed a mass of clouds arranged in the precise same pinwheel shape you see in high-resolution telescopic photos of spiral galax-ies. There seemed to be some cosmic significance here beyond the mere conservation of angular momentum. From certain distances a galaxy could be mistaken for a hurricane.

No one who has to deal with deadlines is allowed any such mildly cosmic insights. When camping, however, I tend to go right from the turkey tetrazzini to Alpha Centuri. I was thinking about our galaxy—a flattened pinwheel system of stars, gas, and dust—with Earth positioned about two thirds of the way out on a spiral arm. The evening promised to be clear, and I would be able to stare into the galactic center, the Milky Way, spread out across the sky. There the great mass of stars are concentrated, and grav-ity sends them spinning in various figures about one another. If there are planets, they may spin around one sun for a time until the gravity of another takes them on a quick do-si-do.

And if there is intelligent extraterrestrial life, surely it evolved in that galactic center rather than out here in the boondocks of a spiral arm. Life-forms waving at one another as their planets go square dancing around the spinning stars, a federation perhaps, feeding on technical cooperation: Intelligent gas clouds swooping down with visiting comets to see how we're doing here in the outback, thinking we're just as cute and cunning as can be with our hydrogen bombs, waiting for us to finally come to it, the insight that unites life, the Universal Principle that, I imagined, could be deduced in the similarity of shape between galaxies and hurricanes.

The note in my journal about this little flight of science-fiction fancy is a drawing of a pinwheel and the words "galaxy" and "hurricane" followed by several emphatic exclamation points (!!!!!!!!!!). Which, apparently, indicated that this concept, whatever it was, when properly elucidated, would change the face of physical and astronomical science as we know it. Without putting too fine a point on it, I have to report that the face of physical and astronomical science remains unchanged. On the other hand, three days later, back home, I started the book, working from my finished outline.

The writing went well, better than it had in months, and it occurred to me that my trip to the Beartooths had helped. Helped a lot. Some folks sleep on a problem, but you can camp on one as well. Camping is for the mind what a high-speed run on the highway is for a car. It tends to blow out all the sludge that accumulates in the type of urban driving most of us are forced to do in order to earn a living.

TOOTH
AND
CLAW

▲

Bear in Mind

▲

A breeze rattled the bedroom windows and jerked me out of a dreamless half-sleep. It was still dark, 4:00 A.M. The last time I had looked at the clock, it had been 3:15. Forty-five minutes of sleep. My stomach was bad. The small, hard knot that had been with me an hour earlier had expanded. There was a burn to it and a bile that I could taste at the back of my throat. I would have liked another day to think about this particular project, to gear up for it, but the real world has a habit of presenting us with now-or-never situations.

I pulled on a pair of shorts, walked into my office, and unlocked the drawer where I keep my gun. It was a .38-caliber revolver, fully loaded. I had bought it years ago, when I lived in California and some people I'd written about had reason to hate my guts. I'd suggested that they were cowards, back shooters consumed by insane hatred, and I believed what I wrote, believed it enough to buy the gun and spend weeks learning to shoot accurately and well. Some of those people are in jail, others are dead, murdered. There are a lot of reporters who have written other, more recent stories about them. A decade has passed, and I don't suppose I've even looked at that gun more than twice in the last five years.

But here it was, and I was holding it in my hands at four in the morning with a cool Montana wind beating against the windows and one dim lamp burning against the night. I emptied the cylinder, cocked the hammer, and aimed at the light. "This is stupid," I said aloud. "Useless." I locked the gun away and walked into the living room. My pack and boots were laid out on the floor, where I'd put them the night before.

What I needed was a few more hours of sleep, but even the TV at 4:00 A.M. didn't have its usual somnambulant effect. There was a man selling financial security through real estate, another selling salvation through Jesus, and a cartoon about a boy with large, perfectly round eyes and no pupils who could fly. I flicked off the set and sat on the couch in the darkness for two hours, fully dressed.

Tom Murphy rang the bell promptly at six, as I knew he would. We got into his car and drove south, through Paradise Valley, toward Yellowstone Park, fifty miles away.

"I thought about bringing my pistol," I said.

"What have you got?"

"A .38."

"Not much use."

"I know."

The sun was rising over the Absaroka Mountains, rising behind some high, thin clouds so that the light that spilled into the valley was shadowed and broken. It was a moving watercolor of a morning: Waves of subtle pastels were flowing gently across golden August pastures.

"Nice sunrise," I said.

"It's pretty," Tom allowed.

"Should we tell someone where we're going? I mean exactly. In case he leaves us bleeding."

"Bonnie knows," Tom said. Bonnie is Tom's wife, and she's used to this sort of thing. We drove in silence. The light reached the river, and for a moment the living expanse of water was a rippling mirror of shimmering pink and gold.

"For bleeding," Tom said, "you know about pressure points?"

"I don't know where they are."

"Well, the best thing is direct pressure. If that doesn't stop it, press on the pressure points."

He showed me where they were as he drove: under the arm, up by the armpit. "You can feel that real strong pulse there. Press it against the bone." For the legs the pressure point was up front near the groin, and you pressed it against the pelvic bone. "Tourniquets are out completely," he said. "People lose limbs they don't have to lose with tourniquets. And, of course for head wounds, direct pressure is the only thing. You wouldn't want to use the jugular as a pressure point, cut off the flow of blood to the brain."

"No," I said, "you wouldn't want to do that. Or worse, use a tourniquet." We laughed—a tourniquet around the neck, wahoo, what a knee-slapper—but the laughter sounded brittle and a little forced in the car.

"You pretty sure he'll be there?" I asked.

"He'll be there all right," Tom said. "He had something buried, a bison carcass, I think. The hole was deep. I couldn't see into it from where I was, but he was feeding on it all day."

"What's the land like where he is?"

"It's a prairie situation," Tom said. "Rolling hills and sage."

"No trees to climb in case he, uh . . ." I didn't know what he might do. Nobody knows what a grizzly bear might do. They are entirely unpredictable. One grizzly might simply ignore a man on foot, while another one could feel obligated to rip him to shreds. A popular theory holds that because grizzlies evolved on the plains, where there is no place to hide, their flight-or-fight mechanism is heavily weighted toward fight.

The bear possesses two football-sized slabs of muscle on either side of its head and these power jaws that can, according to Tom McNamee in *The Grizzly Bear*, "crush a Hereford's head like an eggshell." Additionally, "the large shoulder hump—the grizzly's most distinctive feature and the one which usually distinguishes his appearance from that of the black bear—is . . . an enormous wad of muscle, the engine that powers the mighty digging and death-dealing machinery of the front legs." And they're fast, grizzlies. A National Park Service employee once clocked a running subadult Alaskan grizzly at thirty-six miles an hour. I didn't like the idea of standing behind a two-foot-high tangle of sage in the middle of the prairie a couple of hundred yards from five hundred pounds or more of thirty-six-mile-per-hour grizzly. There would be no place to run, no place to hide.

"There're some trees," Tom said, "but they're about a quarter of a mile away."

"We have binoculars," I said. "We could watch him from the trees. It'd be safer." Grizzlies have long, slim claws that will not hold the weight of a full-grown bear. They can't climb, the big ones anyway.

"I don't think we want to be in those trees," Tom said. "First, they're directly upwind. The bear is sure to scent us there. Second, this is a big bear, a mature male with a little bit of gray on him. . . ."

"So?"

"Well, my guess is that he's the boss bear in that area."

"Yeah?"

"You think some other bears haven't winded that carcass?" Grizzlies have been known to scent a carcass—even a newly dead animal, its flesh not yet putrescent—from several miles away. The animal's sense of smell is more acute than that of a bloodhound. More acute by an order of magnitude.

"So," Tom reasoned, "maybe this bear isn't going to let the other ones in until he's done. And if there are other grizzlies around, where do you suppose they'll be? You think they'll be out in the open? Or hiding in the trees?"

"Point," I said.

Tom had almost walked into the bear the day before. He is a photographer and guides people on photographic safaris in and around Yellowstone Park. Some of his Wilderness Photography Expedition clients had written in with their requirements: They wanted a short walk, no more than two miles, on flat land, and they wanted to see lots of big, hairy mammals. Tom knew of several places that would fit the bill, but he wanted to scout them out first, be sure the animals were there. He had gotten a little carried away on his walk and was five miles in when he topped a rise and found himself 175 yards from the bear. He dropped to his belly and didn't move for three hours until the grizzly took a nap.

That evening Tom stopped at my house and asked if I wanted to join him the next day. He was going back armed with his longest lenses. He swore that he was not about to take any chances to get good shots.

Last year, in Glacier Park, a grizzly killed a photographer who was said to love the bears, to know their habits. Tom had seen the shots.

"It was a sow, with three cubs," he told me. "I think the guy might have been as close as a hundred yards. And she definitely saw him. You could see she saw him. I think he followed her. This should be a safer situation. It's not a sow with cubs to protect. It's not a young male liable to strike out at anything. This is a big, mature male with plenty to eat. If we're quiet, if we're careful, he'll never even see us. I'm sure he didn't see me yesterday."

We parked by the side of the road and began walking toward the grizzly. The valley floor was a rolling, treeless plain, punctuated by stands of sage. At one point, three miles in—two miles from the bear—we saw several ravens perched on a ridge ahead of us. Tom thought they might be attracted to some carrion below but were afraid to approach it. He thought the birds on the ridge might mean there was a bear below, feeding on something. We belly-crawled to the top and peeked over. We saw a few bison, grazing peacefully, but there, not too far away, was some grizzly dung.

Tom broke the scat apart with his boot. It was soft and very black. "He's been eating meat," Tom said.

"You can tell because it's so dark?"

"Yeah," Tom said. "And here's another clue." He bent over and picked a porcupine quill from the dung.

"This bear"—I couldn't believe it—"this bear ate a porcupine, I mean he literally ate a porcupine? And he passed the quills?"

"Must be a mean motor scooter," Tom said.

He handed me the quill, and I stood there with the white needle in my hand, and it scared me just about as badly as anything I'd ever heard or read about grizzly bears, ever. I couldn't imagine any animal—even a grizzly bear—eating a porcupine, quills and all. We walked down a hill and across a marsh that was full of meandering streams and land that moved like stiffened gelatin under the boot. There was a ridge ahead of us, and the bear, if he was there, was on the other side. The wind was brisk, and it came out of the southwest. We crawled to the top of the ridge—on the northeast, downwind side.

The bear was in a bowl-shaped depression about 250 yards away from us. He was standing on a mound of dirt where he had buried something. The freshly dug mound was perhaps two feet high and ten feet long. I made a mental note to forever avoid mounds of dirt in bear country. The grizzly was black, and he glistened in the sun. In proportion to his massive body, his claws were almost delicate, each as big around and about as long as my little finger. They were bone white: the mark of an older bear. His right ear looked a little ragged, as if it had been bitten and torn in a fight.

There were trees to the west, as Tom had said, but they were a quarter of a mile away and almost directly upwind. Where we were, there was only sage, and no one plant was over two feet high.

Tom and I heard, very faintly, the sound of a cracking branch from the stand of trees. There was a dark shape, moving slowly deep in the woods. With the binoculars I could see that it was a bison. The bear stiffened and stared into the trees, like a dog on point.

It is said that a grizzly's hearing is far more sensitive than a man's, and as proof, scientists point out that a grizzly will begin blindly digging in one spot and come out with a mouse or vole he's located by sound alone.

The grizzly stood there for some time, visibly sniffing the wind. A raven flew over the bear, and he looked up in what appeared to be annoyance as the bird's shadow passed over him. The movement brought him around so that he seemed to be staring directly at us. Some people believe grizzlies don't see well, and in fact, they may not see as well as humans, but experiments with brown bears proved that they could recognize their keepers at 360 feet. We were crouched down at 750 feet. McNamee, in *The Grizzly Bear,* warns that "it should not be assumed that a squinting, blinking, head bobbing grizzly bear is having trouble picking you out of some kind of blur." With the binoculars on him, however, I was absolutely certain that he did not see us. I could see his eyes, and I knew he didn't see us.

The bear began digging in the mound of dirt he was standing on. In less than two minutes he had uncovered the front half of a cow bison carcass. We could hear him snuffling and sneezing in a cloud of dry dust. He reached into the hole and lifted up the head and the front quarters of the bison with a movement that seemed to cost him almost no effort at all. The carcass probably weighed somewhere close to a thousand pounds.

He could, I saw, use his claws—the same front claws he'd used to dig—very dexterously, almost like fingers. There was a disconcerting sound of breaking bones as the bear gnawed away on the bison's shoulder area. He was standing sideways to us, and I could see that his belly was distended. There was a lot of meat on the bison, and the bear had probably been feeding on it for several days.

In point of fact, this grizzly didn't seem very hungry at all. He uncovered a bit more of the carcass, flipped it halfway over, and examined the new arrangement. I had an image of a rich guy counting his money: The bear seemed to have a kind of Scrooge McDuck attitude toward the carcass. "Mine, ha-ha-ha, all mine." He scented something in the woods and turned toward the new odor, then dismissed it. Probably the bison in the woods. A second later the bear was back chortling over the carcass.

After an hour or so he began digging a second hole adjacent to the first. He used the dirt to cover the carcass. Then he lay down in the second hole and took a nap in the sun. He was on his back, and you could just see the tip of his nose sticking out of the ground. It looked silly, and I wanted to laugh, and I knew I shouldn't laugh, so a series of muffled giggles came snorting up through my nose. I felt like a kid in church. The fear that I'd been living with for twenty hours had stretched itself to the breaking point and finally snapped. The bear couldn't see us, and now he was taking a nap. With his big-bear nose sticking up out of the ground.

Tom needed to move in closer now that the bear was asleep. I chose to stay where I was. Murphy would retreat back over the ridge and come back over the top closer to the bear. He didn't want to crawl down into the bowl because the breeze could swirl around down there, and the bear might wind him. Tom began packing up his gear.

Tired of staring at the bear's nose through my binoculars, I moved behind a small wall of sage and lay on my back, feeling just a tad bearlike. The wind was driving wisps of high cirrus clouds across the sky, and I thought, Storm tomorrow. A dim drowsiness began a slow descent. Couldn't really focus on the sky anymore. Only forty-five minutes of sleep last night. Was I really falling asleep? Now? Two hundred fifty yards from a grizzly bear. In the wild. What was wrong with me?

Tom whispered, "I'm going now."

I heard myself mumble, "Bear's got the right idea." And I fell asleep. Went out like a light.

When I woke, Tom was within one hundred yards of the grizzly. A few minutes later the grizzly woke up—there was a full half hour of stretching and yawning involved in that process— and he uncovered the bison again. We watched him feed for four more hours. Then he took another nap, and it was safe to leave.

And when we got back to town, the first thing Tom told people is that I took one look at the grizzly and fell asleep. Which is true . . . essentially . . . but, you know, I mean, it's not in context, because, uh . . .

Well, hell, I can't explain it. I'm just going to have to live with it. I'm the guy who spent twenty sleepless hours being so terrified of a grizzly bear that when I finally saw him, I fell asleep.

The Bird

▲

"Falconry," I might have written a month ago, "is that extinct medieval sport wherein guys in metal suits throw birds to fish."

I admit to a large measure of ignorance regarding birds in general and falconry in particular. Tragically, I am afflicted with the agony of ornithological dyslexia. Ignorance, however, if it is sincere and pure of heart, sometimes functions as a knowledge vacuum. Which, I suspect, is the most obtuse and metaphysical explanation of how I ended up attending the 1988 North American Falconers Association Field Meet in Amarillo.

Not two hours after I arrived in Texas, I found myself creeping through a dusty field, sneaking up on a small pond in order to ambush a handful of migrating ducks. The sun had just touched the western horizon, and a full hunter's moon was rising in the east. The colors of the setting sun—pastel oranges and reds—shimmered on the surface of the water. It was a clear, windless day, and the mirrored image of the moon glittered on the shining water as well, so that it seemed as if all of heaven and earth was encompassed in this farmer's stock pond.

The falconer slipped his bird—released her from his fist—and the peregrine took a pitch above, several hundred feet over the pond. I was given to understand that the bells, little jingle bells the falcons wear, are necessary to locate a bird feeding on fallen quarry in high cover, though there is something the least bit anticipatory about them. A hunting falcon rising from the fist sounds a bit like Christmas morning.

When the falcon had taken a pitch of about two hundred feet, various humans charged the pond and flushed the ducks. And suddenly, there she was, a peregrine falcon diving at perhaps two hundred miles an hour. I now know that falconers call this power dive a stoop, as in "She stoops to conquer." (The female falcon is a third again as big as the male, and most falconers fly females).

The peregrine's wings were folded in against her body, and the wind through her brittle feathers—through the bell slits—sounded in a rising whistle. Two lines of flight, one horizontal, one vertical, intersected at a moment of savage radiance above the sun and the moon shimmering below.

And that, I learned, is falconry. It is a form of personally engineered bird-watching.

From the outside falconers themselves appear to be a flock of fairly odd ducks. There were over three hundred birds at the NAFA Field Meet, both hawks and falcons. On sunny days, often at midafternoon, most of those birds could be seen out in back of the Amarillo Hilton, sunning themselves on blocklike perches—weathering—while the falconers stood around arguing proudly.

Falconers argue as a matter of course. A falconer argues, I think, because the sport requires him to bend his will to that of the bird. There is no disciplining an unmannerly falcon. A disgruntled bird will simply fly away next time it is released. Therefore, falconers take out their frustrations on others and bicker endlessly over the fine points of their sport.

They are, I'm obliged to state, monomaniacal in their frenzy. Often they take their birds with them on social occasions, and invariably the bird will mute, which is to say, it will engage its impressive waste-disposal system. When this happens in someone else's house—when the mutes are spread across the couch and new carpet like the contents of several tubes of toothpaste—the falconer does not discipline his bird. This is simply not done. Nor is he likely to help clean up. Typically, a falconer in such a situation will examine the mutes and proclaim, with great satisfaction, "Now that is a healthy bird."

Perhaps the strangest characteristic of the falconer is a complete lack of trousers on the male of the species. I have not yet observed such conduct in the female falconer, though I intend to be patient in this regard.

The male falconer oftentimes runs around without pants because he forgets them in his frenzy of monomania. There is, for instance, a falconer of my recent acquaintance who lives in Winifred, Montana, not far from the breaks of the Missouri River. I'll call this fellow, oh, let's say Ralph Rogers.

One day Ralph decided to hunt the breaks with his falcon. He packed up the essentials for the bird—food, the weathering block, the hood, the jesses, the lure, the bells, the electronic transmitter and receiver—all the paraphernalia necessary for the comfort and safety of his peregrine. Being an experienced outdoorsman, Ralph packed quickly for himself.

It was a warm day, and the falconer was wearing running shorts. By the time he got to the breaks, the weather had turned cold. The experienced outdoorsman discovered that he had not packed any pants. His partner lent him the only conceivable thing he could wear to cut the wind and blunt the chill. Since the other man was about a foot shorter than Ralph, and not nearly so, uh, muscular, the thermal underwear our falconer now wore had that fashionable over-the-calf look that so fascinates clothiers everywhere. Inevitably, the bird rode a particularly strong thermal, rose out of sight, caught a whiff of the jet stream, and got lost. Ralph had fastened a small transmitter to his bird, and he was using a black box with an antenna—the receiver—to find her.

The signal—it always happens this way—took the falconer through a small town. Now when a man is searching for his bird with a receiver of this sort, he must constantly listen to the beeping of the machine and turn in a complete circle, carefully blocking one point of the compass with his body in order to isolate the signal.

Falconers understand such antics at a glance. The rest of us find it bewildering. I mean, here's a man running through your backyard, a little frantic, sweating in the chill, holding a little black box with an antenna on it. Every once in a while he performs a slow-motion ballerina twirl, then goes hysterically galloping off in one direction or another. The man is wearing what seems to be a pair of long johns, bursting at the seams. Naturally, seeing such an individual whirling through your backyard, you might be inclined to inquire as to the nature of his business.

"The hell's going on here?"

"Sorry," your falconer in lingerie is going to reply, "can't talk now. I've lost my bird."

Now, for the average outsider, this translates out to: "Can't talk now, I've completely lost my mind."

The ancient field sport of falconry has been the subject of some controversy over the past few years. There are a number of people who simply can't stomach blood sport of any variety, and they are people of good heart. It is wise, I think, for falconers to point out that they have had a guiding hand in bringing the majestic peregrine falcon back from near extinction. In 1965 there were fewer than twenty known pairs of peregrines in the wild. DDT was killing them. In 1970 the Peregrine Fund, a nonprofit organization supported by scientists, ecologists, hunters, and especially falconers, began raising peregrines in captivity and releasing the young. A dozen years ago, for instance, there were three known pairs of peregrines in the southern Rocky Mountains. Today there are thirty pairs. It is difficult for those of genuinely good heart to take issue with these statistics.

Similarly, hunting falcons are not taken from the wild: all peregrines, by law, must be captive-bred.

Some observers feel that falconers are invariably successful in their hunts. This is not so. A man with a shotgun is a more effective predator than any peregrine.

Indeed, the point of falconry or hawking is not merely to take game; the important issue is the manner in which game is taken. One bright Amarillo morning, for instance, I was out by a duck pond with some falconers and noticed that the man flying the bird had it wait on, which is to say, hover, several hundred yards from the pond. When we flushed the ducks, the falcon stooped, but she was far out of hunting range. The ducks flew off unharmed. Later, I asked the falconer why he had set his bird up for certain failure.

"I want her to learn that she has to take a higher pitch," he said. "If she was over the pond, it would have been a simple slaughter."

And I understood that falconers require a certain perverse elegance in their sport. They are rather like the sexually obsessed in this regard: "Well, if I can't do it with whips and midgets, I'd rather not do it at all."

Most hunters—all but the most doltish fringe—speak about respect for the hunted. A falconer's concern for the quarry is legendary.

One example of my point: There is an individual who is a pillar of moral authority in his community, and who, for that reason, has asked me not to reveal his identity. Let's just say that one fall day, on his annual hawking vacation, he was out flying Harris hawks with several friends. This was in Colorado, and the friends were flying the Harrises from their fists.

Now Harris hawks, I discovered in Amarillo, are rare raptors in that they hunt in groups, using strategy. I imagine the scene was rather like the one I witnessed out in the corn stubble near the Amarillo airport. I recall a rabbit—an animal weighing perhaps seven pounds—being pursued by the Harrises. Once again it occurred to me that if game were the purpose, a shotgun would have served us better here. We scared up a rabbit, and then it was "Ho ho hawk," and the Harrises sprang from four fists as the rabbit bolted toward high cover. Two of the hawks were slow off the mark. One of the pound-and-a-half hawks was coming in high, one low. The rabbit—there were several ferruginous hawks cruising the field, and my guess is that the local bunnies were used to this sort of thing—stopped short so that the high hawk overflew him. The second Harris came in only inches off the ground, but the rabbit leapt a full four feet into the air. Then it disappeared in a series of sharp angles and lost itself in the corn stubble. There was, on the part of the falconers, some small, grudging applause for the rabbit.

The scene was something similar in Colorado that day: four men walking through a field, hawks on the fists. A rabbit broke, the hawks flew. The rabbit bolted toward the gravel road. Between the road and the field, however, there was an irrigation ditch. The day was cold and turning colder. A thin skim of ice had formed over the water in the ditch.

The rabbit had no time for caution, and it attempted to run across the ice. Which broke. Now we have four men standing around with hawks on their wrists looking down into a ditch with some consternation. The rabbit was drowning. It attempted to crawl up on a ledge of ice, which immediately gave way so that the rabbit fell back into the water. When it surfaced the third time, ice was forming on its head. The men were abashed.

Now it is true that only moments before these men had earnestly desired the complete annihilation of the rabbit. But this—this drowning, struggling, pathetic scenario—wasn't nearly what they had in mind.

Someone, it was decided, would have to save the rabbit. The gentleman in question—a moral pillar of his community, remember—took the task upon himself. First he removed his boots and socks. He was going to get wet, and it was no use being miserable all day. Then it occurred to him that he didn't actually know how deep the water in the irrigation ditch was. It could be two or three feet deep. A man could spend the rest of the day wearing wet pants. No, best to take them off. But now his shirt and his parka hung down past his waist, and for all he knew, the water could be chest-deep.

The rabbit was weakening.

No time to waste. Get the clothes off and save the rabbit. Hurry.

Imagine the scene. Four guys standing around with vicious-looking hawks on their fists and one naked man shivering on the subfreezing, wind-whipped plain.

This was the tableau that greeted the elderly couple as they drove down the lonely gravel road that paralleled the ditch. There was a slowing of the car: Our falconers had an enduring impression of two pairs of eyes, and felt much of what a driver feels when a deer is frozen in the headlights.

"Geez almighty, Madge, it's some of them devil worshipers Geraldo was talking about."

A squeal of tires, a spray of gravel, and loneliness on the road.

The postscript to the story is that the rabbit was saved. It trembled in the men's hands, badly chilled. If they released it, this rabbit was going to die of hypothermia. The hunting trip was cut short, the hawks were hooded, and the rabbit was driven back to the motel. The most efficient and least traumatic way to dry the animal and warm it up at the same time involved a blow drier. The rabbit was released in large field where—if the coyotes haven't gotten it, if the wild hawks or foxes have somehow missed it—it is still alive, fat and sassy.

Nonetheless, I have a persistent vision of the maids in that motel gossiping.

"Don't know who they are, but they come here every year. Capture rabbits and style their hair. I think they're mad *hare*dressers."

Finally, the man who swam naked for the rabbit was foolish enough to tell his wife about it. Now, every time he comes home from a hawking expedition with some matter of grave or amusing import to relay—"Honey, guess what happened to me today" —she replies in the world-weary tone of one who has experienced much in life and is not often surprised.

"You didn't get naked again, did you?"

A week in the company of avid falconers has considerably broadened my horizons. "Falconry," I can now confidently proclaim, "is that flourishing contemporary field sport in which frenzied, monomaniacal men (and some frenzied monomaniacal women) soil their neighbor's living rooms with bird droppings and run around naked in the snow."

The Bison Ballet

▲

There's an old Roger Miller song that concerns itself with a series of intuitively inarguable philosophical negatives, one of which is that "you can't roller-skate in a buffalo herd." I yield to no one in my admiration for the man who sang "Dang Me," but it is my experience that, given the proper circumstance, an extremely stupid or suicidal person could indeed roller-skate in a buffalo herd.

The song was running through my head one day last summer when, for reasons that seemed compelling at the time, I found myself on foot in the midst of the largest buffalo herd to roam America since the 1880s. Some twenty-five hundred buffalo range over the 2.5 million acres of Yellowstone National Park, and I was strolling through an aggregation of animals known as the Mary Mountain herd. They were stretched out across the extent of the Hayden Valley, bulls, cows, calves all together in this, the end of the rutting season.

My neighbor, Tom Murphy, and I had been on a day hike through the park, and the buffalo blocked our path to the road and our car. We might have avoided them: scaled the mountain to our left and dropped into the next valley, but that drainage was closed to hikers. Several grizzly bears, the Park Service said, were bickering over a buffalo carcass there. To the right there was only a low rolling ridgeline. The sun was low in the west, and the late August grasses looked softly saffron, aureate. A line of buffalo stretched out over the ridge, and there was no way to know how many there might be on the other side of the hill.

The choice seemed to be grizzlies to the left, a midnight stumble through a herd of unseen buffalo to the right, or a tense straight-ahead sunset stroll through the buffalo we could see. Tom and I set off across the treeless expanse of Hayden Valley, directly into the herd.

"Must be a couple of hundred of them," I said.

Tom, who grew up on a cattle ranch in South Dakota, began stabbing at the herd with the first two fingers of his right hand. "Three hundred sixty-five," he said presently, "not counting that line against that far hill."

To say that buffalo can be pesky is understating the case. Statistically, a Yellowstone hiker stands a greater chance of being injured by a buffalo than of even seeing a grizzly bear. Being stupid ups those bad bison odds considerably. Being very stupid around bison can get you killed.

The bison graze peacefully, stolidly, and they seldom take notice of humans. Indeed, if a bison looks at you, you're already too close. Some people interpret the bison's indifference as stupidity and meekness. A man with the good sense to be afraid of a domestic bull will try to touch a buffalo, to say he's done so. Some people have actually tried to feed bison. Walk right up to the largest animal on the North American continent—bulls can weigh in excess of one ton—and jam a handful of grass in its face. Other people have thrown rocks at bison, just to see what they might do. The enraged one-ton animal might demonstrate its ability to outrun a horse over a quarter of a mile.

One park ranger I talked to thought too many people have a Disneyland mentality about the park. They see an animal up close, are appropriately thrilled, and reason that, since these beasts live in an area administered by the United States government, they must be bound by the same laws of courtesy that apply to petting zoos. In point of fact, over the last four years, at least twenty-seven people have been injured by buffalo in Yellowstone Park.

Most of the injuries are Instamatic in nature. They are the result of someone edging just a bit closer for "a really good picture." And then there are folk horror stories that attain the status of truth, regardless of the facts involved. There's one about a French tourist who wanted a picture of himself with a bison, but the animal in question was lying down. A very unsatisfying picture: Frenchman with dozing bison. He walked over, kicked the bull until it stood up, then he turned toward his friends, and smiled. The bull turned, hooked, gored.

I've checked this story out, and the incident report only mentions the tourist getting close to the bison and turning his back so friends could take his picture. The severely injured man was eventually transferred to the Utah Medical Center, where it took him two months to die. Two months.

The other story involves a father who tried to put his three-year-old daughter on a bison's back, again for a picture. "I've heard that story," a park biologist told me. "I'm not sure I believe it. I think the animal would hook you if you got that close."

And that may have been what happened. The incident report says that a little girl was injured when her father tried to take a picture of her and a large bull. Often these reports are sketchy because otherwise-loving fathers don't care to admit that they wanted to give Grandma in New Jersey just the cutest gol-darn picture of Missy riding a buffalo.

Some incidents don't count in the park's tally: In 1987, for instance, three people were injured fleeing from charging bison. There were twisted ankles, sprains, and face-first falls in that count. These people were injured simply running away, and therefore don't count in the bison-human interaction tally.

In the year 1800 there were over 40 million bison in America. One hundred years later that number had dwindled to a few hundred individuals. Five hundred forty-two in 1889, to be exact.

Hunters were not sportsmen. They were executioners. A man

with a good buffalo rifle could watch the herd for a time, shoot the dominant animal, and pick off a hundred others as they milled about in confusion. All this in a single afternoon. General Philip Sheridan, among other authorities, described the slaughter as a clever way "to settle the vexed Indian question." Buffalo hunters were "destroying the Indian's commissary."

The few hundred bison, orphans of the Indian wars, were sheltered on private ranches. In 1905 the bison's numbers had grown to eight hundred, with seven hundred on private ranches. There was a growing sense of something lost: something wild and valuable and innately American. In the next few years the federal government established several public herds. Today there are one hundred thousand bison in America, and ten public herds.

It's a horrifying and inspiring history, an innately American story. Strolling through the Mary Mountain herd, however, I found myself contemplating gored French tourists. Park regulations prohibit approaching within twenty-five yards of any bison. Twenty-five yards seems entirely too close to me. There is a bison cow on the Wichita Mountains National Wildlife Refuge in Oklahoma that has charged humans from three hundred yards. Her name is Belligerent.

The Mary Mountain bison were sensitive to collision courses, so Tom and I walked in meandering zigzags through the sage on the flat valley floor. Several of the cows had new calves with them. The calves retained their golden color and were not yet resigned to the fact of their bisonhood. They frolicked and ran— "I'm going to be a gazelle!"—and acted not at all the stolid beasts they would become.

This was something of a problem, because the calves were curious. They began following us. Cows followed the calves. And, because it was the season of rut, bulls followed the cows. They sniffed at the back portion of their various intendeds, rolled their upper lips, and shook the great strings of drool that hung from their mouths. The bulls were so deeply in love that they were literally groaning. It was a short "uhhhhh" sound that lasted for a second or two and sounded like rumbling of a Mack truck. The constant groaning played like the sound track of the movie *Night of the Living Dead,* specifically the scene where the cannibal zombies are feeding. It occurred to me that males in love are seldom pretty.

The groaning bulls were inclined to fight another bull that drew too close to his cow. A man on foot could easily be trampled in the melee. Occasionally, Tom and I were forced to split up and separate the cows with the most ardent suitors. We walked for several miles through the herd, each of us doing a 360 every few minutes.

We watched their eyes. And their tails. When a bison lifts its tail, it means either charge or discharge. Or both. An agitated animal often defecates. Then charges. The bulls, however, were intent on the cows and took no notice of us at all.

"You know," I said to Tom, "you could actually roller-skate out here."

"It's going to be dark pretty soon," he pointed out.

"Just clump through the high grass . . ."

"We've got another mile. . . ."

"You could actually do it," I said again.

Alternately, you could throw rocks at the bison, or try to feed them, or run over and kick a dozing bull. You could do that. (You could also spend two months dying.) It might cost you your life, but you could do it.

We had another fifteen minutes of walking and a couple of hundred bison to go. I spun around to see what was behind me: an awkward sunset pirouette in a buffalo herd.

A Missive on Moose

▲

I was thinking, Moose are not very smart. This is the wisdom of popular culture. In Raymond Chandler's *Farewell, My Lovely*, for instance, Detective Marlowe is hired by a huge ex-con named Moose Malloy. Well, Moose turns out to be a mush-head, a real pea-brain. In comic strips—"Archie" and "Funky Winkerbean" come to mind—gentlemen nicknamed Moose wear team jackets, are bigger than everybody else, and are fond of the witty exclamation "Duh!"

The two bull moose I was watching through the trees occasionally said, "Humph." The larger of the two might have weighed fifteen hundred pounds, the smaller perhaps two hundred pounds less. They were standing belly-deep in a marshy pool at the edge of Yellowstone Lake, in the far southeastern quadrant of Yellowstone Park, and they were feeding on aquatic plants. I was standing stock-still in a grove of trees—spruce and lodgepole pines— surreptitiously watching the big fellows dine and edging closer for a better view. The larger bull stared at me for a time, then plunged his head into the pond so that only the top half of his antlers was visible. The other was feeding as well, and while the two were blindly intent on their underwater meal, I moved to another tree five feet closer to the pond.

It was just twilight, the end of a long summer day, and the pond was a shimmering luminescence, a mirror to the fading pastels of the sky. The smaller of the two bulls raised his great, goofy head, and there was the sound of falling water. Streams of it, pinkish silver in the dying light, fell from the animal's immense, palmate antlers.

There was a great inhalation of air: "humph." Then the larger bull came up for air, and the sound was like that of a marlin breaking water in a calm sea. "Humph," the animal said. A fleshy dewlap, the bell, hung from his neck. A string of mossy-green subaquatic foliage dangled limply from his mouth. Color bled across the sky in long, fingerlike streaks, and there was a momentary quickening of the light on the surface of the pond.

The moose stared directly at me, without a great deal of interest. I stood in the shadows, still as death, attempting to look like a stubby lodgepole pine. This was dull entertainment for the feeding moose: I felt like the outdoor equivalent of some inane dinner-hour television offering. The thought festered in my mind for a bit, and I didn't know why. Suddenly, unbidden, I heard in my mind's ear the voice of Lorne Greene narrating a nature documentary I had recently seen on cable TV, the kind of thing you watch while munching on a bad burrito. The show was a fine one, all about bears scooping salmon out of various streams. Mr. Greene, by way of capping things off, said—I swear it—"People don't give bears enough credit for fishing." He sounded peeved about this.

That sentence brightened my life, and for a week I bored nearly everyone I met with my effusive accolades for the fishing ability of bears. "They catch more fish than anybody, and don't you forget it," I'd tell puzzled people over a beer at the Owl Casino and Lounge. "Bears are damned fine fishermen, and people just don't give them enough credit for it."

I wondered what Lorne Greene might have to say about the feeding bulls before me. No doubt the sight would make him indignant. "Moose can eat tons of food with their heads totally under water, and not one person in ten thousand gives a rat's ass."

* * *

There was a slight crackling of branches behind me and to the right. Both bulls turned to the sound. Long ears stood erect on their skulls and swiveled toward this new entertainment. My camping partners, Tom Murphy, a professional photographer, and Lee Hutt, a talented amateur one, were moving down a sloping trail two hundred yards away. They had set up their cameras high above, on a fragrant, sage-covered hillside overlooking the glittering marsh, anticipating that the full moon would rise over the distant mountains of the Two Ocean Plateau, where the imaginary line of the Continental Divide meanders through the high country before snaking down into Wyoming's Teton National Forest. My companions hoped the moon would rise with the colors of the setting sun still on the marsh.

I had dithered around with Tom and Lee for a bit, decided that the hillside shot was beyond my technical capacity, and had gone off with my friend Karen Laramore to fill the water jug at a spring on the edge of the marsh. The path took us past the pond where the moose were feeding. The moose and the color on the pond: It had all seemed a once-in-a-lifetime photo opportunity. We thought Tom and Lee might want to seize the moment, so Karen had gone to get them. Now, for perhaps twenty minutes, I had been alone with the moose, and that was my moment.

I edged closer—it seemed smart to move only during those times when both moose had their heads under water—and eventually found myself standing at the edge of the pond, perhaps thirty feet away from the larger bull. He broke water and stared at me. I took a few pictures. The animal seemed alert: He wasn't disturbed by my presence, and he wasn't ignoring me, either. There was a sense of immense power here, and my heart began thumping hard inside my chest. I felt suddenly weak, impotent— and stupid for being so close. The two moose, huge and sleek, fed in a pond that reflected the sunset, and I didn't think about their intelligence at all. I suppose a clinical psychologist could run a few moose through some sort of giant maze and give you a reading on their IQs—"These guys are dumber than a sackful of hammers"—but the sort of intelligence that could be measured wasn't at issue here. The moose seemed another order of life altogether.

There was, of course, a chance they would charge. I had

planned it all out, the worst-case scenario. The pond was surely muddy, and when the moose moved, they had to pull their legs out of the ooze with a gesture that would cost them some effort. The tree I was standing behind was stout, with several low, step-ladder-type branches. I could get up the tree before the moose could get out of the pond.

Besides, I knew there would be a signal. A moose will likely bristle at the neck, like a hissing cat, before it charges. I had seen this once when, driving in Yellowstone, my skiing partners and I stopped the car to let a moose cross the road. It was cold, and the snow was deep. The moose wanted to walk on the plowed road, and it wanted to walk in our direction. We were in a small Japanese car. This was an American moose. The ruff around its neck stood on end, and it came toward us in the strange, gangling walk that makes moose look so ridiculously uncoordinated. A great hoof, the size of a pie plate, came down toward the window on the driver's side, and we took immediate evasive action. Several hours later, when we tried the road again, the moose was gone.

Once again I decided on evasive action, moving back into the darkness of the trees as Tom and Lee moved in for some pictures of their own.

The moose grazed for another twenty minutes. Tom and Lee shot a few rolls of film, and I sat on a log thinking. This time we were spending, it was a moment of special beauty, with the spice of small but certain danger to it. Some prize such a moment because it gives them a sense of superiority: others are such fools, none of them give bears enough credit for fishing. It's a poor treasure, though, this spiteful superiority. These moments are the currency of our physical and emotional lives. They are what we tell our friends about in the art that comes to each of us. We write or we paint or we tell stories. Photographers prize the moment for the shot. And I don't know why I prize the moment at all, except that there is little enough left in our lives to awe us.

The Llama Dilemma

▲

I was leading, walking past some nameless pond in Montana's Mission Wilderness, when Pancho began humming. At first, the sound could be taken for the gentle creaking of a wooden ship at anchor.

"Uhmmmm."

It was almost a sigh. Pancho might have been saying, "Caramba, this pond is a loveliness, no?"

"Uhmmmm."

The sound was a little louder now, a little more nasal. I turned, and Pancho gave me one of his patented llama looks. His head was precisely on a level with my own, and his face was strangely angular under the ridiculous rabbit ears. Pancho's eyes were flat brown from lid to lid. He looked like something sentient from another planet—not a Peruvian pack animal at all.

"Uhmmmmnnnn," Pancho said, and he swiveled his head on that long, curving neck in order to survey the empty trail behind us. There were no human beings where there should have been five following us. Most distressing to Pancho, there were no llamas back there. His pals—Switchback, Doc, Snowman, Houdini —were nowhere in sight.

"Uhmmnnn," Pancho said, and his long ears swiveled forward on his head in the manner of a man cupping his ears to hear a distant sound. I stepped in close and put a comforting hand on Pancho's woolly neck. The llama edged an arm's length away. Pancho was entirely placid, but he didn't like being cuddled or petted. No llama does. It is beneath their dignity.

"Uhmmmmnnn," Pancho hummed, in mild distress. "*¿Donde están mis amigos,* anyway?" he seemed to be saying.

"Uhmnnn," one of the other llamas replied from around a bend in the trail. *"Aqui, Panchito."* Pancho seemed satisfied, and we stood there waiting.

"You all right back there?" I yelled to the various unseen humans.

"Hooty's taking a pit stop," Steve Rolfing called. Steve and his wife, Sue, own the Great Northern Llama Company just outside Columbia Falls, Montana. They breed the beasts and run commercial llama-packing trips.

Steve was telling me that his youngest llama, Houdini, had stopped to relieve himself. Unlike horses or mules, llamas must stop to heed the call of nature. Their droppings are small oval pellets, without much odor, and look rather like something a large deer or small elk might have left on the trail. Anyone who's ever done the apple dance behind a string of pack horses will understand why llama owners, alone among packers, point with pride to the droppings of their beasts. It is minimum-impact packing.

Another advantage: Llamas are not hoofed animals, like horses or mules. The bottom of each foot consists of two large pads, like those on a dog. While a heavily used horse trail can sometimes be worn down to a depth of two feet, the llama's pads leave less impact than a hiking boot. A kind of horny toenail above each pad curves down to a point that can grip into the slick ice of a glacier or snowfield. Llamas can carry packs there, in spots where horses would be sliding forever, falling into crevasses to be imprisoned throughout time, like mastodons frozen in ice.

Steve and the rest of the pack string came around the bend. I put the rope from Pancho's halter over my shoulder and fixed it to a Velcro tab on my jacket, leaving both hands free. Pancho liked to walk two feet behind me, no more or no less, and we could have strolled along for an hour like that, at whatever pace I chose, without pulling loose from each other.

"When am I going to see one of these guys spit?" I asked Steve Rolfing. I liked the llamas so much I was looking for some drawback to packing with them. Investigative journalists aren't paid to go around liking stuff.

"My llamas," Steve said, a bit defensively, "don't spit. Zoo llamas spit." Llamas, like cows, have several stomachs. Foraged foods—bear grass, alfalfa, fallen leaves, pine needles—are broken down by a bacteria in the first stomach, then brought back up into the mouth in a cud that is thoroughly chewed before being swallowed a second time. Unlike cows, which are doltish and bovine with their cud, llamas, in the process of digestion, seem wise beyond the capacity of their species, even philosophical.

"In petting zoos," Steve said, "people crowd the llamas. They try to touch their face." Llamas hate that. "So they spit."

You can see it coming, this warning gesture: The animal swallows once, and then you can see the cud from the first stomach working its way up the long, graceful neck. Folks who continue to insist on cuddling llamas, those who mistreat them, find themselves doused in a fire-hose blast of odorous green bile.

Llamas are the New World equivalent of camels, relatives of those foul-tempered ships of the desert whose owners can often be seen running from their own animals. Llamas—these camels of the clouds, woolly buggers that evolved on the cold, fifteen-thousand-foot-high plains of Ecuador and Peru and Chile—are regular sweethearts in comparison. They don't spook, shy, or kick; and because they have teeth only in their lower jaw, they couldn't bite even if they wanted to.

"One lady asked me if you can go blind if you get the spit in your eyes," Steve said. "The answer is no. The real answer is to pack the llama properly, give it an arm's length of respect, and it won't spit anyway."

In a further gesture of respect to the animals that earn his living for him, Steve has resisted the impulse to name any of his animals Fernando, Dalai, or Tony.

While llamas can weigh four hundred pounds and more, Steve thinks the smaller animals, those weighing 325 to 350 pounds, have more stamina. "A general rule is that a llama can comfortably carry about one third of its own weight." With properly weighed and balanced packs, a llama can put in a good twenty-mile day. An overloaded or exhausted animal will simply lie down on the ground. It will spit and refuse to budge. No amount of pulling on the halter will move it.

As far as I could see, anyone who'd overload a llama, or walk it to exhaustion, has to be an ogre. The animals gently let you know if they are uncomfortable about something with a nasal hum. Ignore the hum and live for hours with a sordid sense of guilt.

We camped for the night near the alpine lake. I unloaded Pancho and buried that night's beer in a north-facing snowbank. Common sewers of the hop, such as myself, know that all beer tastes better in bottles. Backpackers, such as myself, frequently omit bottled beer from their gear in favor of more mundane survival items, such as warm clothes or food. My usual pack, for instance, weighs about fifty pounds. Pancho was comfortable carrying twice that, and the extra weight was the difference between serious comfort camping and a survival trek. In addition to the beer, we had a two-burner cookstove, camp chairs, fishing gear, tackle boxes, bottles of wine and cognac, and a pineapple upside-down cake in a large tin.

While the night's batch of cutthroat trout was baking on the campfire, Steve whipped up a fondue on the stove. He said that he had hurt his back a few years ago while working at a ski resort. "I hammered moguls all day long for a whole season. Then the next year I had a desk job. My back gave out, and the orthopedic surgeon said the best thing for me was walking." Without a backpack.

Steve, an avid outdoorsman with a degree in forestry, thought that he was doomed to day hikes until a friend suggested he try llama packing. The Rolfings bought their first llama, Pancho, in 1979. Now they own thirty of them, and Steve guides weeklong treks into the Glacier National Park region.

While Steve stirred the fondue, I went through a large scrapbook he'd brought along for my edification and education. I read an article about a sheep rancher in Wyoming who hasn't lost a single lamb to coyotes since he installed a pair of llamas in his pasture. The animals are alert and curious, and they come running up to a visiting coyote humming, *"¿Qué pasa,* hey, what's going on, *Señor?"* The coyote, for his part, sees a couple of really strange-looking beasts, both nearly ten times his size, and he departs, in haste, thinking, "Perhaps this evening I'll dine on rabbits."

Every journalist who had gone packing with Steve Rolfing seemed to adore llamas. There were articles in the scrapbook about "llama llove," about minimum-impact packing, and nobody mentioned any drawbacks at all. I worried about that, about writing a balanced article on llamas, as I sat in my tent with a last cup of coffee and cognac. Pancho was tethered just outside the front door: my own personal watch-llama. It was grizzly country, and Steve said Pancho would make a sound like a cold car engine turning over on a subzero morning if something unwelcome visited the camp. "I haven't had any grizzly problems," Steve said. He thought that llamas might smell dangerously weird to bears. Mostly though, he figured that all the "big, warm bodies around camp" are something of a threat to the grizzlies.

The possibility that hungry bears might avoid llamas, for whatever reason, didn't seem to be a drawback to camping with a few of them.

I figured up the expenses. Steve said a bale of hay will last a llama about ten days, so that it costs about $120 a year to feed one. Not bad.

A trail-trained male costs $1,200 to $1,500. With an import ban on the animals and only about eight thousand llamas in all of America, a female can cost six thousand dollars or more. But the animals, Rolfing assured me, are earnest and frequent breeders—

females are in season all year long, and the gestation period is about eleven months—so that purchase of a young female and a stud is an investment that should pay for itself several times over.

Steve's llamas require only half an acre of pasture apiece. "You can even house-train them," he told me. "They always go in the same spot, so all you have to do is show one some pellets by the back door. When the llama's gotta go, he'll stand by the door." Steve had kept Pancho in the house for a while. "They're graceful," Steve had said. "They don't bump into furniture or knock anything over. Of course, they're hell on houseplants."

That's it, I thought, finishing the last of the cognac Pancho had carried: the fatal drawback to owning llamas. I unzipped the tent flap and glanced out at the watch-llama guarding my door. "You're hell on houseplants," I said. The llama gave me a calm, flat-brown philosophical glance.

"*Es verdad*," Pancho hummed, ruminating over his cud, "but as for myself, at this moment—how do you say?—I could give a pellet." He lay on his belly with his legs folded under him in a contemplative posture. The full moon seemed very bright above, and the lake was a shimmering expanse of cold, molten silver.

Last Stand of
the Mountain Gorilla

▲

Mount Karisimbi is fifteen thousand feet high, and pretty much of a walk-up in mountaineering terms, but there was tragedy on the upper slopes some fifty years ago. In those days foreigners in central equatorial Africa habitually traveled with porters, and when the snow began falling on that simple summit attempt half a century ago, the African porters seemed to sense the awful gravity of eternity. These were men who had never seen so much as an ice cube, and now frozen water was falling from the sky. No one has ever satisfactorily explained why they did what they did —it may have been a matter of religion, or superstition, or the sure, sudden sense that the world had gone to hell in a handbasket—but the porters simply lay down in the drifting snow and waited to die.

The English climbers were courageous. They literally carried several of the porters down out of the storm to a blazing fire not all that far below. The Africans would not walk down of their own accord.

I see that scene in my mind's eye: I see moisture rising like steam out of the jungles of the Congo basin to the west, rising and coalescing into clouds, the massive dark towers of equatorial Africa. I see those clouds colliding with the chain of volcanic peaks known as the Virungas, dumping their rain and snow on Visoke, on Sabino, on the highest of them all, Karisimbi.

It must have been beautiful then. Just below the summit of twisted rock and black volcanic sand, Karisimbi is covered with thick, green, clinging grass, a mossy sort of grass that holds the imprint of a boot for an hour or more. The porters lay down on that lush, living carpet as the snow began to fall, as the green disappeared beneath an alien layer of brilliant white, first two inches deep, then four, then six.

Below the steeply sloping grasslands leading to the summit there is a forest of lobelia: twelve-foot-high plants that look like massive candles set in stemmed holders. A funereal fog would have been rolling off the mountain there, and it would have followed the climbers down into an African alpine meadow below. The fire was built there, in among the giant senecios, with their broad green leaves and brilliant yellow flowers.

The Englishmen had to leave many of the porters on the upper slopes: It would have been suicidal to risk a rescue in the dark. And so those men died there, on that soft white slope. They must have huddled together for warmth and comfort. Certainly, they spoke to one another at first as the snow drifted over their bodies. And, because the people who live in the valleys below the Virungas are, to this day, stoic, and even fatalistic, tragedy sometimes elicits a response many Europeans and Americans find inexplicable. They laugh. The sheer inevitability of pain, of a lifetime full of pain, is funny, and the final pain is the funniest of all. I hear those men on Karisimbi: Before the snow and ice silenced them, I hear them laughing among themselves, a soft, rich sound, muffled by falling snow.

I sat on the black sand atop Karisimbi, endured the dive-bomb attack of a huge African raven, and thought about the last two hundred wild mountain gorillas alive in the world.

Photographer Nick Nichols and I had been in the central equatorial African country of Rwanda too long, and on the last few days of our visit, we decided to climb Mount Karisimbi. We had been studying the habits of the mountain gorilla for nearly a month, and my thoughts about the animal, and its chances for survival, were bleak, claustrophobic, frigid. There was about them the faint sound of laughter, muffled by falling snow.

Rwanda's Volcano National Park is the last refuge of an estimated two hundred mountain gorillas. They live on the jungled slopes of the Virungas, between about seven thousand and eleven thousand feet, where they feed on the writhing vegetable riot that erupts out of rich volcanic soil.

The gorillas weren't all that difficult to find: A family of six or ten animals moving on all fours through a dense, wet meadow of nettles, or a thick stand of bamboo, makes a wide and easily identifiable trail. The family group is led by a dominant male, called a silverback because of the wide patch of gray across his back, a silver saddle that denotes sexual maturity. Immature males, blackbacks, will quickly develop a silver saddle when they are forced to lead a family after the premature death of a reigning silverback. One thinks of men who have had "greatness thrust upon them," of presidents who are said to "grow into the office."

In the month I had spent with them, I had learned the simple rules one adheres to when approaching a family of browsing gorillas. Staying low signifies lack of aggressive intent. Smile. Gorilla faces read like human faces, and a smile is a friendly gesture. Just don't show your teeth. This is impolite at best; at worst, it signals a desire to attack. And don't stare. A direct, unwavering stare is a sign of aggression, as it is for both dogs and men.

There is a proper distance to keep, but it varies with the individual gorilla, and the circumstances, so that sometimes fifty yards is too close, and sometimes the gorilla will allow you to move within arm's reach.

These are mere matters of etiquette, not to mention self-protection, and they are applicable to any number of situations in human society. Take your typical barroom fight. Here's a big, nasty Hell's Angel minding his own business and sitting on a low stool over in the corner. A man with peaceful intentions would not signal them by hulking over to this guy, by standing inches away, by frowning down on the man with gritted teeth, by staring at him for minutes on end.

Do something like this to the Hell's Angel and he's likely to nail your head to the floor and tap-dance on your face. Do it to a mountain gorilla, and he'll charge.

Mrithi is the silverback presiding over the family known as group 13. From the summit of Karisimbi, I could see across to the lower slopes of Sabino, where I first met him. It was down there, below the mossy grass, the eerie lobelia forest, the senecios, even below the nettle fields and hygenia meadows, all the way down into the bamboo forest. Mrithi's path had been plain enough: The closely spaced bamboo stalks, ten and fifteen feet high, had been smashed to the ground along a sort of trail. The gorillas had peeled the stalks to get at the white pulp inside. The trail was littered with these peelings, which looked like discarded sandwich wrappers.

Mrithi was sitting in a small clearing. We approached on our bellies and announced our presence with a double-belch vocalization, a double clearing of the throat that passes for a polite "hello" among mountain gorillas. We followed the rules, but he regarded us with some suspicion. His face was shiny, almost iridescent in its blackness. He was frowning slightly: a look I can best describe as tolerant annoyance. There were creases above the heavy ridge of his brow, and the corners of his mouth were turned down, like a child's drawing of an unhappy person.

He stood for a moment on his short bowed legs, but we lay motionless, avoiding his stare. His chest was massive, and the long black hair on his huge arms looked rich, regal, like mink or sable. He stared at us for a minute or two, then sat back down and scratched his head. (George Schaller, in his pioneering work on the mountain gorilla twenty years ago, noticed a lot of this head scratching. Schaller supposed that the gorilla was pondering his options—fight or flee—and thought that the head scratching was a sign of indecision, just as it is with humans.)

Mrithi pounded his chest with his cupped palms, and he stared at us in a challenging manner, but the display was halfhearted, and entirely unintimidating. We lay still and silent as stone. Mrithi peeled a bit of bamboo, keeping a wary eye on us.

We crawled a bit closer. His odor was strong, like burnt rubber and vinegar, though not so unpleasant as that sounds. The great animal seemed almost to sigh, as if in resignation, and we took the sigh as an invitation. We crept closer still.

Mrithi ignored us for some time. He seemed ready for his afternoon nap, and the ten members of his family gathered about. Mrithi fell onto his back and yawned elaborately. Mtoto, a three-year-old female no bigger than a collie pup, crawled up onto his absurd potbelly and yanked at the equally absurd goateelike growth under his chin. The two frolicked, lazily. They glanced over in our direction frequently, smiling slightly, and I had the impression that they had passed beyond resignation and into acceptance, that there was, somewhere in the frolic, a desire to entertain.

Eventually, Mrithi led his family deeper into the bamboo. We followed for a time, but Mrithi was clearly getting tired of us. When he pounded the flat of his palms on the ground several times, we took it as a sign that we had overstayed our welcome.

It was on another visit that Mrithi charged me. I had gone into the bamboo with some researchers. Mtoto had caught her hand in a poacher's antelope trap, and it was necessary to assess the extent of her injuries. We had been aggressively impolite, over-staying our reluctant welcome an hour or so, and Mrithi came at me faster than I could run. But the first thing the experts tell you about such a situation is, "Don't run," "Never run." Anyone who has ever been walking along the sidewalk on a strange street and had some dog come snarling out of a yard knows the principle. Stop. Face the animal. Run and you'll be bitten. So it is with gorillas, and I discovered that holding one's ground in the face of a charge is, for one simple reason, a good deal easier than it sounds. A mature mountain gorilla can weigh up to 425 pounds and stand almost six feet tall. A charging gorilla will bare finger-sized fangs, scream, topple small trees.

Mrithi was charging with a bearlike four-legged gallop. I lay there, holding my ground—Nick suggested that I was paralyzed with fear—and the big silverback stopped about five yards away. He turned abruptly, and strode into the darkness of the bamboo.

A week later, another gorilla, Brutus by name, screamed and charged one of the researchers. The scream was awesome, high-pitched at first, then dropping down into a lower register and reverberating off the surrounding hills. The researcher held his ground—my experience suggests he was probably paralyzed with fear—and Brutus stopped, as all mountain gorillas will stop when a man holds his ground. For whatever reason.

When Nick and I set up camp on the lower slopes of Sabino, near the small village of Karendage, I began to identify strongly with the gorillas. Instantly, or so it seemed, hundreds of people burst out of the earth and gathered to watch us set up our tent.

We had been learning some Swahili, but everyone in Karendagi spoke Kinya-rwandan. We could not communicate, apart from shrugs and other friendly gestures. The Rwandans were both fascinated and polite. They kept their distance—about two feet—and smiled in various reassuring manners.

We regarded the smiling horde with what amounted to tolerant annoyance.

"How long do you think they're going to stand there, staring?" Nick asked.

"I don't know. There's no television. . . ."

Time passed. After about half an hour, we became accustomed to the presence of the others. The Rwandans were not threatening, only honestly inquisitive. I began to worry that we were a dull show.

The desire to entertain lasted perhaps an hour and a half. I cooked some dinner. "Freeze-dried lasagne," I said importantly, and I prepared it with extravagant magician's gestures. Dinner was a big hit, and the urge to entertain drove me to ludicrous lengths. I sang. I told knock-knock jokes in English. I knelt on one knee and diagrammed football plays in the black muddy soil. People stared, smiled uncertainly. They seemed puzzled, contemplative. I imagine they thought much the same thing I thought as I watched Mrithi: that this strange creature was very different from myself, and yet, disturbingly, very similar.

Our mood—Nick's and mine—went through a subtle transformation. We were exhausted, tired of entertaining, tired of being watched. And still the Rwandans stood there, smiling and staring. We sat in the tent. People knelt to peer inside. It was seven at night, and neither of us would be able to sleep for several hours.

Suddenly—unconsciously, I think—Nick screamed. It was a thirty-second howl of frustration, a plea for privacy, and though it lacked the authority of a roar from Brutus, the intent was precisely the same.

A cold wind sprang up on Karisimbi, and in the sudden chill I found myself thinking that it wouldn't do to identify too strongly with the mountain gorilla.

Sometime in the distant past it is possible that a creature that was to become the gorilla shared the forest with a creature that would become man. As the equatorial forest began to shrink, the forebears of man moved out of the forest, onto the broad plains and savannahs, or so one theory has it.

Food was not plentiful on the plains, and the new creature was forced to hunt animals larger and more powerful than itself. Survival was a process of constant adaptation. Language was essential to the hunt, as was cooperation, and the invention of tools.

The gorilla stayed in the forest, where it reigned unchallenged up until the beginning of the last century. Food was everywhere —mountain gorillas consume some seventy-five different plants— and there was no need for language, for the invention of tools.

It's not that the gorilla is incapable of doing these things: Gorillas in captivity have been seen using tools, using a stick to bring a bit of food into their cage, for instance. And at Stanford, a lowland gorilla named Koko has been taught to use sign language. She knows six hundred words, invents some of her own, and can construct coherent sentences.

Twenty years ago, Geroge Schaller wondered whether the life the gorilla chose, the provident life of the forest, was not an "evolutionary dead-end." I put this question to Sandy Harcourt, the director of the Karisoke Research Center, which stands in the shadow of Karisimbi, on the slopes of the dormant volcano called Visoke. "No," Sandy said, "the gorilla is not an evolutionary dead-end. The animal is perfectly adapted to the forest." True enough, but now it is the forest that is endangered.

Rwanda is a nation of subsistence farmers. There are over 5 million of them in a country the size of Maryland. If the rate of population increase remains constant, the population will double shortly after the year 2000. And there is simply no more land. Already some Rwandans are going hungry. The people who cut down the forests of Rwanda in order to survive are now looking to the forty-six-square-mile Volcano National Park for more land.

The government is committed to the park. It understands well enough that the decimation of the remaining forest will destroy the Virunga watershed and cause drought below. It knows that the gorillas can be habituated to the presence of man, and that they are a potential source of badly needed tourist revenue.

Still, the press for more land is going to be almost irresistible in the next few decades. "The gorilla will survive," Sandy Harcourt said, "if we just leave his habitat alone." Twenty years ago there were just about twice as many gorillas in Volcano National Park as there are today. The world lost half of them when half the park was turned over to cultivation about twelve years ago. It's a very simple equation.

The gorilla cannot, or will not, adapt to a life other than that of the forest. Other animals adapt: Coyotes manage to survive in Los Angeles; lions learn to herd their prey into newly constructed fences in Africa's game parks; and the people who live in the villages below Volcano National Park know how their fathers' fathers died on Karasimbi half a century ago, and that tragedy will never be repeated.

It was very cold atop Karasimbi. I thought of Mrithi and Mtoto, of Brutus and Beethoven, of the forty or so individual mountain gorillas I had met in the last month. The wind shrieked and howled among black twisted boulders, and I heard in it the soft sound of laughter, muffled by falling snow.

If the mountain gorilla survives, it may very well be due to the Mountain Gorilla Project. This organization provides funds for training park guards and pays for antipoaching patrols. The project feels education is its most important goal. Workers go out to the villages and schools around the Virungas, where they stress the importance of the forest watershed. The project also takes paying customers out to observe one of three habituated gorilla groups. This money goes to the Rwandan Office of National Parks and is funneled back into such activities as antipoaching training. Last year, for the first time in its history, the park made a small profit, and the government—one supposes—began to look more favorably on the idea of preserving the gorilla, if only as a source of badly needed revenue.

The international organizations that fund the Mountain Gorilla Project are the Flora and Fauna Preservation Society, the People's Trust for Endangered Species, the World Wildlife Fund, and, in the United States, the African Wildlife Leadership Foundation, which accepts donations at 1717 Massachusetts Avenue, N.W., Washington, D.C. 20056.

The Clam Scam

▲

The Tongan customs officer found something in my backpack that bothered him. He called over a man who appeared to be his superior, and as they sorted through my gear, the word *ratbag* passed between them.

Ratbag?

The first officer, a big huge powerful Polynesian giant of a man, had been shuffling through my underwear, swimsuits, diving equipment—all pretty much standard tourist gear—when he came upon a number of file folders located in the bottom of my backpack. The folders contained articles about Tonga, the idyllic South Pacific island kingdom located south and west of American Samoa and east of Fiji. It was this printed material that occupied the customs officials.

There was an article about the proud history of Tonga, the only South Pacific nation that has never been colonized by a European power. It all seemed pretty innocuous: a country of 170 islands located almost directly on the date line; a population of one hundred thousand people living on forty of the islands; four major island groups, with the government located on the island of Tongatapu.

I had also brought along several articles about Polynesia in

general, a few of which contained certain anthropological mus-
ings. Polynesian people, one theory ran, tend toward a certain
physical immensity due to their history of seafaring. Five thousand years ago the ancestors of the man currently pawing
through my effects had to cross vast expanses of empty seas in
open canoes. Survival, the theory went, favored men and women
of great upper-body strength: good paddlers. Additionally, a certain degree of fleshiness was necessary to withstand bitter wind
and cold rains.

Was I going to be denied entrance to the country because some
anthropologist had decided to comment on the size of the people?
It wasn't as if the article were titled "Tongans Are Great Big Fat-
ties." In addition, I had thought that physical size and prowess
were matters of some pride to Tongans. The current king,
Taufa'ahau Tupou IV, once weighed a properly regal 460
pounds. His Majesty—the first man in his nation's history to
graduate from college—is now in his seventies. Concerned about
his health, he has begun an exercise-and-diet plan and, according
to a three-year-old magazine piece, has lost at least one hundred
pounds. There were pictures of the king riding a specially made
bicycle, with panting bodyguards jogging alongside.

"You are interested in our government?" the customs official
asked, or words to that effect. Tongans speak Tongan, a Polynesian language of many vowels, few consonants, and plenty of
glottal stops. Most everyone in the kingdom speaks some English,
although not always with precision.

"I am here," I said, "to study giant clams."

The officials conferred together for some time. They spoke in
Tongan, but I gathered they were concerned about the fact that I
had a beard, carried a backpack, and was in possession of information relating to His Majesty, the king. Occasionally, in the
midst of a tangle of Tongan, I heard again, in English, the word
"ratbag."

Other people, those who hadn't thought to bring any reading
material about Tonga, were being waved through the line. I, on
the other hand, had taken pains to inform myself about the country and was, apparently, a ratbag.

Whatever that meant. Better, in this case, that the officials believe I was a scientist. I attempted to direct their attention to a number of scientific papers: "Prospects for the Commercial Cultivation of Giant Clams *(Bivalvia: Tridacnidae)*"; "*Tridacna derasa* Introduction in American Samoa"; "The Gastropod *Cymatium muricinum,* a Predator on Juvenile Tridacnid Clams."

Giant clams exist throughout the Pacific and Indian oceans. The largest, *Tridacna gigas,* can reach more than three feet in length and weigh in excess of two hundred pounds. In black-and-white movies, swimmers wearing sarongs get their feet stuck in giant clams, which, my experience would later prove, is sort of like grinding your arm all the way up to the elbow in a kitchen garbage disposal. It could happen to anyone—anyone at all with the brains of a cabbage.

At any rate, *T. gigas* doesn't exist in Tongan water. There are some *T. derasa,* which are about half the size of *gigas,* some smaller *T. squamosa,* and, smallest of all the Tongan giant clams, the oddly named *T. maxima.*

The customs officials examined these scientific papers, laden with bar graphs and pie charts, and seemed to relax a bit. Ratbags, I imagined, weren't interested in giant clams.

One of the officials was reading about the sexual habits of tridacnid mollusks, which are exceedingly complex, if not actually perverse. Giant clams begin their mature lives as males, but by about the age of four will produce eggs as well as sperm. As the clams get larger, they settle into a state of ecstatic female fertility: A single full-grown *T. derasa* can produce at least forty times as many eggs as a clam at first female maturity. I wondered if this kind of filth—a treatise about hermaphrodites—was the sort of thing ratbags had in their possession, and so I sought to divert the officials' attention by gibbering about other clam-related subjects. A giant clam, I explained, has symbiotic algae living in its mantle, a lining much like skin inside the shell. Unlike lesser clams, a giant lies on its back, open to the sun, which nourishes the algae. The algae live on sunlight and the clam's waste products; the clam lives on the algae's waste. This is probably why a giant clam becomes so big: The animal actually incorporates a handy photosynthetic food system into its own tissues. Giant clams literally farm their own algae.

"Good to eat," one of the officials said.

That was a problem I didn't want to get into at all. Because the clams grow best in shallow water, where the sunlight is brightest, they are easily harvested. In Tonga, one species of giant clam, *Hippopus hippopus,* was already extinct. *T. derasa* was endangered. Both these species had been an important source of food for the islanders since at least 1500 B.C. And now they were in danger of extinction. Which, I thought, said something depressing about the life of the sea in these parts altogether.

After successfully avoiding a discussion involving the decimation of an entire form of life, not to mention the disturbing sex life of bivalve mollusks, I was admitted to Tonga. I lugged my pack out into the humid night. What the hell, I wondered, was a ratbag?

Tonga's capital city, Nuku'alofa, on Tongatapu, has a main street of about six blocks lined with wooden buildings once painted white. There is the Sincere Variety Store, Tonga Radio, and John's Takeaway, where people sit on picnic benches and eat bowls of curry washed down with Coca-Cola. The name Nuku'alofa means "abode of love."

Several days after my arrival I had the good fortune to meet Tevita Helu in the best of the local bookstores. Mr. Helu, who had received a college degree in New Zealand, directed me to a number of books I might not have purchased on my own, including *The Life of the Late George Vason of Nottingham,* published in London in 1840. In 1796 Vason, an emissary for the London Missionary Society, traveled to Tonga, where he was to educate the heathen in the Christian faith. Vason chronicles a typical day among the Tongan men: "As soon as the morning dawned, they arose; and then took place the important ceremony of drinking kava and eating yams . . ."

Kava is a beverage derived from the root of a pepper plant and drunk for its tranquilizing effect. "They often drink kava from break of day to about eleven o'clock," observed Vason. "Then they go and lie down and sleep for two or three hours; when they rise, they bathe, walk among the plants, or amuse themselves in wrestling, boxing," or "an amusement" called *"furneefoo,"* which, as described by Vason, seemed to be a form of bodysurfing.

Because foreigners are known in Tonga as *palangi,* literally "skybreakers," some early visitors flattered themselves with the notion that Tongans regarded them as gods from above. Vason had no such illusions: "They called us 'men of the sky' because, observing that sky appeared to touch the ocean in the distant horizon, and knowing that we came from an immense distance, they concluded that we must have come through the sky."

Vason—and I think this is the reason Tevita Helu recommended the book—changed his name to Balo, wore native dress, took a number of wives, and lived the life of a Tongan chief. The book, written by missionaries after Vason's death, has him sermonizing at the end of each chapter in a manner that rings entirely false. To wit: "I lament to say that I now entered with the utmost eagerness into every pleasure and entertainment of the natives."

Personally, I don't think George did much lamenting at all. The pace of events in Tonga plods along pleasantly through the vastness of geologic time. It's *faka tonga,* the Tongan way: seductive, relaxing, easy.

Much has changed since the days of George Vason, but the people are still attractive and athletic. They revere their king and seem to delight in royal rituals. The best way to do something is the simplest and most obvious way, the Tongan way. Large, complex operations are seen as jarring to tradition. They are not *faka tonga.*

I had come to Tonga because of a hopeful article about giant-clam conservation in *Earthwatch* magazine. Earthwatch, a non-profit organization out of Watertown, Massachusetts, is involved in conservation efforts worldwide and helps preserve endangered species and habitats; it also supports archaeological digs in Mexico, Spain, Japan, and Chile. According to an Earthwatch promotional pamphlet, the programs "work a bit like the Peace Corps. We organize expeditions to research sites all over the world for leading scholars and scientists. We then recruit interested men and women like yourself who are willing to lend a hand by serving as staff volunteers."

Earthwatch also has its magazine. In the April 1990 issue there was a quarter-page article about the giant clams of Tonga, along with a picture of a snorkeler regarding a clam that looked to be several feet long.

The community giant-clam program, as funded by Earthwatch and supervised by Dr. Richard Chesher, was, it seemed, a good idea: simple, inexpensive, imminently workable, very *faka tonga*. Fishermen would collect endangered giant clams from outlying waters and arrange them in circles, in shallow water, in plain view of a village. A clam would issue sperm into the water, followed by eggs, which would trigger other clams to spew out sperm, then eggs. No matter which way the currents were flowing, the circular arrangement of the clams would make for fertilized eggs.

The village would be able to collect smaller clams in perpetuity, provided the larger clams in the sanctuary—the brood stock —remained unmolested. Honest fishermen would be warned off by the circles, which would be obviously man-made. Poachers would avoid taking clams because the circles were in plain sight of the village and belonged to the people there.

It seemed a hopeful story: an endangered species preserved at no cost to the Tongan people. And not only were the giant clams being preserved, but breeding success meant food for the people in the form of baby clams thrown off by the circle. The short article, entitled "Turning Around Extinction," was very nearly ecstatic about the project:

> For four seasons Earthwatch teams have monitored giant clam circles and encouraged a conservation ethic on these South Pacific islands. Now Dr. Richard Chesher has some extraordinary news: Tonga's endangered giant clams are breeding like crazy. Tongans had arranged the giant clams in circles to improve their breeding success several years ago but until this summer the circles that Chesher helped establish off the island of Falevai [actually Falevai is a village on the island of Kapa in the Vava'u island group] pro-

duced no offspring. Now Chesher reports 'a dramatic increase in both *Tridacna squamosa* and *Tridacna derasa*. . . .'

More importantly, the concept of community stewardship of the clam circles—central, in Chesher's view, to the clam circles' success and the environmental education of Tongans—seems to have caught on.

A biologist friend of mine believes some animals are naturally "fubsy," which is to say, in less than scientific terms, cute. The public at large loves fubsy animals. When our fubsy pals are endangered—when people go around braining baby harp seals with clubs—something snaps inside us. Some ancient instinct is outraged.

The great naturalist Konrad Lorenz tried to define that impulse and to quantify cuteness. He suggested that certain features of human babies, when evident in other creatures, trigger our maternal and paternal instincts, our need to care and protect. Among those features are "a relatively large head, predominance of the brain capsule, large and low-lying eyes, bulging cheek region, short and thick extremities, a springy elastic consistency, and clumsy movements."

By this definition, koala bears are fubsy. Baby seals are fubsy. Pandas. Puppies. Decidedly not fubsy are spiders, snakes, fleas. People the world over are not easily moved to preserve the odd endangered invertebrate.

More to the point, giant clams rate lower on the fubsy scale than even snail darters. Giant clams do not have large heads, or indeed any protuberance at all that we might identify as a head, which effectively eliminates a predominant brain capsule or bulging cheeks or low-lying eyes. Giant clams do not possess thick extremities, and they do not move in a clumsy manner. After the first week of life they generally don't move much at all. By the time they are adults, they just lie there, effectively headless. They are, for all intents and purposes, the very antithesis of fubsy.

And yet every one of the dozen Earthwatch volunteers I met on Vava'u (the main island in the group of the same name) was highly enthusiastic about giant clams. They actually used the word "cute." It was, I suppose, a case of "to know them is to love them."

Some of the volunteers were keen divers in their late teens and early twenties. Others were pushing seventy, but they all worked together. The volunteers had paid their own ways to Tonga—besides donating nearly two thousand dollars apiece to Earthwatch—and were living in a less-than-luxurious guest house that reminded me of a dormitory at a particularly Spartan Bible college. Most of these people had regular jobs and were spending their vacations working on this project. Most, like a former Peace Corps volunteer I met, were people who loved to travel and thought they needed to "give something back." By their example, these people thought, they were imparting a larger message about the life of the sea.

The best Earthwatch snorkelers combed the reefs around the Falevai clam circles on neighboring Kapa, where the first of the community circles had been introduced. They looked for juvenile giant clams, measured them, and made underwater notes on a chalkboard. The divers surfaced to signal the shore party, which used surveying equipment to take coordinates and positions. Because clams can swim for the first week or so of their lives, the teams were mapping clams for miles in every direction.

Everyone was excited about the work. They were finding dozens upon dozens of juvenile *T. derasa,* the most endangered of the clams. In 1987, before the clam circle was established at Falevai, Earthwatch teams had worked the very same reefs, establishing baseline data to see exactly how many baby clams might be found in the area if there were no clam circles. During that season divers had found no juvenile *T. derasa.* Not one. Zero.

The Tongans I met on Vava'u had come to respect the Earthwatch volunteers. Originally, during the initial stages of the experiment, Tongans had seen people diving, taking notes, working long hours, and they wondered, these Tongans, what sort of wealth comparatively rich Westerners planned to extract from their sea. That's why people worked in the sea: to take things from it. But over the years the people had come to appreciate the Earthwatch divers. The Tongans were even impressed, albeit in a vaguely amused manner, by the Earthwatch team's "conservation ethic."

It was a nice inspiring story, except that a distinguished scientist in the field, Dr. John S. Lucas, an associate professor of zoology at James Cook University of North Queensland, in Australia, seemed to have taken immediate and violent exception to Chesher's findings as noted in *Earthwatch* magazine. He fired off a letter to Mark Cherrington, the editor of *Earthwatch,* in which he questioned whether the clam circles of Falevai were turning around extinction. Indeed, he charged that they might be contributing to it.

One of the Earthwatch volunteers on Vava'u had a copy of the letter. In it, Lucas identified himself as coordinator of an international project investigating the mariculture of giant clams. He had, in that capacity, worked with the fisheries department of Tonga to adapt an existing clam hatchery in Sopu, near the capital, to the needs of his project. (In such a situation clams are raised in cement "raceways" in a shore-based laboratory, then released into the sea.) More to the point, Lucas and a scientific liaison officer, Dr. Rick Braley, had visited Tonga in April 1990. Braley had traveled to Falevai and inspected the clam circles, where, Lucas said, "There was certainly no evidence of 'dramatic increase in both *Tridacna squamosa* and *Tridacna derasa*' nor of 'breeding like crazy' as was reported in *Earthwatch*."

Dr. Lucas complained that "several giant clam circles, which I understand were established with Dr. Chesher's involvement, resulted in the clams being poached. If there has only been a slight recruitment [increase in baby clams], if any, as a result of the surviving giant clam circle, the net result of Dr. Chesher's efforts so far may be that there are fewer giant clams. . . .

"My concern here is accurate reporting," Lucas wrote, and went on to point out "another misleading aspect" of the *Earthwatch* article. "The species pictured in the photograph . . . has not been reported from Tonga. It is *Tridacna gigas* and this species is much larger than the species that occur in Tonga."

I asked a few of the Earthwatch volunteers if the letter wasn't a bit disheartening. They each had shelled out a lot of money to bring these clams back from the brink of extinction, and here was Dr. Lucas, a man who really ought to know, suggesting that they were getting bamboozled by a charlatan, a fraud preying on their demonstrably good hearts.

No one was upset by the letter, and in point of fact Chesher had given it to them along with a stack of scientific reports and general articles on giant clams. The volunteers were convinced that their work was both important and successful.

"We're finding juvenile *derasa*," one woman said. "Lots of them."

"Okay," I said, "but what about this charge that Chesher's faking pictures?"

There was some general laugher.

"That clam's still here. It's out in the circle at Falevai," someone said. There were, I was shown, a number of easily identifiable differences between *T. gigas* and *T. derasa*. See for yourself, the volunteers said.

Which is what I decided to do.

When we first came here," Richard Chesher said, "the Tongan attitude was essentially that God put the creatures there on the reef and that people could go and take what they wanted and God would replace it."

It was an easy way to think of the sea. It was *faka tonga*.

We were sitting on Chesher's boat, the *Moira*, a forty-four-foot cutter anchored just off the island of Vava'u. Chesher, an engaging and tireless talker, was talking clams.

As fishermen began to avail themselves of certain technologies — outboard motors, diving equipment, reef-walking shoes—the resources had dwindled. "So the attitude was," Chesher said, "if I don't take it, the next guy will. As a result of this, the giant clams rarely get to a size where they are breeding females."

Chesher, an American, had been sailing around the Pacific since 1969, working on various environmental and scientific programs. The *Moira* was a research vessel, sure, he said, but that didn't mean he and Frederica Lesne (known as Captain Freddie) couldn't anchor in some private cover and swim naked with the dolphins. And, looking back on it, the time they had to outrun pirates off the Chinese coast made a good story. Chesher's tales— lots of them—involve that kind of rollicking adventure. He seems to be a man who likes a challenge, and some of his campaigns have been political as well as scientific. Several years ago, for instance, he spearheaded a successful effort to end dolphin shows in part of Australia. The media were helpful, and Chesher spoke out on the subject at many public meetings—at which he was often introduced, to his embarrassment, as "the controversial Dr. Chesher."

A Ph.D. marine biologist and a former Harvard professor, Chesher refuses to collect and dissect animals for study. Oh, he dissected his share of marine life on the path to his doctorate. And sure, he learned in the process. But there came a time when he began to see the dissection as a sort of science at odds with his sense of the sea. Freddie helped him out a little on that. Not being a Ph.D. marine biologist, she didn't understand why you had to kill something to study it. Every time Rick tried to explain what he was doing, his words rang hollow. So he simply quit killing animals in order to save them. It was, in a way, a spiritual decision.

Many of the projects Chesher has been involved in have had to do with the conservation of life, the future health of the sea. The more he thought about programs and the waste often involved in aid and funding, the more he realized he needed a formula to evaluate the success of an environmental project. That formula seemed self-evident: "A successful environmental program is one that alters the behavior of the people in such a way that you have measurable improvement in the flora and fauna."

Altering the behavior of the people: not something ordinarily taught in marine biology. Chesher was a scientist, but, especially in developing countries, he saw no way to separate biology and sociology.

In the South Pacific the traditional measure for success of aid programs is a report at the end of a workshop. It's paper. But in Tonga the government had sponsored an environmental-awareness week since 1984. During that week the islands were cleaned up and trees were planted. It met Chesher's definition.

A Tongan official in the Ministry of Lands, Survey, and Natural Resources, however, fretted that while much was being done for the land, nothing was being done for the sea. Did Chesher have any ideas?

Indeed he did. Once, in the Solomon Islands, he had come across a place where villagers kept large concentrations of mature, breeding giant clams. "They went out to get the clams in calm weather," said Chesher, "then put them near the village. When the wind kicked up, they had these clams as an emergency food supply. But what happened was, over the years, having all these large adults in close proximity to one another, there were so many small ones everywhere that the people never had to touch the big ones."

Something like that, Dr. Chesher suggested, might work in Tonga. No one else thought it would. People believed that big tasty clams placed in close proximity to villages would be promptly eaten. Indeed, in nearby American Samoa, the principal cause of "clam mortality" in a mariculture program was theft. The Tongan official himself was skeptical.

"Our goal," Chesher said, "was to change the cultural behavior of the people and leave. Walk away. Leave a big population of giant clams sitting in shallow water protected by the will of the community."

"Community" is the operative word. The government couldn't do it; individuals couldn't do it. The clams could be protected only by the will of the community.

It was decided that there would be a contest in the Vava'u island group. Divers from each island would go out and get clams, and local businesses would pay market value for them, plus small cash prizes for the fishermen who brought back the most *T. derasa*. "That meant," Chesher said, "that when they came in, the whole community bought the clams, and they belonged to everyone."

There were so few clams near the populated islands that the fishermen had to travel hours to scour far outlying reefs. Meanwhile, Chesher and several groups of Earthwatch volunteers were doing baseline studies, counting the number of clams to be found in waters around the near islands. Only four adult *T. derasa* were found in seven months of surveys. And not a single juvenile.

In January 1988 some fifty big *T. derasa* were arranged in the first community circles, just off the shores of Falevai. Twenty more adult clams were added later. Chesher, with help from the Tongan government, launched a cultural offensive. There were newspaper articles about the importance of clam brood stock. There were town meetings. One problem was that the Tongan language has no polite word for sperm. Every time the substance was mentioned, there were guffaws to the degree that people lost the thread of the argument.

Then Chesher hit on the idea of a professionally produced videotape. About 30 percent of Tongan homes have VCRs, and one estimate has it that there is one video rental store for every twenty-five hundred Tongans. A video, Chesher reasoned, could put across complex biological ideas with pictures.

The video was an immediate success. There were no Hollywood stars in this production, no *palangi* at all, only Tongans explaining reproductive biology. His Majesty, the king, appeared at the end of the video and said, in his great resonant voice, that with a project like clam sanctuaries, "everybody wins." It was all so easy, so *faka tonga.*

The tape was played in schools, in villages, and it was rented with astounding regularity. People wanted to see their friends. They wanted to see a professional video that had to do with them, with Tonga. They especially enjoyed seeing the king chuckle in the middle of one comment. That section was rolled back and replayed constantly. Most people see the king only at ceremonial events, at which tradition requires that he be appropriately solemn. But here he was endorsing the community clam-circle idea, admonishing people to protect the brood stock, and laughing at the same time.

In October 1988, ten months after installing the sanctuary at Falevai, Earthwatch volunteers found the first juvenile *T. derasa* they'd ever seen in the inner waters. It was within thirty feet of the giant-clam circles, but there was no definite connection between the juvenile and the circles. The clams, remember, can swim for the first week of life, which meant that this one might have started miles away.

A year later, Chesher's Earthwatch teams, returning for another survey, found sixteen juvenile *T. derasa* right smack in front of Falevai. "They were all of a certain size that indicated they'd come from the first spawning," Chesher said. "Clams grow at about five millimeters a month, and these were all between eighty and one hundred millimeters long. They had to come from the first spawning in January of 1988. Right number of months, right size."

I asked Chesher about Dr. Lucas's charge that there was "no evidence" that the clams were "breeding like crazy."

"Well," Chesher said, " 'breeding like crazy' is not how I'd put it. But there is evidence that they're breeding."

I asked to see that evidence, the raw data, in his field notes. Chesher handed me eleven notebooks of the kind sold in Tongan bookstores: "Friendly Islands School Exercise Book." One was labeled "Finders, '90." The raw data was entered in several different colors of ink, and a few notes were penciled in. On July 13 Earthwatch volunteers had found a 78.5-millimeter *T. derasa* at Port Maurelle. I flipped through the pages: On August 23, at South Mala, near Falevai, ten *T. derasa* juveniles, ranging in size from 48 millimeters to 115 millimeters, were found. At least two different spawning periods were represented in that batch. In all, seventy-four juvenile *T. derasa* were found in 1990, where none had been discovered in the baseline surveys conducted in 1987.

I gave the notebooks back to Chesher and asked him about the letter Lucas sent to Earthwatch. From that followed a long, convoluted tale of what Rick Chesher saw as a case of scientific sabotage in the South Seas.

"But," he said after several hours, "you can ask Dr. Lucas about all that."

"I will," I said. "I also want to see the clam in question, the one Dr. Lucas said is not from Tonga."

"Tomorrow," Rick Chesher said. He was all smiles.

The night before my visit to the clams of Falevai, I sat in on a kava circle. Kava is completely legal in Tonga, and there is sometimes a full cup of the stuff sitting in official offices, there for the visitor afflicted with a *palangi*'s unseemly swiftness of manner.

The kava club was a single-story cement building; in it were a dozen men sitting in a circle on the floor. I recognized a shop-keeper and a cabdriver I had met. The men accepted me immedi-ately and passed a wooden bowl containing a light gray liquid that tasted a bit like dirty dishwater and set my lips buzzing. Other than that, it had no effect on me whatsoever.

What did I think of Tonga?

Loved it.

The women?

Beautiful.

No trouble?

No, no, not a bit. *Faka tonga* all the way. Well, except for the airport. There had been some problem with my reading material. The officers, I informed the men of the kava circle, were talking about ratbags.

And the word sailed around the room in ever-decreasing circles so that, in the kava-colored silence, I asked, as politely as I knew how, if someone would please tell me what the hell a ratbag was.

My mouth was now tingling in the frozen manner I associate with the dentist's office. We had been drinking kava, which didn't affect me at all, for hours. I wanted to say something else, but it suddenly occurred to me that my tongue was a huge fat flap of flesh that occupied my entire mouth. I couldn't seem to get any words out around the great globular thing. The effort made me drowsy.

The men of the kava circle, I realized simultaneously, were the very finest men who had ever lived. They were talking to me about ratbags, and I heard them through a somewhat distant echo chamber. They spoke of a number of young men from New Zealand who had been members of some strange religious orga-nization. They had worn beards and carried backpacks. They had known something of the government of Tonga and had gone about spreading rumors that there would be a coup. Which was ridiculous, for people revered and even loved the king. Tevita Helu, my bookstore friend, had said that while other island na-tions were changing rapidly, often not for the better, Tonga had retained much of its traditional culture—the weaving, the singing, the dancing, the feasting—because all these traditions were incorporated into royal rituals. Tongans, Mr. Helu had said, liked that.

The kava men agreed that the king was cherished and said that this reverence was why the rumors of a coup had upset people and why the bearded backpackers had been asked to leave the country. Someone mentioned that it was the men themselves who had referred to their rumor-mongering as ratbagging. A ratbag, the extremely wonderful gentlemen of the kava circle explained through the echo chamber, was in their opinion someone whose methods were aggressive, disruptive, and altogether something less than *faka tonga.*

It was raining hard, and I was hunched over in an open boat on my way to Falevai to interview the clam in question. From a distance the island of Kapa was an undulating delight of shimmering green hillsides, with limestone cliffs at the waterline. The village was set on a narrow sandy beach with the jungle rising up behind it. About two hundred people lived in Falevai.

The man who had taken charge of the clam circles was a former district officer named Vanisi Fakatulolo. He was a large, intimidating man with a sweet smile and biceps the size of my thighs. Inside his cement house he brewed me up a cup of tea on a kerosene stove. There were chickens clucking and muttering in a back room with a mud floor. Shiny paper stars and crosses hung from the wall, giving the house a festive, Christmasy look. Somewhere, in a back room, a baby fussed.

Mr. Fakatulolo said that, for the first time in his life, there were baby giant clams all over the reef in front of his house.

How many?

"Plenty, plenty."

He said that a year ago a few men from the village had gotten swacked on kava and had poached five giant clams from the sanctuary. Fakatulolo had gotten angry and had "raised a big force." He was a lay preacher at the church and had excoriated the men from the pulpit. For a time these men had lived in shame, a powerfully corrosive emotion in a small Tongan village: People accused in such a way sometimes actually commit suicide.

Since then there had been no other thefts, but it was because of the poached clams, five out of seventy-two, that Dr. Lucas of Australia had written Earthwatch and suggested that Chesher's project might be hastening the demise of the giant clams.

Not long after the poaching, Fakatulolo said, a man from Australia had come and asked to inspect the clam circles. The man dived for less than thirty minutes. (This man, I gathered, was Dr. Rick Braley, who, according to Lucas, had found no evidence that *T. derasa* were "breeding like crazy.")

Braley told Fakatulolo that "maybe the baby clams he see come from the rock." Fakatulolo did not speak good English: By "rock" he meant "reef." Dr. Braley was probably telling him that the new baby clams might have swum over from elsewhere on the reef, from other adult clams not in the circle. (Braley, I later learned, had not seen the baseline studies indicating that there were virtually no other adult clams nearby.)

Fakatulolo got the idea that Braley was telling him the reef had spit up the clams by some sort of spontaneous generation. This irritated him, and he put the Ph.D. straight in no uncertain terms. "The man," Fakatulolo said, "he borned the man. The fish, he borned the fish. The clam, he borned the clam. The rock, he no borned the clam."

Rick Chesher was still furious about the visit. "This goes beyond academic bickering," he fumed. "When you go to the villagers who are involved in this awareness project and tell them it's not working, what happens? What can you expect will happen? People will simply go take the big clams. Luckily, Vanisi knew better."

Indeed, Fakatulolo had noticed over the past few years that fishing was getting better and better in front of the village. In his opinion it had to do with the clam circles. There was no reason people couldn't fish with a net over the circles—that was acceptable—but no one did. "They think," Fakatulolo explained, "that if someone sees them there in the day, and then later maybe someone takes the clams at night, they will get blamed." So the people of Falevai had created, almost accidently, a small marine reserve. And now they were catching more fish, closer to the village. The "conservation ethic" was paying off.

"We used to break the rock," Mr. Fakatulolo said. People had used iron bars, he explained, to break the reef structures and drive fish into nets. "I think now, if you break my house down, I do not come back here to live. Same with fishes."

It was as Dr. Chesher had said: The community clam sanctuary was "a beginning, a way of raising consciousness."

I dived on the Falevai Circle and counted nineteen juvenile *T. derasa* in two breathhold dives. I visited the clam in question: the one Dr. Lucas had identified as *T. gigas*. No doubt about it, it was *T. derasa:* the smoothness of the shell, the number of interlocking teeth, the size.

The largest *T. derasa* lay open on their backs, exposing their mantles to the light. Some of the mantles were bright or dark blue, with a yellow pattern that looked a bit like the whorls of fingerprints. Most had yellowish tiger stripes on the rims of their shells. They were colorful and interesting and not very cuddly.

Later I dived at nearby Port Maurelle, looking for more juveniles thrown off by the Falevai circle. The water was shallow, and I could see waves breaking above me as I drifted through multicolored corals where such scenic fish as Moorish idols, butterfly fish, and great schools of blue jacks were busy making a living.

I was scanning the bottom for juvenile *T. derasa,* concentrating fiercely and ignoring the schools of jacks that were swimming past my face in the way that flocks of birds sometimes swoop in front of your windshield. Suddenly, the bottom dropped out of the ocean, and a black abyss opened up below. Whoa . . .

After the first few hours I found myself not really looking much anymore. Searching for clams a couple of inches long and buried in deep coral is hard work. I listened to the rain hiss on the surface above, powered out over the drop-offs for a quick adrenaline rush, and swam at top speed toward coral knobs, pulling up at the last minute like a jet just clearing the trees at the end of the runway.

That's what I was doing, pulling up with my mask inches from the coral, when I saw a tiny *T. derasa* everyone had missed. Rick Chesher swam over, measured it with calipers, mapped its position, and said that this six-month-old tridacnid bivalve mollusk would be known, henceforth, as Tim. Tim, as might be expected, was not a fubsy individual.

I spoke with Dr. Lucas on the phone. It took quite some time to explain Rick Chesher's ideas about sabotage. Chesher had told me that he had no objection to the Lucas-led clam mariculture project and indeed believed that a mariculture program and the clam-circle concept complemented each other. He had, however, been stunned when Lucas wrote to Earthwatch.

"Dr. Chesher," I said, "wondered why you didn't write him, instead of his funding organization."

"I was interested," Lucas said, "in journalistic accuracy."

"But you were wrong about the picture of the clam," I pointed out. "It was *T. derasa,* not *T. gigas.*"

Lucas said that he had made a mistake, and that the photograph, taken with a wide-angle lens, had made the clam look larger than it was. He seemed to regard this as some kind of trick, although he said that after another look at the picture, he had written a second letter to Earthwatch apologizing for his earlier inaccuracy. (Mark Cherrington, the editor of *Earthwatch* magazine, described that letter as "one of the most ungracious apologies I've ever read.")

The meat of Chesher's accusations, I explained to Lucas, came down to money. Chesher's own project wasn't cheap: $106,000 from Earthwatch for the four-year start-up. But his was not, he said, like many traditional South Pacific aid programs that "recycle" money between the aid program and the donor governments without much of it reaching the people. His project was simple, it involved the community on a grass-roots level, and now that the clams were breeding, he could do what he had said he would do: walk away and leave it all to the people.

Lucas's mariculture project, funded jointly by the Australian Center for International Agricultural Research (ACIAR) and James Cook University of North Queensland, was, Chesher charged, somewhat more complex. I knew that the initial research-and-development phase of the project (involving Fiji, the Philippines, and Papua New Guinea) had been approved in March 1984 and that expenditures for the first three years were estimated at \$836,245 Australian (about \$650,000 U.S.). Lucas's current budget for another three-year phase was reportedly \$1.8 million Australian (about \$1.4 million U.S.), split among mariculture facilities in five South Pacific nations. Chesher thought that this was a lot of money—even if the Tongan hatchery in Sopu received only a portion of it—and that Lucas saw any successful clam-conservation project as a threat to his funding.

The reasoning went like this: Mariculture works, but it is expensive and complicated. There are a land-based hatchery and cement raceways to be built, maintained, and guarded twenty-four hours a day. Clams grown in the raceways must be returned to the ocean in plastic-mesh containers ("predator exclusion trays") to grow a bit larger before being released onto the reef. But any time you put an unnatural concentration of living things on the reef, you will attract predators. In addition, the little buggers in the ocean nurseries are susceptible to certain parasitic organisms that must be picked out by hand, twice a week in some seasons. These clams, as the experience in American Samoa has shown, are also objects of temptation to local people. They get pulled up in their plastic boxes and eaten for lunch.

These are problems Lucas's mariculture project would address. But research money is hard to come by. What if ACIAR saw a relatively cheap, effective alternative that, not incidentally, raised the awareness of the local people and created a de facto system of marine reserves? Chesher believed that Lucas saw the clam sanctuary concept as a threat to his funding, to the millions of dollars that had been put into the program in Tonga and elsewhere.

To defuse that threat, Chesher believed, Lucas had attempted to discredit Chesher with Earthwatch and, most galling, to undermine the program with the people it would benefit.

Dr. Lucas denied these allegations and said his actions involved scientific credibility and journalistic accuracy. Truth was very important to him, he said. And indeed, after consulting with Rick Braley, he said that Braley had never spoken with Vanisi Fakatulolo, aside from asking him for permission to dive at Falevai.

Then who was this Australian scientist that Fakatulolo had been talking about?

Lucas didn't know. But, he wondered, what did it matter, anyway? "If Dr. Braley had seen little evidence of giant-clam recruitment and reported this to a local authority, would it have been wrong for him to be telling truthfully what he had seen?"

Well—completely aside from the fact that Dr. Braley had never seen the baseline studies and that he would be basing his report about a four-year program on one half-hour dive—yes, one would think it would be wrong.

I spent my last day in Tonga back on Tongatapu with Tevita Helu, who took me to the southern coast of the island to see the magnificent Houma blowholes just at sunset, as the tide was pounding into the shore. The beach was a raised coraline limestone platform that extended ten feet above the level of the sea. As the waves came in, they pounded into the cliff face, where there were a number of natural vents. Great plumes of water erupted out of the top of the limestone bench. There were hundreds of them, some a hundred feet high. They reminded me of the eruptions at Old Faithful in Yellowstone, except that they all fired at once, all up and down the deserted beach for miles. When the sea fell back from the wall, the spouts faltered, and there was the sound of a hard rain falling.

Mr. Helu wanted to know what I had learned in Vava'u. I told him about the clam circles and about Dr. Chesher and Dr. Lucas. Helu had once taught in the Tongan school system and felt he knew something about Tongan attitudes. People would simply take the clams, for that's the way it was in Tonga. He said this with some sadness. The people just wouldn't understand. It would take a generation before Tongans grasped the concept of a marine reserve, much less the idea of an inviolable brood stock.

But, I explained, the sanctuary at Falevai was intact. People were not taking the clams. Indeed, the success of the project at Falevai had been noted throughout Vava'u. Ten other villages had asked the government for assistance in creating their own clam circles. On the island of Taunga, one village had arranged its brood-stock circles in such a way that they spelled out a word.

"What word?" Helu asked.

"Ongomatu'a," I said.

Helu stared at me for some time, shaking his head, as if in disbelief. A slow, proud smile pulled at the corners of his mouth, and suddenly his face lit up brighter than the setting sun.

Ongomatu'a.

Parents.

Another breaker hit the cliff, and hundreds of waterplumes took on the gaudy tropical colors of the sky.

"This Dr. Lucas," Helu said, "I think he is an evil man."

There was the hard patter of falling water as the sea pulled back from the land.

"No, not evil," I said. "Just a bit of a ratbag."

THE NATURAL WORLD

▲

Lechuguilla

▲

I loved this little room, one thousand feet below the surface of the earth. It had been my home for four days, and these last black seven or eight hours would be my final chance to savor the wonder. Alone.

The passage itself was tubular, about eight feet in diameter, and it was perfectly white, very crystalline, so that the walls and ceiling all shone glittery bright in the light from my helmet. The heat from my body loosened a few of the crystals from the ceiling so it looked as if it were snowing in Lechuguilla Cave.

The crystals were talclike gypsum, and the room was composed entirely of the stuff. I was sitting on my bed, an inflatable mattress, waiting until I stopped sweating.

Lechuguilla is a hot cave. The temperature is a constant 68 degrees, and the humidity is over 99 percent. The smallest effort causes a caver to burst into a sweat, and I had found, over the past few days of strenuous exploration, that the sweating process continued for about forty-five minutes after I stopped moving.

Because almost nothing lives in the cave—there are a few crickets near the entrance, no bats at all, and a host of invisible microorganisms—Lechuguilla was devoid of the familiar odors of life and death that permeate the outside world. The air smelled clean, wet, and sterile, like freshly washed laundry, and it had a weight and feel to it, like the gentle caress of damp black velvet.

I liked camping alone in the cave, in the gypsum snow. I had never had any trouble sleeping in the silence and absolute darkness of Lechuguilla, probably because I was always so exhausted at the end of each day. There were, I knew, seven other cavers nearby. Some slept in groups; some, like myself, preferred solitary camping on the hard, sloping rock floors.

We had all eaten dinner together: freeze-dried food that we rehydrated and spooned up straight from the foil pack. My companions were among America's most noted cavers, and the topic of conversation was Lechuguilla Cave. We talked about "new leads," which might open up into huge undiscovered rooms. Such rooms could contain geological wonders that might keep the scientists at their microscopes for decades. These were quite realistic expectations.

Lechuguilla was discovered only four years ago, and it was unique in its size, in its origin, and in the strange formations found in its immense caverns.

I have been caving, in a desultory fashion, on and off, for about ten years. Still, Lechuguilla had been a surprise. It was so big, so hot, so intimidating, that it had taken me several days to come to something close to full comprehension of its marvels: Crystals the size of small trees, forests of aragonite flowers, huge-domed pits, rooms as high as a thirty-story building. That so many wonders existed in such profusion in one cave boggled the mind.

My dinner companions gibbered on about what further marvels Lechuguilla might offer. For the eight thousand or so active cavers in the United States, exploring caves is often a life-consuming passion. Men like the legendary Colorado caver Donald Davis describe it as the only activity in which a person of modest means can actually explore the unknown. Davis, who has personally mapped much of Lechuguilla, calls it "the cave I have been looking for my entire caving career."

It was, I thought listening to just this kind of talk over a gluey freeze-dried macaroni dinner, as if someone had discovered the Grand Canyon in this day and age. In the summer of 1990 it was a staggering idea. The entire surface of the earth has been mapped. Some few areas are little known, but they have been photographed from planes or satellites. The moon has been mapped.

But here, under the surface of the American desert, on national park land, only three miles from Carlsbad Caverns, a new cave had been discovered. The only entrance to Lechuguilla is set in a spare desert canyon alive with low scrub: with creosote, prickly pear, and lechuguilla, which is a foot-high plant with pulpy green leaves so sharp they can cut through a pair of pants. The canyon takes its name from the lechuguilla plant, and the cave takes its name from the canyon.

This new cave is big: It drops 1,501 feet and is the deepest cave in America. When I made my first descent, 48.1 miles of it had been mapped, but explorers—pioneer cavers, my dinner companions—add more passage to the map with each expedition.

Exploring Lechuguilla Cave requires some technical rope work. There are free-fall rope ascents and descents of two hundred feet and more, and all this work is done in the dark.

The entrance is a seventy-foot rappel followed by another very short rappel, and a downhill walk that culminates at Boulder Falls, a 150-foot rappel that drops free—the rope merely dangles in the darkness of underground space—for most of the way.

Just past Boulder Falls, about hour or so into the trip, there is a block of gypsum the size of a twenty-story building laid on its side. From below, looking up, I could see that the hard white mineral followed the descending flow of the cave, like a glacier dropping out of a mountain valley. Smaller blocks of gypsum were falling away from the central mountain, falling away in the slow-motion vastness of geologic time; falling away like icebergs calving off a tidewater glacier. The room itself is called Glacier Bay.

In ten years of caving I had never seen anything at all like Glacier Bay. My companions, Rick Bridges and Anne Strait, were veteran Lechuguilla cavers, and they dashed by the glacier with hardly a second look. There was, I thought, a clear implication of other, more awesome treasures below. In most American caves, Glacier Bay would be a destination, not just a sight to be contemplated in passing.

The trail dropped out of Glacier Bay, and the big passages ended abruptly. Ahead, there was a great cleft in the mountain, a split that was often no wider than a man's shoulders. This area, the Rift, is set at an angle that varies from sixty-five to eighty-five degrees. I moved through it leaning to the left, climbing up over rocks that were wedged along the way. Where there were no rocks under us, we moved across narrow ledges, and when I looked down, my light was swallowed by the darkness. It was better not to look down.

Nothing about the cave was terribly technical—not the rope work, not the climbing—but it never let up, never gave me a break. A typical move might be likened to, say, getting up on a small table, crawling across, then getting down. Easy, unless you have to do it fifty times in a row, in the dark, with a fifty-foot drop under you. My forty-pound pack was hateful.

I found I required two headbands to soak up the sweat dripping into my eyes. There were sharp gypsum crystals under my soaking-wet T-shirt, and, worse, there were more crystals in my shorts. My eyes were already red-rimmed from salty sweat. I was, I realized, four hours into the first trip, badly chafed, and already totally exhausted.

The passages led downward through a series of rope drops, a painful crawl-through passage called the Tinsel Town Maze, and a long stand-up passage that opened up into an enormous cavern, the Chandelier Ballroom. Immense crystals of gypsum hung from the sloping ceiling like baroque drunken stalactites. At their base the crystals were as thick as the trunks of small trees, and they swept down off the stone in ragged arcs. Some of them were eighteen and twenty feet long. They were powdery white at their thickest upper reaches, but down toward the tips, some of which were at eye level, they began branching out, like elk antlers or claws. The tips were clear, crystalline, and there were tiny globules of water hanging from the ends of most of them.

It is estimated that there are about fifty of these formations over ten feet long in the cavern called the Chandelier Ballroom. They are the largest such crystals to be found anywhere. The chandeliers are like the geysers of Yellowstone Park: They are the jewels of this cave, its world-class wonders.

That first night I collapsed in my gypsum-snow cave, not far from the Chandelier Ballroom. Alone in the darkness, in the silence, I lay in a light jungle sleeping bag and slept for twenty hours. Lechuguilla required, I discovered, stamina as well as certain technical skills.

When I was finally able to walk again, my companions and I set off to look for "leads" in some of the known rooms. Rick Bridges and Anne Strait took me to a cavern called Darktown, below the bright layer of glittering gypsum.

"Look around you," Bridges said, and when I did, I could see hints of shimmering metallic glitter in my light. There were, I finally saw, thin strands of clear gypsum crystal, called angel hair, hanging all across the expanse of this huge dark room. The angel hair looked a bit like the tinsel you might hang on a Christmas tree, but it was clear, and some of the strands were thirty feet long. It was an incredibly fragile room, and walking too rapidly through it could create a breeze that might snap the delicate strands of angel hair. Nothing at all like these elongated crystals is known to exist anywhere else.

On another day we left the Chandelier Ballroom through a low-crawling passage that led to the Prickly Ice Cube Room. The ceiling of the room was as high as a twenty-story building. The floor was littered with gypsum blocks that had calved off of another gypsum glacier perhaps thirty-five feet high. Drops of water falling from the ceiling had eroded away the tops of the blocks, creating little spikes that stuck up eight and ten and twelve inches. From above, the white blocks looked like huge prickly ice cubes.

We caught up with another team of cavers, including Patty Kambesis, Chris Stein, and *National Geographic* photographer Nick Nichols. The combined teams were crawling through what is called a boneyard maze, a series of dry, dusty passages that wound around and over and through each other like tunnels in an anthill. At one point there was a walking passage that skirted a funnellike pit that dropped off into darkness. I slipped, fell, and began sliding rapidly.

The funnel was a foot deep in powdery "rock flour," and I was sliding down on my belly, not entirely uncomfortable, although the events of the immediate future concerned me. Patty Kambesis was below me, and she reached out a hand. Patty weighs one hundred pounds. I weigh two hundred, and had gathered a bit of momentum. It occurred to me, in passing, that if I took Patty's hand, I'd pull her down with me, and she would share my uncertain future. I declined her offer, rather gallantly, I thought.

A sharp rock ripped through my T-shirt and gashed my chest. I could now see that there was a low archway just below. I got a leg up and managed to stop myself—bam!—like that.

Everyone was looking at me, and the combined force of the lights on their helmets felt hot, like fire. I wasn't badly hurt, only embarrassed.

Cavers wear message T-shirts that emphasize the individual's responsibility to move through passages safely: IF YOU DIE, WE SPLIT UP YOUR GEAR.

And yet, had I so much as broken an ankle, the two teams would have struggled for days to pull me up the ropes and through the Rift. It wouldn't have been any fun for anyone, but they would have done it.

"I'm okay," I said quickly.

Chris Stein, who was closest, took my hand and pulled me out of the rock flour. "Hey," he said by way of comment on the acrobatic nature of my fall, "the Romanian judge gave you a nine-point-six."

After two hours in the dry, dusty boneyard maze, we ducked under a stone archway and stood on the shores of Lake Castrovalva. It was sixty feet to the opposite shore. The water was twenty feet deep, and it glittered and shimmered in my light like a pool of liquid sapphire. We stripped off our filthy clothes so as not to foul the pool and swam to the far shore. The banks were smooth and reddish brown, so delicate and crystalline that we walked over them barefoot.

The ceiling was hung with white stone icicles and with long, thin white columns that looked like giant soda straws. To my right, the far reddish-brown bank rose up in a sloping hillside that was guarded by huge formations that looked like otherworldly pagodas or huge melted Buddhas.

The most fantastic formations, however, were under water. Circular stone lily pads, some of them ten feet in diameter, stood just under the surface of the turquoise water. They were balanced, like tables, on stone columns that extended from the floor of the pool. These shelf stone lily pads were reddish brown, but their outer edges were scalloped in a slightly thicker smooth white stone, like buttery frosting.

I stood barefoot on the smooth bank and thought that Castrovalva was the most beautiful place I had ever been.

That night, I sat on my inflatable mattress in my snow cave and waited to stop sweating. The conversation over dinner had been a familiar one: cave preservation, and what explorers can do to minimize their own impact on the cave.

The cavers wear nonmarking boots—the kind of shoes you must wear on a gymnasium floor—rather than mar flowstone floors. In places like Castrovalva people go barefoot or wear clean sneakers they carry in their packs for the purpose. The pools, which are still and clear, are not for bathing. The project even puts clean pitchers nearby so the water isn't fouled by organic material in a canteen. (The only exception to the no-swimming policy is when a pool must be swum for the purposes of exploration.)

Cavers moving through Lechuguilla routinely—I saw it over and over again—take difficult handholds on crumbly rock rather than grab a sturdy stalagmite and dirty it with muddy gloves.

Because there is little organic life in the cave, human waste does not biodegrade. It must be carried out. We all developed our own methods for dealing with the problem. Some cavers didn't want to talk about waste disposal; others found it necessary to discuss the matter over dinner. Every night.

I thought about conservation in the gently falling gypsum snow, then slipped into my bag, put my head on my pack, and slept for eight hours without moving.

We left about noon the next day, and long before I was in the entrance pit, I could smell the sweet odor of life in the desert canyon above. Rick Bridges and I climbed out of the pit on separate ropes, side by side. We wore mechanical ascenders on our feet that allowed us to literally walk up the rope.

We pulled ourselves over the lip of the pit and sat in the moonlight, savoring the odor of life. Rick and I discussed our plans for the next few weeks. As the director of the Lechuguilla Cave Project, a group formed to study and explore the cave, Rick had organized an expedition of exploration for the week after next. The goal was to explore and map enough of Lechuguilla to bring the total mapped miles to fifty. Two dozen cavers from all over America were expected to help "push" Lechuguilla the necessary 1.9 miles. Rick was a bit nervous about the expedition: He had already invited the superintendent of Carlsbad Caverns National Park and the mayor of Carlsbad to the gala fifty-mile celebration.

Most of the world's caves were formed in a gentle, timeless process.

Water flowing on the surface of limestone hills passes through the topsoil, where it absorbs carbon dioxide from rotting organic material and forms carbonic acid. This is a very weak acid: It is present, for instance, in carbonated soft drinks.

But limestone is slightly soluble in carbonic acid, and over the millenia, this rather anemic acid, seeping into the cracks and fissures of humped-up limestone beds, melts out caverns and chambers and passages and pits in the solid rock. Most of the dissolved limestone is carried away in mineral-rich "hard" water.

Lechuguilla, however, is one of a very limited number of limestone caves formed by a very different and much more violent process. Lechuguilla was born of sulfuric acid.

"Lechuguilla is dominated by a totally different chemistry than a typical cave where water comes in from the surface," Art Palmer told me. Palmer is a hydrologist and director of the Water Resources Program at the State University of New York in Oneida.

Speleogenesis, the process by which caves are formed, is Art

Palmer's special area of interest. The fact that it was powerfully corrosive sulfuric acid rather than carbonic acid that melted the rock and carved out the caverns of Lechuguilla is what, in Art Palmer's words, "electrified the caving community. It's like talking about a new planet whose atmosphere is methane or something. It stretches the imagination. Lechuguilla is dominated by sulfur rather than carbon dioxide."

I asked Art Palmer if he could explain the origin of the cave, its speleogenesis, to me.

Palmer took me back to the Permian period, about 250 million years ago, when parts of Texas and New Mexico were covered over in a stagnant inland sea, something like the Dead Sea or the Persian Gulf. At the northern edge of this sea a limestone reef formed.

Twenty to 40 million years ago, the earth shuddered, and the northern portion of the basin was uplifted and then lifted again 2–4 million years ago, forming the Guadalupe Mountains. As the reefs of the northwest rose, the southeast portion of the old sea sank slightly, forming what is called the Delaware Basin. Today the Delaware Basin contains vast deposits of gas and oil.

The boiling oil-field brines in the basin are tapped in huge underground reservoirs, along with hydrogen sulfide, which doesn't exist on the face of the earth. When the gas encounters oxygen, it forms sulfuric acid. "In order for the hydrogen sulfide to come up to the surface," Art Palmer said, "you've got to have some kind of unrest in the earth's crust. A fracturing will release pressure sort of like a flat in a tire."

So, millions of years ago, hydrogen sulfide, released from its underground reservoirs by a fracturing of the earth's crust, rose through a series of cracks and fissures into the bedded limestone of the Guadalupe Mountains. When it reached the water table, it combined with the oxygen in the water to form sulfuric acid.

Because sulfuric acid is so powerfully corrosive, it dissolved the limestone very rapidly, in geologic terms, forming huge caverns and rooms.

Aside from big rooms, another characteristic of caves formed by sulfuric acid is the presence of great quantities of gypsum. The chemical process is a simple one, easily seen in the laboratory and sometimes demonstrated in high school chemistry classes. Drop enough limestone (calcium carbonate) into a beaker of sulfuric acid, and a white precipitate, gypsum (calcium sulfate) drops to the bottom, like snow in the enclosed glass winter scene on Grandma's table.

"So," Art Palmer said, "the limestone is converted to gypsum. And you can see places where whole walls and ceilings and floors are white with the stuff. You can see bedded gypsum in Glacier Bay and the Prickly Ice Cube Room."

The gypsum in Lechuguilla takes on many different forms. It can produce the fantastic eighteen-foot-long chandeliers of the Chandelier Ballroom, or glacierlike blocks, or delicate flowering tendrils, or strands of angel hair thirty feet long.

"Think of ice," Art Palmer said. "Ice can form filigrees on a cold window in the winter. Ice forms differently on the surface of a frozen lake or in an iceberg. It's all ice, but it looks different. And in Lechuguilla, different outlines of how the crystals are put together, different origins, give you gypsum in cottonlike puffs or massive beds.

Movements of air inside the cave have also influenced its formations and size.

Larger caves tend to breathe: They inhale and exhale great quantities of air. When the barometric pressure on the surface changes, when a low-pressure system lumbers over the land, for instance, air rushes out the entrance as the cave attempts to reach barometric equilibrium. If a high-pressure cell is present aloft, the cave inhales.

The winds that sometimes flow through the cave, according to Kim Cunningham, a geologist with the USGS and chairman of the Lechuguilla Cave Project Science Committee, carry tiny organisms that eat away at the rock. "Lechuguilla," Cunningham told me, "is a microbiological forest." There are bacteria in the cave that are chemosynthetic, which is to say, they are able to oxidize and feed off of mineral compounds like sulfur, manganese, and iron. A type of fungi can live on the bacteria.

What this means is that microorganisms, swept through the

cave by currents of air, eat away at the solid rock wall. The indigestible residue created by this process often looks like a kind of brown, greasy, loose-packed mud and can sometimes be felt falling like a gentle rain. The rock flour I had slid down on my 9.6 acrobatic plunge was just such material.

The idea of a cave being modified by microbiological means is, according to Cunningham, "confounding and a delight to study. It seems atypical on the planet."

Lechuguilla had existed undiscovered until 1986, because it lacks a natural entrance. There was a ninety-foot-deep pit in the desert, but it offered no opening into the cave below. For a time the pit was known as Misery Hole.

But occasionally, in the calm before a Pacific storm lashed the land, great clouds of dirt could be seen swirling out of the hole like dust devils. Winds of forty miles an hour and more whistled out from under the rocks in Misery Hole. A number of people concluded that there had to be a large cave breathing somewhere below the pit. Winds of fifty miles an hour do not blow out of solid rock.

So, over the decades, cavers with shovels and pickaxes dug in the cave. On Memorial Day of 1986 a Colorado group calling itself the Lechuguilla Dig Project broke through. In two days the Lechuguilla Dig Project had mapped its find all the way past Glacier Bay to the Rift. It was obvious that a major new cave had been discovered.

From the start the project had cooperated with the Park Service. Ronal Kerbo, at the time the Park Service's only cave specialist, was told of the breakthrough immediately.

The Park Service quickly installed a culvert to shore up the breakthrough hole. There was a locked gate at the top of the culvert to protect the cave from the curious and the curious from the cave.

The breakthrough group, now calling itself the Lechuguilla Cave Project, is a self-funded volunteer organization. A memorandum of understanding with the Park Service states that the LCP will be allowed to conduct exploration and scientific research under certain guidelines. Anyone who has the requisite caving skills, however, can obtain a permit to visit the cave provided he or she has a valid scientific reason.

The caving community was buzzing with the news of the discovery, but there was little mention of Lechuguilla in the conventional media. And the good people of Carlsbad, New Mexico, began to feel as if the Park Service was keeping a secret from them. Tourism is New Mexico's number-one industry, and Carlsbad benefits greatly from the 750,000 people a year who visit the nearby caverns.

Mayor Lyle Forrest was aggravated to hear that the cave would be managed as wilderness. "No one," he recalled, "said a thing to us about what the future of that cave should be or how it should be handled. So that's when I formed the Mayor's Task Force on Lechuguilla Cave."

Mike Currier was appointed chairman of the task force, which met weekly from March to August of 1989. "We had some people who were very strong proponents of commercialization and some who were opponents," he told me. The purpose of the task force was research, pure and simple.

Still, there was misunderstanding all around. Lyle Forrest received angry anonymous calls: "Are you the mayor who wants to put a McDonald's at the bottom of Lechuguilla?"

Mike Currier believes that the turning point came when members of the Lechuguilla Cave Project made a presentation to the task force and the Carlsbad Department of Development.

The Mayor's Task Force decided that "after listening to the various opinions about Lechuguilla Cave we believe . . . it is in the best interests of all concerned not to seek development for general use at this time."

A year later, Mayor Forrest told me that "the more we see of Lechuguilla, the more we're convinced that maybe this is one cave that can't be developed and shouldn't be developed. We want to do what's best."

In the summer of 1990 the three groups most concerned with Lechuguilla Cave—the town of Carlsbad, the caving community, and the National Park Service—were in agreement about the future of what has been called the finest underground wilderness in the world.

The hurricane of controversy, Ron Kerbo thinks, has dissipated. The undeveloped wilderness of Lechuguilla, Kerbo says, "is significant in that it continues to foster the spirit and the heart and soul of exploration."

I suggested that the exploration of the cave was really very similar to what happened during the Lewis and Clark Expedition.

"You know," Ron Kerbo said, "I used to use that analogy myself. But then I realized that everywhere Lewis and Clark went, there were people. Exploring Lechuguilla is entirely different: No one's ever been in those virgin passages. It's Neil Armstrong stuff."

I was on my third trip into the cave, sometime near my 28oth hour in Lechuguilla, during the final fifty-mile push. Patty Kambesis and I were sitting on a sloping block of gypsum just above the lower end of the Rift, and we were scooping booty, which is to say, we were exploring a section of the cave where no one had ever been. The new lead was found by Rick Bridges at the lower end of the Rift. Beside the marked trail, there was a hole called the Death Pit. On another expedition, Rick Bridges and Buddy Lane had descended the pit, looking for leads. A huge rock had dislodged itself from the wall and thundered past them in such a way that observers above were certain they were dead, "flatrocked" at the bottom of, hey, let's call it Death Pit.

About thirty feet down, a natural bridge, three feet wide, spanned the pit. The bridge led to a rabbit hole "lead" in what appeared to be a solid wall. In fact, the hole did "go"—it emptied out onto a sloping ledge below a nearly vertical flowstone cliff about sixty feet high. A climber named Dave Jones scaled the cliff face and rigged a rope for Patty and me to climb.

Rick Bridges and Anne Strait were mapping the approach to the rabbit hole, just beyond the Death Pit. Patty and I went ahead to see how far this new lead might take us.

Atop the cliff face there was an upward sloping room with a

slanting roof, perhaps four feet high at its lowest. A forest of pearly-white stalactites and stalagmites made me feel as if I were trapped inside the jaws of some great beast. We could not see through the formations, in the same way you can't see through a thick forest. We knew we had to go on. (That's what we told ourselves.)

Where the ceiling was highest, it might have been possible to walk upright, but Patty rejected the idea. There were too many delicate formations.

I was not surprised that Patty would not take the easiest but the most damaging route onward. Cavers who accidentally damage a formation live for weeks in a state of self-flagellation. But Patty scouted the room and found a narrow side fissure that looked as if it might take us above the formations. We chimneyed up the crevice, backs against the rock, our feet braced on the opposite wall. It took half an hour of hard, dangerous work before we rose out of the cleft in the rock.

Because Lechuguilla is sweaty-hot, heat exhaustion and heatstroke are very real dangers. Most cavers choose to wear short pants and short-sleeved shirts. Knee and elbow pads are worn for protection, but no one escapes unscathed. Patty was bleeding from her right thigh. My shorts had ripped against the jagged rock. I was scraped in a sensitive area but had not yet begun to bleed.

The fissure gave way to a junction room perhaps ten feet high and forty feet across. There were at least five good leads that I could see. The best one, I thought, was a man-sized keyhole-shaped opening in the rock that was completely rimmed in gypsum.

We had climbed the fissure, Patty and I, precisely to see whether there were any leads. Our job was done. It is bad form to scoop booty and not map.

Patty Kambesis, who is the chief cartographer of the LCP, was particularly sensitive on the issue. Mapping an area that has been scooped is not nearly the same as mapping "virgin passage." The "map as you go" policy was sometimes annoying—no caver I know is a great fan of rules—but it meant that difficult passages had to be mapped before people could get to the more spectacular rooms.

Still, we would map this room later, and I couldn't help myself: I had to see what was on the other side of the gypsum rim.

"You want to come?"

Patty shook her head and smiled.

And so I scooped the rim, alone. There was a concave block of gypsum on the other side of the keyhole. When I glanced at it from the side, I saw that it was very thin, sculpted by the wind into an upward-sweeping curve. It looked like a cresting wave. Beyond that was a small room with one high lead that didn't look promising. I sat and studied the cresting wave for ten minutes. Something that felt very much like victory expanded inside my chest, and I thought I could hear my own heartbeat echo off the walls. Neil Armstrong stuff.

When I came back, Patty asked me what I had seen, and I told her that there was a block of gypsum that looked like an ocean wave.

Later, along with Rick Bridges and Anne Strait, we mapped the area. The fissure Patty and I first climbed (first climbed!) intersected with a passage that ran above the Rift and slightly parallel to it. Some clever cavers named it the Parallel Universe. When Patty sketched the area beyond my (my!) gypsum-rimmed keyhole, she nodded to me and named it the Ocean Wave Room.

Several days later, Rick Bridges entered the information from Patty's sketch pad into the Lechuguilla Cave Project's computer, using an ingenious program written by LCP member Garry Petrie. It was Friday night, the last day of the LCP's weeklong summer expedition. There were now, Rick Bridges said, 51.6 miles of cave mapped.

And the next night, we sat at the gala fifty-mile celebration dinner in good conscience. Mike Currier was there, representing the mayor, who was away on business. Members of the Mayor's Task Force on Lechuguilla were there. Wallace Elms, the superintendent of Carlsbad Caverns National Park, spoke, and he congratulated the cavers on their achievement. Rick Bridges spoke.

Ron Kerbo gave the most moving speech. He talked about knowledge and poetry; he talked about the heart and soul of exploration. I felt gooseflesh rise along my arms and across my back.

The Ocean Wave Room.

The Big Open

▲

The first thing I told them at the Hell Creek Bar was that the Big Open wasn't my idea. "Hey, I'm just here to see what you guys think of the plan." The Hell Creek is one of two bars in Jordan, Montana, population 485, and national reporters have not fared well here in the past. Several years ago, Geraldo Rivera was in town doing a story on a farm foreclosure. In the course of his research Rivera became involved in a physical altercation at the Rancher's Bar, which is a few doors down the street from the Hell Creek. Locals didn't think it was much of a fight.

"Nobody even punched the guy," a hefty fellow wearing an old canvas coat told me. "It's just . . . see, he was poking into affairs that was none of his business, and he got his head runned through the wall."

"Well," I said, "Geraldo deserved it." I wasn't sure whether Geraldo actually needed to have his head runned through a wall or not, but it seemed wise to agree with these gentlemen. They were, all of them, farmers and ranchers, hardworking men with big, hard callused hands.

You have to work hard to wring a living out of the land around Jordan. It is, for the most part, a vast, rolling unpopu-

lated prairie, littered with sage and bereft of trees. It is said that
the turn-of-the-century photographer L. A. Huffman was the first
to call this combination of marginally fertile prairie, high desert,
and badlands the Big Open. The distances seem vaguely hostile,
alien to outsiders, and the major river is called Big Dry Creek.
Buttes, like great wind-whipped symbols of erosion, rise against
an impossibly immense expanse of indifferent sky. Except for a
pair of two-lane paved highways that "T" at Jordan, the roads
are cruel graveled jokes. When it rains, pickups founder in the
greasy red clay of those roads. It is a clinging mud locals called
gumbo. Infrequent rain pounds the land, and water runs on the
surface in violent washes, forming small canyons and gullies
called gunions. In places gunions carved into the earth seem to
swirl around some bit of land left standing like a misshapen pillar. These badland formations are called gumbo knobs.

It's been a hard decade for ranching and farming in the Big
Open. The bad winter of '78–'79 killed off hundreds of stock
animals; there was a plague of grasshoppers in the summer of
'86; and there has been drought around Jordan since 1980.
Worse, while expenses have risen with exponential absurdity,
farmers are getting less today for a bushel of wheat than their
fathers and grandfathers got during the Depression. These are
hard times around Jordan: Four counties in the Big Open area
have been named "hunger counties" in a Harvard School of Public Health report. Many farmers, deeply in debt, are facing imminent foreclosure. It's called getting bucked off the ranch.

In late February Robert Scott, a Hamilton, Montana, man, a
former petroleum engineer who was bucked off his own ranch in
central Montana, proposed a bold plan that would allow the
farmers and ranchers to hold on to their land and nearly double
the average household income. Under the Big Open proposal,
people would sell off all their sheep and cattle, tear down the
fences, and reseed fields with natural grasses. The Big Open—
about fifteen thousand square miles of it: an area the size of Con-
necticut, Massachusetts, and Rhode Island combined—would
become, over a period of perhaps fifty years, a vast prairie game
reserve rivaling those in Africa.

There are, at present, 363,000 sheep and cattle grazing this land, or about a hundred head for each of the three thousand people living in the area. Scott estimates that the Big Open would support wildlife herds numbering 320,000 animals, including 75,000 bison, 150,000 deer, 40,000 elk, and 40,000 antelope. The hunger counties of the Big Open would become again the land that staggered Lewis and Clark with its bounty in 1805.

A game reserve of this magnitude would draw tourists from all over the world. According to Scott, "Huge herds of free-roaming buffalo would be an unrivaled attraction." The game park "would be unequaled by any other place on earth, save possibly the Serengeti plain of East Africa," which, not incidentally, produces annual gross tourist receipts of $300 million a year.

The Big Open might be operated as a wildlife-range cooperative system that would incorporate both private ranches and the five thousand square miles of land that are government-owned. Receipts of $50 million annually would be generated from hunting fees alone. And while farmers and ranchers would retain their land, the average household income would rise from $15,000 annually to about $28,000.

Scott presented his proposal in late February at a conference sponsored by the Institute of the Rockies, a Missoula, Montana–based nonprofit organization of academic and business leaders. The idea was so appealing—to those of us who don't live in the Big Open anyway—that it was widely reported. One area rancher told *The New York Times* that local folks were likely to be suspicious at first. He suggested that Scott "play this scenario in the Hell Creek bar in Jordan."

So I was sitting in the Hell Creek one Saturday in March, talking with farmers and ranchers about the idea. It was hard to convey the idea that this plan was not something to be imposed on them by the government. "If they want my land for a park," John Cooly said, "they can buy it out from under me, and I'll go somewhere where ranching's fun." I tried to tell John there was no "they" involved. "It's supposed to be your choice."

"Look," Cooly said, "I don't want to deal with tourists. I don't want 'em around. If I wanted to see people every day, I'd move to town. And I'm not the only one feels this way. People here are furiously independent. You'll never get the ranchers together."

Terry Murnion, sitting on another stool, was a good example of Cooly's point. Terry's cousin, Nick, was getting married that night, and there was a reception at a hall down the street. Terry didn't go, "because I been to one marriage in my life, and I expect to go to one funeral."

Terry heard me out on the economic benefits that would accrue to him under the Big Open plan. Scott had estimated that a twelve-thousand-acre farm like Murnion's would clear a minimum of fifty thousand dollars on hunting permits alone. The numbers didn't seem to impress Terry Murnion. "If my old granddad was tough enough to come here broke," he said, "I should be tough enough to stay here broke." It's been hard, Terry said. "One old Ford pickup and a pissed-off wife is all I got," he said. Still, "I got a lifetime here, and I'm paying taxes." As for the foreclosures looming on the horizon, well—"There's more heart in this country than the bankers can handle."

Terry was drinking beer, and others in the bar were drinking bourbon neat. The most popular drink in Montana has always been a "ditch," bourbon and water, but no one drinks ditches in Jordan. The water is alkaline, it causes diarrhea, and most people distill their household water before drinking it.

And while there is little locals can do about the water they get from their wells—the century-old problem has something to do with minerals in the bedrock—they can do something about the quality and quantity of the surface water. The land around Jordan suffers from heavy erosion, the result of drought and a century of overgrazing by cattle and sheep. They are destructive grazers, these domestic animals, and the native plants that once held moisture, that provided a spongelike watershed, are gone. Creeks that once ran almost all year are now mostly dry. Those that do run carry great loads of sediment. In contrast, elk and antelope and deer, wildlife species that evolved on the prairie, consume native flora across all species and seasons. They are biologically in tune with the area: Their modest foraging does not destroy the watershed. Additionally, dryland farming in the area, it can be shown, exhausts the surface organic material as well. Overgrazing, dryland farming, and the resultant erosion combine to produce a process scientists call desertification. They point out that the Sahara was once the granary of the world, until human mismanagement turned it into dunes.

This is the kind of argument, however, that is not to be advanced in the Hell Creek bar unless you want your head runned through a wall. Several men in the bar suggested that instead of using eastern Montana prairies as a game reserve, the western part of the state should be "turned into a zoo." Most of these gentlemen saw the mountains of western Montana (where I live) as a place full of colleges, liberals, and people in waffle-stomper boots. Sierra clubbers and coyote lovers. Maybe tourists would pay to see a zoo full of such weirdos.

One man, John McKeever, made a telling point. "You want to be a farmer?" he asked me. I told him I didn't have the knowledge, the skill, the grit. Most of all, I had no desire to work a farm. "It's been twenty years since I bucked a bail of hay, and I hope I never buck another," I said.

"You like what you're doing then?" McKeever asked, and I told him I did. "I like what I'm doing," he said. McKeever raises prize bulls. "You're asking me to stop doing something I like and start up on something I don't know anything about. Something I don't want to do. It's like me telling you, you have to be a farmer, you'll like it, and it's for your own good."

So the scenario didn't play well in the Hell Creek bar. At least not the first time around. It would take some time for the idea to sink in.

The next day I drove forty miles through the gravel and gumbo to Claude Saylor's ranch. He was out in the barn, castrating pigs, but knocked off for a chat. Like a lot of other area ranchers, Claude has always worked a second job to make ends meet. For a time he traveled Montana and Wyoming shearing sheep in the way that other ranchers work as carpenters or mail carriers. Then, several years ago, Claude discovered that some city dwellers envied his life. There were people who would come out to the ranch and work ten-hour days mending fence with him. "And they'd pay me sixty-five dollars a day for the privilege," Claude said.

He stopped shearing sheep and turned over part of his ranch to a tourist operation. "I run two hundred head of cattle," Claude said, "and I make about fifteen thousand dollars. In the fall I get between twenty and forty hunters, and I average about twenty thousand dollars off of them. They're here five days a week, and then they're gone. The cattle cost me money every single day."

Claude's grandfather had come out to Montana in a covered wagon at the turn of the century, and that old Studebaker wagon was still around. Claude spent about two thousand dollars restoring the wagon, then went looking for the remains of others, old wagons you can find rusting in piles on the prairie. He now has twelve of them, and runs wagon-train trips for paying guests. The nostalgic summer trips have been featured on national television, and *The Wall Street Journal* recently ran an article about Saylor, about how he was using recreation to save his ranch.

Somehow, the very idea of paying guests annoys many of Claude's neighbors. A letter in the *Jordan Tribune* about *The Wall Street Journal* article asked if maybe there wasn't "too much recreation and not enough riding or too much play and not enough work."

Claude showed me the letter and said that anyone presenting the Big Open plan would have a hard row to hoe. "People around here are tough," he said, and mentioned that there seemed to be more foreclosures west of Jordan, on much more fertile land. "That's because people around here have always had it tough, and they know how to weather bad times. They think they can hold on to their ranches." Claude shook his head sadly. "They'll think that right up to the day of foreclosure."

Maybe. Sitting here in the safety of western Montana, I can say the Big Open proposal looks like a good deal for local ranchers. For many, it may be the only way to save a ranch that has been in the same family for three generations. I think, as the idea sinks in, many—especially those in the deepest trouble—may even welcome the idea. These ranchers and farmers don't want to change, but they are not suicidal. If it comes down to losing everything or turning the ranch into a wildlife range, many of these independent, hardworking people are going to opt for survival. In the end it's their choice. You could get your head runned through a wall telling them that, but it's their choice.

Look Natural

▲

I was hanging from a rope affixed to a diaper, which was, in fact, a ten-foot-long runner made of nylon webbing wrapped about my legs and crotch in a manner most familiar to mothers and climbers. The ends of the runner were hooked into a pair of carabiners, which, in turn, hooked into a small device called a figure eight.

With my diapers and carabiners in place, I could run a doubled-over climbing rope through the figure eight, step backward off the lip of a cliff, and slide safely down the rope. This is the fastest nonfatal way to get down off a mountain. Since most cliff faces are higher than the average climbing rope is long, numerous slides are required to reach flat land. Ropes are expensive, however, and in order to retrieve them after each slide, they are usually wrapped around an anchor—a tree, a horn of rock, a sling affixed to a chock—and dropped double down the face of rock below. The ends of the rope should at the very least dangle over a stand-up ledge. There the climber can pull on one end and bring the rope down after him. The process is called rappel, a French word meaning "recall."

I was out recalling over the side of a cliff this spring day because the summer was shaping up heavy on rope work. I'd been invited to help some people place a pair of peregrine falcons on a rocky ledge rising high over the Pacific Ocean. I'd also promised to join a caving expedition where we would be expected to slide down a rope in absolute darkness some four hundred feet. "You can rappel, can't you?" I was asked in both cases.

The last time I slid down a rope was six years ago. As I remember, it seemed a painless procedure after the first-time terror of trying to scale a 5.7 climb called the Grack in Yosemite. Slide down a rope? No problem. Rappel off a cliff while holding a delicate peregrine falcon in a sweatsock? Piece of cake. Drop off into the darkness of the earth's abysmal depths? I could handle it. But what the hell, a little practice with the rope wouldn't hurt.

My friend Paul Dix, a photographer, has been climbing for almost thirty years and owns all the requisite ropes and hardware. As it happened, Paul didn't mind taking an afternoon off for some rope work. In fact, he said, I would be the perfect subject for "some rappelling photos." Paul said he would be happy to supervise my practice sessions if he could shoot pictures of me.

Which is how I came to be hanging over the lip of a cliff in Yankee Jim Canyon, just above the rapids of the Yellowstone River. Other men have hung from the neck until dead: I was hanging from my diapers and dying of boredom. This is the curse of going anywhere with an outdoor photographer.

"Just hold it right there," Paul said, diddling with his Nikon. "Okay, now drop down about two feet. Good. Now turn your face out of the shadow. Lift your right foot about four inches. Perfect. Hold it. Look natural."

For me, a natural look would have been one of intense apprehension, but after hanging for some time in a position one sees only in East Indian sex manuals, a certain ennui takes hold of the soul.

"Can I go now?" I called. The diapers were beginning to chafe.

"Uh, wait just a minute, please. I'm changing film."

Using Paul's gear and relying, as I was, on his expertise, I was in no position to argue. I was in no position at all. I was hanging by my diapers, thinking uncharitable thoughts about photographers.

"Oh my God," Paul called. "Could you hang for another few minutes? Five more minutes. There's a couple of kayakers upriver." Paul was in a lather of anticipation, scrambling up the side of the cliff, dragging thirty pounds of camera gear in a frenzied quest to find the perfect angle. "If I can just get you and the kayakers *in the same shot* . . ."

Someday Paul will be sitting at home, in his office, and his agent or some magazine art director will call and ask, "You wouldn't have a photo of a fat guy rappelling down a cliff with a couple of kayakers paddling by below, would you?"

And Paul Dix will say, "Of course," in a way that suggests all good photographers have that shot.

There was a nice little stretch of rapids upstream, and the kayakers had no idea that I was hanging in the wind, waiting for them to pass so that Paul could be nonchalant with art directors about his rappelling photographs. The kayakers were probably nice guys. I bet I'd like them if I met them at a bar. What I didn't like about them from this angle was the way they kept fooling around. Drop into a big hole and paddle furiously in order not to move. Anybody who would work that hard to go nowhere, I thought, twisting slowly in the wind, was an imbecile of heroic proportions.

"Can you drop below the overhang so you hang free?" Paul asked. So I hung there, working hard to go nowhere and feeling as vapid as a kayaker in a rapid. The diaper was cutting into my thighs, and paralysis had overtaken my legs. I mean, I was hurting. I began to think of Paul as a Kodachrome sadist.

Okay, I admit that photographers, as a rule, are probably wonderful people, as likable as the idiot kayakers no doubt were, but while at work the average outdoor photographer is not to be trusted. Once, in South America, I stood under a heavy waterfall wearing raingear made of a "new generation" fabric while photographer Nick Nichols took shots for a catalog, shots designed to show that this stuff was impervious to water. It was a cold day on the high plateau known as El Mundo Perdido, the Lost World, and the fourth time I walked through the falls, I called up to Nick that I was soaking wet and cold.

"This stuff doesn't work," I screamed, "not even a little bit."

"Gimme one more walk-through," he shouted back. "I haven't got the shot."

"But the stuff doesn't work." A bit of logic and fine good sense howled into the empty space between a working photographer's ears. "It leaks like a sieve."

"I don't know that," Nick shouted. "Gimme one more walk-through."

"This stuff is the fabric of betrayal. . . ."

"Looks great," Nick yelled, "real good. One more walk-through."

Nick has actually asked people to give it one more walk-through over a bed of coals. That was in Surinam, where he was working on a story about the people who live deep in that country's tangled jungle. Nick spent three weeks in one jungle village, long enough to count the people he met there as friends.

The villagers finally agreed to perform their fire dance for the camera. "I still don't know how they do it," Nick told me. "Whether they go into a trance or whether their feet are just so callused they can stomp the fire out. Anyway, the head dancer goes first, then his assistant comes out, then a trainee comes and stomps out the rest of the fire."

It was a difficult lighting situation—shooting into a fire at night —and Nick was worried about the shot. He asked his friends to give it one more walk-through the next night.

"I think," Nick recollected, "they thought I was disappointed in the size of the blaze, because this time they built a bonfire. The head dancer didn't stay in very long, and neither did his assistant. The magic wasn't there that night. Something. When the trainee came in to put the fire out, it was still blazing away, and I could tell he was definitely getting burned."

And so they learned in Surinam what it means to have a photographer as a friend.

* * *

Far and away the worst of the breed are underwater photographers. I've had enough scuba experience to know that, in any given group, the person with the camera is likely to be the best and most knowledgeable diver. Just don't get buddied up with him. The scuba photographer drops down the anchor line, swims ten yards, and finds something to engage his or her interest. As likely as not, the fascinating stuff involves a couple of tiny organisms the size of your thumbnail swimming around a coral knob no bigger than a coffee cup. The rest of your group is off hanging on the backs of manta rays or watching green turtles mate, but the inflexible rules of diving won't let you leave your buddy, the motionless photographer. No use even swimming over to see what the camera sees. You'll stir up the sand, frighten the organisms, and spoil the shot.

After the dive the photographer will be in a state of near sexual excitement. "A feeding phenomenon no one has," he'll mutter in ecstasy. "No one's ever seen it before."

"Especially not me," you point out.

"Hey," the photographer says, "I've got it on film," as if photography is somehow superior to experience. "I'll send you a copy." The shot, when you get it, will be beautiful, suitable for framing, a photo you could label "The Conservation of Underwater Experience."

I was thinking about the treachery of photographers when Paul said it was okay, I could go ahead with my practice rappels. When I was just about at the end of my rope, he called, "Hey, Tim, could you hurry back up here? There's a big raft coming down the river."

I clipped out of the rappel rig.

"They're coming pretty fast," Paul called. "Could you run, please?"

Antarctic Passages

▲

I am sitting on hard snow and ice here at Cape Evans, on Ross Island, in the Ross Sea, and this Antarctic beach feels like the last beach on earth. I sense a prophecy: This beach will encompass the earth at the end of time when the sun is a feeble glow, without heat, and the world a ball of ice hurtling through infinite space.

There is a beauty here, at the edge of Antarctica, at the end of time. A high wind rips a line of wispy clouds into shreds that flutter under a cold silver sun. The white plain that backs the beach takes on the color of the sky. The snow is vaguely pink, like watermelon. Ahead, across gray waters littered with ice floes, looms a high headland of ice and snow. A brisk wind blows loose, dry snow over the lip of a two-hundred-foot-high cliff like a pale pink waterfall. More clouds mass under the sun, and the powdery snowfall in the distance has become a dark, vaguely purple curtain: falling snow like inky dusk.

Above, a royal albatross, a great white bird of good omen, soars past the purple snowfall and over the watermelon plain. Skuas, gull-like seabirds, shriek overhead. Fifty yards away, a fat gray seal basks on a seaside snowbank. It has the characteristic upturned smiling mouth of a Weddell seal. The animal blinks once, flirtatiously. The black eyes are large and gentle, doelike, adapted for hunting in dark waters under the sea ice.

Not far behind me is the hut where Captain Robert Falcon Scott prepared for his ill-fated march to the South Pole, about 820 miles away. Everything inside is perfectly preserved in the perpetual deep freeze of the continent. I saw a table where scientific experiments were conducted; beakers and electrical wires littered the shelves nearby.

It had been dark and gloomy in the hut: Windows let heat escape. Reindeer sleeping bags lay on wooden bunk beds arranged around a metal stove. There were English magazines from the turn of the century, discarded gloves, and provisions stocked on the shelves: Colman's mustard, Fry's Pure Cocoa, Huntley & Palmers biscuits, Belmont Stearine candles "made expressly for hot climates."

Antarctica is not tolerant of mistakes. In front of the hut, on a beach of icy volcanic rock, is a ship's anchor tailing a length of frayed rope. In 1915 Ernest Shackleton used the Scott hut to prepare depots for the first transcontinental overland crossing. Two parties in two ships were supposed to land on opposite sides of the continent and then trek until they met, but Shackleton's ship was crushed by ice and sank. His men survived. The other ship lost its mooring in a blizzard and drifted to sea, leaving ten men marooned ashore. Only six lived. The annals of polar exploration are filled with dozens of sagas like this.

Up the slope from the cabin is the mummified carcass of one of Scott's sled dogs, covered in drifting snow. Above, on a commanding hill, is a cross commemorating the death of three members of Shackleton's Ross Sea party.

It is a sobering scene, here on Cape Evans, the very edge of mortality. I have wandered off to sit between two hillocks of snow, on a small plateau that overlooks the sea. In the midst of all these symbols of death and hope and glory, I feel a need to savor the nobility of living things.

I have plunked myself down near a series of meandering tracks in the snow. I am waiting for the creatures that made them: Adelie penguins—stout, ill-tempered little birds about two feet high and weighing perhaps eleven pounds. Soon enough, I hear a few Adelies calling to one another. They sound like indignant baritone crows. And here they come, over the top of the icy drift, five of the robust little birds with the distinctive and clownlike white Adelie circle around each eye. They flop onto their bellies and bodysurf down the slope, struggle to their tiny feet, and then waddle importantly up the near hill. One bird cuffs another with its flipper. All squawk and caw at each other.

These Adelies, so darling in documentary films, are, I see, lusty, powerful birds, very intent on survival. They surround me in a rough semicircle and stare. One lifts its head, beats its flippers, and croaks out a challenge to the sky: "Ahhhh, ahhhh, ahhhh, AHHHHH." The others follow suit. They seem to be saying, "I am a penguin, and what a hell of penguin I am!"

Having made their point, the Adelies waddle off toward the beach, presumably contemplating the dive that will take them out to sea for most of the coming winter. They tend to plunge in large groups. This disorients predators like killer whales. But these Adelies seem to hesitate, as if debating the matter: "After you, my dear fellow."

"Tim! Hey, Tim!"

It is Peter Carey, a penguin biologist currently employed as a lecturer aboard Salén Lindblad Cruising's newly built *Frontier Spirit*, a 365-foot passenger ship anchored a mile offshore. Dr. Carey says it's time to pile into a rubber Zodiac and head back to the *Frontier Spirit* to join the eighty other passengers for dinner. The ship is unusual—an iceworthy vessel that combines luxury and ecological sensitivity. It's filled with all sorts of antipollution gear, including an entire sewage-treatment plant, aimed at minimizing our effect on these waters.

I liked my fellow passengers. They were informed and enthusiastic people of all ages, ranging from those in their mid-thirties to one remarkable man in his early eighties. They included a number of medical doctors from the United States and Australia, a famous Japanese photographer, a pair of journalists from Chicago, bird fanciers from several countries, and one resilient woman in her late seventies who found the entire trip "magical."

They had come to discover, for themselves, the continent of

Antarctica, this glittering wilderness that encircles the South Pole: 5,500,000 square miles, most of it capped by ice so thick that the land beneath may never be seen until some future cataclysm heats up the entire earth. The Antarctic, we soon learned, is a savage place, as soul-stirring as it is unforgiving.

We had not embarked, strictly speaking, on a pleasure cruise. Oh, no. Despite the regal saloon, complete with piano, despite the gourmet meals and well-equipped lecture hall, this trip was billed as an "expedition cruise," suggesting physical discovery and intellectual enrichment. Such a cruise necessarily requires a measure of flexibility and hardiness in its passengers, embracing, as it does, a small degree of physical discomfort and an uncertain schedule dictated by the weather. In this case, on this trip, there were also twenty bad minutes of real life-and-death drama.

It was the expedition's coleader, Mike Dunn, who told the passengers in an orientation lecture that the twelve Zodiacs carried by the *Frontier Spirit* made the difference between a cruise and an expedition. There is no place to dock a large ship along Antarctica's icy shores. The Zodiacs, inflated rubber boats with outboard motors, were our ticket into the continent, ensuring some kind of communion with the awesome land and whatever life we could find there. It would be, Mike explained, no small thing to step from the ship's boat deck into the Zodiacs as they bobbed on swells that were often four and five feet high.

Mike told us all this soon after we set sail from Bluff, New Zealand, and headed south toward the Ross Sea through some of the world's stormiest latitudes—the ones sailors call the Roaring Forties, the Furious Fifties, the Screaming Sixties. We encountered three or four major storms, one after the other, boom-boom-boom, just like that. The Southern Ocean generates the worst weather on earth for navigation, according to Heinz Aye, our captain. He ought to know. This was Captain Aye's sixty-second trip to the frozen continent.

Instead of indulging in conventional shipboard diversions like shuffleboard, we spent our days at sea attending lectures about the history, wildlife, and politics of Antarctica. At the same time the storms raging outside quickly got our attention, lending our studies a surreal quality.

One day I went to the well-stocked library, on the fifth deck, and read a book about penguins. The wind was howling bitterly, and the waves were running about thirty feet, hitting us from the starboard side, where I sat, next to one of the enormous windows that I never could call portholes. For a moment, as we crested another wave, I was staring up into a troubled gray sky—there was a now familiar "top of the roller coaster" sensation in the pit of my stomach—and then the ship began its slow slide into a mammoth trough of water. In that instant the sun, which was low in the sky, bullied its way through the clouds and fell across the tops of waves that ran all the way to the horizon. The sea was a savage morass of gold and gray, both terrifying and beautiful. Then, as the *Frontier Spirit* dropped into the depth of the trough, a great, upwelling mass of gray water filled the entire window.

The radiant and illuminated sea was dazzling, and that was a surprise, something I hadn't imagined in my dreams of Antarctica. It was, in fact, only one of a number of astonishments I was to encounter on the cruise. I had, for instance, been uninterested in the sub-Antarctic islands we would visit on the way down and back from the frozen continent. But our first landfall, on Campbell Island, two days out of Bluff, was a revelation.

The temperature hovered around 50 degrees, and our Zodiac churned through a kelp bed dotted with perfectly round, perfectly purple, pizza-size jellyfish. An escort of Hooker's sea lions, the rarest in the world, frolicked alongside, keeping pace with the Zodiac and staring at us with large dark eyes set in smiling, doglike heads. The island is volcanic in origin, and directly ahead a silver waterfall fell against an ebony wall of rock. Campbell is a New Zealand meteorological base and nature-conservancy area. A boardwalk winds through a boggy stretch of land, replete with ferns and thick vegetation of all kinds. The single tree on the island is distinguished by the *Guinness Book of World Records* as "the loneliest tree on earth."

The boardwalk emerged onto a marshy hillside of green, tussocky grass and low shrubs. Above were black rocky spires and specks of white dotting the treeless hillsides below. The specks were nesting royal albatross, dozens of them, separated from one another by twenty to twenty-five yards. I sat about twenty-five yards from one of the great birds and examined it through binoculars. It was huge, the size of a bald eagle at least, and a brisk wind ruffled its white feathers. The bird had a hooked beak, a dark filigree on the back of its wings, and tubular nostrils, and it stared back at me with a kind of serene awareness.

A heavy mist, driven by the wind, blew off the spires above. One of the albatross stood, spread its wings, caught the wind, and disappeared into the vaporous sky. The bird I had been watching stood for a moment, as if to reveal its rather large chick, and then squatted again with a comfortable back-and-forth motion, like a fat man settling into a soft sofa.

These birds, or birds very like them, circled the *Frontier Spirit* all the way to Antarctica. They rarely flapped their wings but soared on unseen currents of air. We counted them good omens, in the manner of ancient mariners.

Several humpback whales, the most acrobatic and playful of the species, kept pace with the *Frontier Spirit,* swimming only yards off the starboard bow, then crisscrossing in front of the ship. There was a mother with her calf, and when the young one breached, I could see the underside of its scalloped flukes, as white as the good omens sailing overhead.

Far in the distance I saw strange, coffin-shaped icebergs that had calved off the continent and swirled in a slow-motion outward spiral. The *Frontier Spirit,* Captain Aye pointed out, was not an icebreaker, but it did have the next-to-highest ice classification that can be given to a passenger ship.

Dawn the next day was brilliant, and the sea appeared somehow sluggish under a cold golden sun. The water glittered strangely, and it seemed gelatinous, viscous. The entire surface was now covered over with closely spaced shards of forming ice the size and shape of knitting needles. The sea rolled slowly, thickly, and for the first time in days there were no whitecaps, even though a wind of perhaps twenty miles an hour was hitting us from starboard.

And then, later in the day—just that much farther south—the world changed again, from horizon to horizon. The sea was covered over with perfectly round medallions of ice, some of them the size of pancakes, of phonograph records, of coffee tables. There are names for the various kinds of ice encountered in the Southern Ocean: names for slushy water and fast-moving pack ice, and a name for the ice I had seen earlier in the day: frazzle ice, the spiky crystals that formed on the surface of the sea. This lily-pad arrangement was called pancake ice. The edges of each frozen, shimmering plate of ice were turned up neatly, and the sun lay across the icy medallions in a long, glittering golden tail.

Antarctica is governed by an international agreement, signed in 1959, making the land at the bottom of the world a demilitarized zone preserved for scientific research. Twelve nations—including the United States and Soviet Union—originally signed the treaty, which was renewed in 1989. It was the overwhelming feeling among passengers and crew that the treaty should be made permanent but that no more scientific bases are needed.

There is a Greenpeace station at Cape Evans, and a representative of that organization was invited aboard to lecture. He said that the organization favors ship-based tourism in Antarctica compared with the alternative, a land-based hotel and landing strip. Passengers aboard vessels like the *Frontier Spirit* learn about the continent and leave with a desire to preserve it.

It was the expedition leaders themselves who flipped their Zodiac. They were on a scouting trip, assessing the safety of a landing site, when they plunged into ice-clogged waters no more than a thousand miles from the South Pole. In such conditions, passengers had been repeatedly told, a person has about two minutes to live. I stood on the fifth deck of the *Frontier Spirit* and watched, powerless, as Mike Dunn floated farther and farther from the luxurious ship, carried away on the current. He was in the water for five minutes, for ten, for twelve. Every half minute or so, one of the five-foot swells washed over his head. It was 25 degrees below zero, and a twenty-mile-an-hour wind was driving snow before it on a horizontal slant.

About the twelfth minute, Mike managed to get a hand up out of the water and salute the 140 horrified passengers who were shouting for him to hold on. Help was coming. It had to be coming. Mike dropped his arm back into the water, and skuas circled over his head. Skuas are the wolves of the Antarctic, and they prey on the vast penguin colonies there, pecking the eyes out of the sockets of infant birds, of the sick and dying. Mike Dunn was dying, and the skuas were circling.

The Zodiacs are lowered by crane from the top deck of the *Frontier Spirit*. The drivers ride the boats to the water and then unsnap a simple hook when the Zodiacs are afloat. The *Frontier Spirit* was brand new, and the hooks that fasten Zodiacs to the crane had been equipped with a new "safety" clasp. The intent was to keep the Zodiacs from accidentally dropping off the crane. In fact, these safety clasps had frozen shut, so when Dunn's Zodiac hit the swell, it held fast. The combination of a tight line and a five-foot swell had dumped Dunn and another man into the water.

The same thing happened to the first rescue crew that went after them, and there were now four people in the water. Steve Dawson, among others, was finally able to get a third Zodiac into the water. He could not see the drowning men, because of the high seas, and allowed passengers on the fifth deck, twenty feet above, to direct him. Nothing could be heard above the howl of the wind, and we simply pointed at the man nearest Dawson's Zodiac. We pointed all at once, in the same direction, like a drill team composed of stunned and horrified marchers.

Dunn was rescued from the water after eighteen minutes. So were the others, all of them barely conscious and unable to move. Some time later, while they were being treated by the ship's doctor, Steve Dawson and I had dinner in the elegant dining room. We were pushing roast pheasant around on our plates, contemplating, in silence, this contrast of luxury and deadly apprehension. Then came an announcement. All four men were fine.

Steve Dawson, who had done himself proud during the rescue, burst into tears.

In the fifth-floor bar later that evening, loud applause rang out when Mike Dunn and the three other men appeared, walking a bit stiffly and ready for a snifter or two of Rémy Martin. Several of us took a break from the festivities and walked around the fifth deck. Curtains of green smoke swept across the sky above. Dozens of passengers stood out on the decks, in 30-below weather, to watch the aurora australis color the star-strewn sky.

It had been, I realized, a dazzling and savage trip. The first Antarctic landfall, in Cape Evans, had featured mortality and spectacle in about even measure: a cross on the hill and a watermelon snowfall. Not now. I looked at the luminous sky and tried to see it through Mike Dunn's eyes.

The Moronic Sport, Revisited

▲

The novelist and poet Jim Harrison, an avid sportsman, once penned a perverse essay on the winter diversion of catching fish through a hole in the ice:

"Ice Fishing: The Moronic Sport."

Last February, Jim was visiting my hometown in Montana, and I was invited to have dinner with him at a friend's house in the country. It was also a day that I planned to accompany another friend on an ice-fishing trip to one of the high lakes in the Gallatin Mountain Range.

Aha.

I'd bring fresh trout to dinner, and explain that I had spent the entire day engaged in the Moronic Sport. Harrison and I would argue about the intellectual attainments of ice fishermen. I figured a few tasty fish, caught that day, would tip the scales of cerebral justice in my favor. Triumph.

Now, in the Midwest, where I grew up (and where Harrison lives), ice fishing can seem, to the uninitiated, a somewhat thick diversion. Hardy men, generally in their later years, can be seen catching all manner of fish on hooks baited with maggots. To keep these larvae warm and apparently succulent, the accomplished ice fisherman places them between the cheek and gum, like a plug of tobacco.

It is this sort of thing, I believe, that has skewed Jim Harrison's attitude toward the sport. The novelist is a renowned gourmand.

Or maybe it's the people who drive their vehicles right out onto the ice and fish who amuse Harrison. Every year, in the late fall and early spring, someone sinks his Blazer. Others tow small ice-houses out onto the lake, complete with wood-burning stoves, and they sit on wooden benches, inside, and stare into small holes where very nearly somnolent perch drift listlessly by succulent maggots. You need to "jig" the perch, which is to say, lift the bait up and down in front of them. Sometimes the perch take the maggot.

Ice fishermen, dressed like winos in layer upon layer of jackets and slacks, drink schnapps, play pinochle, watch football on battery-operated TVs, and fail to notice when the red flags snap up on the tip-ups they've installed outside the shack. Tip-ups are fish-ambush devices, small wooden contraptions attached to a line through the ice. The bait, a minnow, swims about, and when a big fish hits it—a northern pike or a muskie—a red flag pops up. In theory, an ice fisherman sees this through the fluttering plastic window of the shack, dashes outside, and hauls in the fish of a lifetime, hand over hand.

In practice, of course, the fishermen never notice the tip-up flags. They are playing pinochle, or dangling spittle-soaked larvae in front of a mesmerized four-inch perch. Some of them are out engaged in political campaigning: On certain lakes, hundreds of fishing shacks are set out side by side, in a kind of town grid, and a mayor is elected. Other men may be engaged in more distracting activities: It is said that an incredibly hardy band of hookers work the frozen ice cities.

In Montana a cross-country skier may drill a hole in a frozen lake and catch a good-sized lake trout on a piece of canned corn. That's what I'd always heard. On the morning of the day I was to have dinner with Jim Harrison, my friend John Olson and I strapped snowshoes on our boots and made for Hidden Lake, which was nestled in the peaks, at nine thousand feet, about three thousand feet above the trailhead. We traded off carrying the ice auger, a fairly light plastic drill three and a half feet long and edged in surgical steel.

Snowshoes are not my favorite form of winter locomotion. They're okay on the flats and all right if the path goes directly up or downhill. On steep side hills it is hard to set an edge with snowshoes. A man tends to fall; he rolls up in a big snowball, with the blades of the auger bouncing erratically, now over there, now inches from his eyes. This process suggests certain unpleasant headlines:

MORON, SLASHED BY OWN AUGER, BLEEDS TO DEATH.

Finally, at three in the afternoon, we hit the lake, which was a frozen expanse just below a series of jagged spires that formed the top of the range. The sun was hidden behind a peak, and the sky was gray. The temperature stood at 20 below zero, and the wind was blowing about forty miles an hour.

John and I stood on the ice, hunched over in misery, staring at a hole it had taken us twenty minutes to drill. The gray water was the same color as the sky above.

"Has the lake been stocked?" I asked through gritted teeth. Sometimes the Forest Service stocks the high lakes with rare golden trout. Sometimes they are stocked with rainbow or brown or brook trout.

"Don't know," John said.

"Just cuts then?"

Cuts are cutthroat trout, our native species.

"Don't know."

Sometimes the high lakes do not contain fish.

"You don't know if there are any fish here?"

"Came here to find out."

The wind was picking up the powdery snow, and it swirled around us in a waist-high ground blizzard.

What we discovered, on this day, was that there seemed to be no fish of any kind in the lake. (This perception may have been caused by frozen maggots.)

It was dark by the time we got back to the truck, and late by the time we got home. A quick shower and I was on the road. The hosts for the dinner with Harrison, longtime friends, said that the milelong road to their home had not been plowed. I was to bring my four-wheel-drive vehicle.

Now, over the years, I have been to this house dozens of times, perhaps hundreds, but in the dark and snow, I missed the turn and drove two miles overland, through crusty drifts, when it occurred to me that the truck was behaving badly. I stopped, with the engine running, and steam erupted from under the hood. It was coming from a rupture in one of the radiator hoses. The wind was howling at sixty miles an hour.

I climbed on top of the cab of the truck and took my bearings. The lights of the house I wanted were off in the distance, about five miles through the snow. I was out in the middle of a field owned by a local rancher who was notoriously inflexible about trespassing. The wind was blowing the steam in such a way that an inch of ice had already formed on the windshield. There was ice in my beard and ice coating the entire front of my body.

One of the many things I thought at that moment was that I was going to miss dinner with Jim Harrison and would not be able to defend the intelligence of ice fishermen.

Instead, I planned to stand there in the freezing steam for another few hours and mold myself into a noble ice sculpture, a heroic figure atop a disabled vehicle, a seasonal tourist attraction: the Moronic Sportsman.

The Moody Waters of
El Petén

▲

El Petén, the northernmost state of Guatemala, is for the most part a tropical forest veined by slow, sullen jungle rivers that bulge into the dark varicose clots of brackish ponds and brooding lakes. In some of these rivers and a few of the more unlikely lakes there are tarpon, the noble, silver-scaled saltwater fish one is accustomed to hooking off the Florida Keys. An odd and ancient breed, the tarpon begin their journey to the heart of the jungle at the mouth of the Río Usumacinta, just below the Mexican town of Frontera, on the Bay of Campeche. The great fishes—some of which weigh in excess of 150 pounds—are driven against the current by instinct, and they fight the Usumacinta for hundreds of miles until they find their way into smaller Guatemalan rivers such as the San Pedro or the Pasion. From the Pasion, the tarpon enter the Petexbatún, a river no more than fifty yards wide for most of its length. The Petexbatún flows into a lake of the same name, a lake so small it is not included on the less detailed maps of Guatemala. There, in the dark waters of that jungle lake, four hundred miles from the ocean, the tarpon spawn as they have spawned for more than 100 million years.

The tarpon's epic journey into one of the most dense and isolated jungles on the face of the earth takes them past the silent ruins of the ancient Mayas, past the massive stone palaces and ball courts of this most advanced pre-Colombian culture. The tarpon spawn in the heart of the low-lying jungles of El Petén, where, in the first thousand years after Christ, the Mayan culture soared to its greatest heights.

Only in the past few years have sport fishermen discovered Lake Petexbatún and the tarpon it contains. Only in the last few years have professional archaeologists penetrated the depths of the nearby jungles and begun excavation of the Mayan ruins.

I jumped at the chance to visit a lodge on Petexbatún Lake and sample both the tarpon and the ruins. A good part of my eagerness had to do with the fact that while others have caught tarpon on spinning rods or casting rigs, no one, as far as I knew, had ever caught a Petexbatún tarpon on fly-fishing gear. With a little luck, and some scientific angling, I would be the first. Fly-fishing is a snobbish affair; a true fly-fisherman, a purist, would rather not catch fish at all if he can't catch them on a fly.

I packed my rods and reels, my collection of saddle hackle flies from Dan Bailey's, my jungle boots, my books about the Maya— *The Maya* by Michael D. Coe is probably the best introductory text—and caught the flight to Guatemala City. Aviateca, the Guatemalan national airline, runs a series of remarkably informal flights to the city of Flores in the center of the state of El Petén. There was a curious amalgam of passengers on the flight: prosperous-looking Guatemalan businessmen on their way to make lumber or oil deals in Flores, elderly tourists and hippie backpackers on their way to the great Mayan temple complex at Tikal, and a number of Indians in sandals, some of whom carried turkeys in wooden crates.

At the Flores airport I was met by representatives of Panamundo, the Guatemalan travel service that owns the lodge at Lake Petexbatún. We stowed the gear in the back of a four-wheel-drive Scout and headed south for Sayaxché. The map said it was forty miles, over an all-weather road, but the drive took two and a half hours. The road was a cruel joke, a rutted washboard, insidiously studded with small, kidney-jolting rocks. A fine, drizzling mist splattered the windshield, and the rain intensified the odor of the jungle, which rose like an endless green wall on both sides of the road. It was not an unpleasant odor; it was, in fact, rather sweet, like syrup and day-old cut flowers combined with a certain distant muskiness.

At Sayaxché, on the Río Pasion, we transferred the gear into a large, canoelike vessel dug out from a single immense mahogany log. The boatman was named Conrado, and he was joined by Liko, a representative of Panamundo. Conrado yanked the twenty-horsepower outboard into life, and we set off up the Pasion and into the Río Petexbatún. The water was dark, black, almost like oil, but with no hint of thickness. The river flowed so slowly that it seemed almost still, and the black water glittered with a metallic sheen. Sometimes, the reflection of thick, low clouds loomed up out of those dark, gleaming waters and, near shore, the river shone with the myriad shades of green in the jungle wall. The odor here was more intense—Liko pointed out orchids growing in absurd profusion—and this heavy greenhouse fragrance was combined with a new smell, something a touch brackish and bracing, like a saltwater marsh. The river was a pleasure after the torture of the road. Tiny deer drank from the river, turtles slipped into the river before us, and snowy egrets rose ahead of the boat. The air was thick, warm, and floral, and we were accompanied by a constant symphony of unfamiliar birdsong.

The sun began to set, unseen behind a dark layer of clouds. Conrado steered the dugout through a small wall of reeds, and suddenly we were on Lake Petexbatún, a small body of water, still and black as onyx against the overhanging greenery of the jungle wall. There were a few thatched-roof huts set in clearings along the shore, and the flickering light of kerosene lanterns shone through the glassless open windows. The sun sank below the clouds, and its light set them aflame so that their color glistened, in the stillness of the lake, and Petexbatún seemed, for a moment, like a great, blood-warm reservoir of light and color in the darkness of the jungle.

Presently, Conrado pulled into a break in the jungle wall. Two dogs erupted into a furious crescendo of barking and yelping as we tied the boat to a tree. A thin, elderly black man stood behind the dogs. His name was Albert, and he escorted us along the stone path to the Petexbatún Lodge.

It was a thatched-roof affair, very much like the huts we had passed—same style, same materials, same workmanship—except that it had two stories and seemed much sturdier. Albert took us up to the second story. My room had a bed, a foam mattress, and a kerosene lantern.

Albert noticed two bottles of rum among my gear—we had been advised that the old caretaker took an occasional dram—and escorted us downstairs for dinner and a drink. He fried some catfish he had caught on fixed lines. The fillets were perfect: Albert is an open-fire gourmet.

He was also something of a raconteur. Originally from Belize (formerly British Honduras), Albert spoke an eloquent nine-teenth-century English with a Caribbean lilt. "We has some heavy fishes in this lake, mon. Ah, they come in on first flood, in September." Albert spoke with the wisdom of age, and, as the night progressed, with the animation of rum. He introduced us to the dogs, Lassie and Jet, and to the parrots, Marie and Lorenzo. Albert declared that Lorenzo spoke perfect Spanish. "He says, 'Lorenzo, *lorito bonito.*'" The words mean "Lorenzo, pretty little parrot," and when, after an eternity of coaxing, Lorenzo finally squawked, "Loreeko loreeko loreeko," Albert smiled like a proud parent. Lorenzo would take your finger along with a cracker, and he had a voice like a buzz saw tearing through a pine knot. Albert, of course, spent most of his time at the lodge alone with this cantankerous bird.

Albert has been caretaker, cook, and resident fishing guru at the lodge for ten years. The place was built by archaeologists who used it as a base during their study of nearby and recently discovered ruins. Albert said he had enjoyed the company of the archaeologists. "Ah, they brought wines of the finest variety from the land of France," he informed me grandly. I felt a bit shabby with my two bottles of local rum. "Whisky from Scotland," Albert went on. "Oh, we had some fine times. . . ."

The night was cool—incredibly, there were almost no mosquitoes or other noxious stinging insects—and it was pleasant to listen to the whisper of rain on the thatched roof and on the jungle canopy. It sounded like sustained applause, like an ovation heard faintly from a distance. Albert held forth on the proper method for catching tarpon, on the Mayan ruins, on the foolishness of civilized man. There was something almost unbearably romantic about sitting there with my glass of rum, quite comfortable in the midst of one of the thickest and most remote jungles on the face of the earth.

The days were alternately sodden and bright. Heavy tropical clouds formed and reformed over the water. They were dark, operatic, even Wagnerian, these clouds, quite beautiful in their own way. For several hours each afternoon the clouds gave way to blue skies and welcome sunshine that glittered off beaded rainwater on the vegetation. Occasionally, drifting near shore in Conrado's dugout, we'd spot large tarpon, rolling indolently. The fish are air-breathers, and they surface much like dolphins, their silver scales stark against the darkness of the water.

Conrado would paddle us into the area, and I'd cast blind into the darkness, while Liko threw out a handline Albert had lent him. The fishing snob in me regarded the handline as unscientific, primitive; Liko couldn't understand why a man would fish with gear that was obviously too light for the fish he hoped to catch. I spent some time explaining the superior and scientific aspects of fly-fishing, but it didn't make any difference: Whether our methods were snobbish or savage, neither of us caught fish. So one day when the rains came again, misting gently over the lake, we decided to visit the old Mayan site called Aguateca.

It was a half-hour ride to the other side of the lake and another fifteen minutes of threading our way through narrow, bayoulike channels until we reached the trail. We walked for half an hour, straight uphill, until we found ourselves on a rocky ridge that overlooked a great green marsh choked with waterfowl.

Aguateca, first discovered in 1957, has six temples that seem to belong to the jungle: odd, almost rectangular mounds, twenty to thirty feet high, covered over with the tangle of the jungle, with wrist-sized vines and twisted jungle trees. During the last thousand years of solitude, wind-driven leaves and other debris had settled on the temples, settled so thickly that they formed a sort of soil as they decomposed. This soil took the seeds of the jungle so that it was difficult to tell the temples from the forest itself.

At this particular site several stelae had apparently stood free in front of the temples. Stelae are stone monoliths, shaped rather like the tablets Moses brought down from the mountain. They stand six feet high or more. Carved into the rock are the images of priests and warriors. These stylized figures are generally accompanied by a kind of hieroglyphic writing that has yet to be fully deciphered. It is the stelae that the archaeologists find most useful in interpreting the vanished culture of the Mayans, and the archaeologists who stayed at the Petexbatún Lodge had uncovered and pieced together a number of evocative stelae at Aguateca.

I stared for a time at the stela labeled No. 2. It depicted a man in battle dress: He held a pike similar to those carried by Europeans in medieval times, and his shield was decorated with a terrifying and inhuman face. Oddly, this warrior, who seemed to be standing on the back of a crouching slave, was staring through a small stone circle. Could it have been some sort of lens? A telescope? The idea of a telescope in the middle of the jungle sometime around A.D. 700 set the mind spinning, sent gooseflesh rising up the spine even in the heat of the jungle.

The Mayas possessed accurate calendars and a knowledge of astronomy; they created brilliant sculpture, exquisite pottery, and architecture we find almost alien in its symmetry. They reached the Classic period of their culture between A.D. 250 and 850. About the year 900, for reasons no one has ever been able to explain, the Mayan leaders abandoned their magnificent structures and the race fell into an inexplicable decline. During the Classic period, experts estimate that there were more than two hundred people per square mile living in El Petén. Today you can divide that number by one hundred.

Early travelers to the region were stunned by the size and complexity of the ruins and concluded that such wondrous structures could not have been constructed by the ancestors of the indigenous Mayas. They were thought to be the remains of a lost and superior culture. Some postulated a wandering Israeli tribe; others assumed the ruins had been built by Tartars or perhaps Welshmen. Even today, a popular pseudoscientific theory holds that these Meso-American Indians were assisted in their labors by extraterrestrials—ancient gods in spaceships.

It is mystery itself that generates such absurdities, or so I thought as we walked back down to the boat. I had already seen a restored temple at Ceibal, near Sayaxché. It stood in a grassy courtyard, ancient and alien, strange in its symmetry, and the hard local stone, newly polished, glittered under the jungle sun. How splendid it was—how splendid the people must have been—but the mystery was deeper and darker at Aguateca. It expanded inside the chest and left me feeling helpless with wonder.

Coming back across the lake to the lodge, I found myself feeling just a bit dizzy. The sun broke through the clouds then, and I saw the tarpon of Lake Petexbatún. They were slashing through a school of baitfish, feeding greedily, dozens of them clearing the water in startling silver leaps. They set the lake aboil. We cut the motor and paddled into the feeding frenzy just as it was ending. I tossed out my line to straighten it for the first cast. A good-sized tarpon took the fly. The fish have bony mouths, and to hook them you must yank hard, but I stood there in an entirely loopy manner while the tarpon rose out of the water and shook the hook from his mouth.

He had been a big one, an inutterably ancient-looking beast; his kind had been alive during the time of the dinosaurs. Tarpon had traveled up the Usumacinta since time immemorial—they had seen the Maya come and go—and now this fish had spit out the best fly I had. So much for the snobbery and science of fly-fishing.

The tarpon simply disappeared. The dark water was silent and the reflections of massive clouds drifted by under the boat. I cast for another hour or two, but the big one had gotten away. This is not unusual for me, and at least I had seen him surface, this great silver anachronism. I would have released him anyway: Tarpon are not particularly good eating. But he had thrown the hook himself, preserving his own mystery just as the jungle had embalmed the mystery of the Maya. Both the tarpon and the Maya, it seems to me, are impervious to the challenge of science. Albert and Conrado and Liko and I drank to that idea that night as the rain applauded, distantly.

Baja by Kayak

▲

Martine Springer was tall and tan, fit as a broadcast aerobics instructor, and she was waist-deep in the resort pool, demonstrating how to get back in a sea kayak once you've fallen out of the son of a bitch. A guy could, Martine said, muscle his way back in, maybe. "Just remember," she said, "if you go over, you've probably been battling some heavy water. You'll probably be tired."

The proper technique involved blowing up a little bag to place on one end of your kayak paddle. Martine laid the paddle out in the water, with the unbagged end on the kayak itself, then lifted a long leg to the shaft, and slithered back into the kayak like a badger into a burrow. She pumped water out of the cockpit with a bilge pump and glanced up at her five clients standing poolside.

"You guys try it," she said.

I looked over the fence and across the road where a heavy morning wind was whipping whitecaps across the surface of the Gulf of California.

"Is this," I asked, "one of those deals where a guy ought to know how to swim?"

*   *   *

Baja (lower) California is a fierce, sun-blasted land, a narrow strip of desert, eight hundred miles long, that separated itself from the Mexican mainland in a slow tectonic slide about 20 million years ago. The Pacific Ocean rushed in to fill the void, forming the Gulf of California, the youngest of the world's deep-water gulfs. This vast arm of the Pacific, two miles deep at its mouth, was once known as the Vermilion Sea, and indeed, under a rising sun, the warm, tranquil waters shimmer like pale blood.

The mountains are stark, ridged, and crenelated and bare. The land supports a variety of obdurate and malicious flora: There are thistles underfoot and cardon cacti towering overhead. Every growing thing, or so it seems, sticks, stabs, or stinks. The sere desert, with its tortured red rock mountains, is little given to agriculture or ranching. There are red dirt roads branching off the paved road that bisects the peninsula, which was built to attract American tourists. The rough, rutted secondary roads lead to dusty towns where generators provide electricity for two hours a day.

The eastern coast, north of the town of Loreto, is unpopulated, undeveloped (for the most part), and harshly serene. A vast, ringing silence owns the land, except where the sea, driven by afternoon winds, explodes against rocky headlands and points.

And the sea is an exuberant celebration of life. Swarms of baitfish go about their business and are pursued from above and below by all manner of predators. Pelicans and blue-footed boobies attack from the air; pods of killer whales roll and breathe on offshore patrol; colonies of sea lions strike out from rocky points. Manta rays, some of them weighing in excess of one thousand pounds, erupt out of the shimmering sea: great black batlike plankton feeders in flight four feet above the surface of the water. They are like images seen in some inexplicable dream, and the water cascades off their huge black wings in iridescent sheets.

The Gulf of California, this great arm of the Pacific Ocean, is a giant fish trap, a fecund sea in the middle of the Sonaran Desert. It is this contrast—the living sea in proximity to harsh, unforgiving land—that so intoxicates the Baja coastal kayaker.

*　*　*

These days, sea kayaking along the coast of Baja is a big business.

I had chosen to paddle with Ageya, an Alaska-based kayaking outfitter, primarily because the company's trip seemed less structured than those of the other operators. They were new in Baja, didn't have a lot of clients, and their itinerary wasn't set in stone. My friend photographer Paul Dix and I could go off on our own, provided the guides felt we weren't putting ourselves into potentially mortal waters.

Paul and I, for our part, had kayaked the Alaskan coast, alone. We had surfed our fragile crafts on waves thrown up by calving tidewater glaciers in Glacier Bay, and camped under the northern lights while wolves howled mournfully through the night. More to the point, we owned a two-man kayak. Neither of us had much experience enduring organized tours.

Still . . .

It was a four-day drive from our homes in Montana to the Baja. We would have to buy food, pack tents and sleeping bags, inquire as to legalities of various campsites, scout the coast ourselves, then arrange for someone to watch our vehicle and to pick us up at our eventual destination. A private expedition would cost us three weeks in return for one week of paddling. The monetary cost would be about the same, but with Ageya, we'd spend all our time—seven days—on the water: in and out, just like that.

That was the lure of the organized tour.

The drawback, as I saw it, was a dismal lack of adventure. I don't much care to have someone else in charge, someone who knows what he or she is doing. The trip goes too smoothly, stuff falls into place, and you never end up, oh, swimming for your life through savage seas. You never wake up half-drowned in some small Mexican village where there are no telephones, where there is no electricity and, of course, no doctor. On organized trips you seldom find yourself being nursed back to health by a beautiful Mexican woman whose long black hair brushes your sweating chest as she feeds you another spoonful of mashed bananas. Her large dark eyes burn with desire, and there is a stirring in . . .

Naw, what happens on organized trips is good, clean, safe fun.
I suppose.

After our morning orientation in the motel pool, Ageya's five clients piled into a van driven by a Mexican cabdriver who drove
with staggering caution (yes, staggering caution) about forty
miles north along the paved road. We turned on one of the red
dirt paths that led to the coast and stopped at a broad, curving
beach that served as a camp for the fishermen of Loreto.

We set up our tents near a place where the fishermen dumped
gutted fish. Sea gulls shrieked in the dump, and they strutted
among feeding vultures. There was a bad odor when the wind
shifted.

Martine said that this would be her first outing as head guide.
Kimmer Ball usually took the head guide's position, and she was
coming along in an advisory position. Kimmer, like Martine, was
in her late twenties. She looked as if she might have pumped
some iron in her time, like a woman who did a lot of reps for
tone. Both women were strong and confident. They seemed competent and likable, thoroughly professional, achingly attractive,
and sadly unavailable.

As we set up our tents for night, Martine warned us to check
our shoes for scorpions in the morning. The little bastards were
nocturnal hunters, and when the sun rose, they sought any available source of shade: a shoe, a pair of pants on the ground, a
sleeping bag containing a sleeping human being. In the day the
scorpions tended to be in the bushes, which meant that a person
had to watch where he walked.

One other thing we should know: The Gulf of California could
be a killer. It tended to be tranquil from the hours before sunrise
until about noon, when the wind picked up and made paddling
hazardous. You only had to look at the sea to make certain deter-
minations. A ten- to twelve-mile-an-hour wind whipped up
widely scattered whitecaps, and such waters were negotiable in a
sea kayak. When the whitecaps were more closely spaced, the
wind was probably blowing at fifteen to twenty miles an hour.
You didn't want to be out paddling in that.

The most treacherous waters were found where rocky points projected out into the sea. Here currents and winds collided, and the sea was choppy, confused, dangerous. Sometimes you found yourself paddling out of a placid bay, around a point, and discovered that the wind on the other side was howling at twenty-five miles an hour. A well-known outfitting group had lost two kayakers in such a situation several years ago.

The sun rose over the Vermilion Sea, and a wispy pink fog drifted up off its mirrored surface. We were paddling north, just beyond the breakers, heading for a point about three miles away. It would have been faster to just cut across the bay, but Martine wanted us to hug the curving coastline. I was in a two-man kayak, paddling with David Risley, a geophysist from Anchorage, Alaska. We were both sealed into cockpits that were covered over with spray skirts to prevent a freak wave from swamping the craft.

In the distance a raft of grebes bobbed on the gentle swell. There were several hundred of the small, drab-looking birds. The paddling party, which included Mo Hillstrand and Eric Hall, two emergency medical workers also from Anchorage, approached the birds, cautiously. They dived, all at once, and disappeared for what seemed like several minutes. And then they surfaced, all at once, a few hundred yards away. We were between them and the sun, and their eyes were an unworldly, lazarlike red.

There were a set of foot pedals in my cockpit that operated the kayak's rudder, but the craft was mushy on all but the fastest turns. Dave felt it as well. We had probably overloaded the rear storage compartment to compensate for the fact that I outweighed Dave by twenty pounds or so.

"We should put both tents in the front," Dave said.

"Food's heavy too."

The grebes stared at us with their lazar eyes, suckers for an existential conversation, I supposed.

We were paddling in a sure, steady rhythm that had tired me for the first half hour or so. Now, I was on automatic pilot and sensed I had hours left. My forearms felt as if golf balls would bounce off them.

Just before noon the wind began to pick up, and we pulled in to a wide beach protected from the wind by a high, Gothic-looking point two miles to the north.

We swam and snorkled and set up our tents. Kimmer came over to give me a hand, and I waved her off. Something about human males that has never been very clear to me. I never ask directions when I'm lost either.

There was another boat in our party, a twelve-foot motorized sailing craft that carried provisions and was available in case of emergency. Steve Audett, the captain, a sometimes musician and electrician out of Anchorage, had brought his family along for the ride. His wife, Shine, was a midwife. Their son, Loghan, was six and his sister, Oceana, was three. The family seemed beneficent and happy, like Deadheads at a picnic, and indeed Shine had once taken the Grateful Dead on a wilderness tour of Alaska.

I ran into Loghan down near a lagoon and tried to show him how to skip stones, but he waved off my instructions. "I know how," he said in some pique. Human males.

Kimmer said that Ageya got all kinds of clients. Some people had never been in a kayak before, others were experts. The experts, she thought, came along on organized tours for the companionship, for the people they would meet.

And so, sitting by the fire after dinner, with the sun setting behind coastal mountains and spreading purple shadows over the beach like great puddles of ink, we chatted amiably. Loghan sat by Martine and explained that he had six girlfriends in school. He named them off in the order that he liked them best, and the women around the fire reacted, in tandem, with amused horror. Human males. They raised their eyes to the sky, which was a dark red-black bruise.

Loghan misinterpreted the gesture, put his arm around Martine, and explained that she could be his girlfriend on this trip. Since she was here.

"It's in the genes," Martine said of human males.

Oceana, the three-year-old girl, was sitting in my lap. "I don't have any boyfriends at all," she said in some sorrow.

"Then," I said grandly, "I'll be your boyfriend."

Oceana laughed a tinkly little laugh that went on for an uncomfortable length of time.

"What's so funny about that?" I asked, aggrieved.

"I can't be your girlfriend," Oceana said. "I'm too little."

The next morning I rose early and walked down a gravelly wash lined with cardon cacti and bushes that were still green in what had been a wet spring for Baja. The wash led into a box canyon whose walls caught the light of the rising sun. In the clean, clear air they looked like pale pink watercolors rising on all sides. Above, the western sky was blue-black. There was a sound I had been hearing for some time, a distant buzz, as of hundreds of people murmuring softly, but now the buzz took on a sharper, harder-edged resonance.

The canyon ended in a kind of expanded horseshoe shape, and I could see green trees and bushes standing against the reddish walls that rose 150 feet on all sides. The buzzing echoed against stone and reverberated and filled me with an as-yet-unspecified dread. Two more steps and I saw them: thousands upon thousands of long, thin wasps swarming around a single tree in such numbers that it seemed to be covered with a thick mass of shifting yellow flowers. In the half-light of early morning, in the cool shadow of the canyon, the wasps seemed slow, nearly somnambulant. They moved on the tree in turgid masses, like viscous globules of some thick liquid. The buzzing seemed to be getting louder, and I abandoned the rest of my walk.

That day we paddled against a brisk wind, north to the point, which was named for a kind of small octopus that swarmed the nighttime reefs there. Dave and I were paddling well together, and we seldom clacked paddles. A kayak paddle is a single shaft with two blades set at right angles to one another. The shaft is twisted in the hand at each revolution so that the upper blade cuts the wind.

There was a small sea stack ahead of us, a spire of rock that rose from the water like the twisted battlements of some ancient fortress. A dozen or more pelicans had taken up positions on a series of ridge lines, and there were hundreds of western sea gulls interspersed among them. Dave and I studied the current a bit, then let the kayak float near these populated spires. A few gulls circled overhead and shrieked at us in their self-righteous manner. Two of the pelicans stood atop the spire, facing the north wind with their wings extended. When the evaporative effect of the wind had dried them sufficiently, they leaned into the wind, fell two full feet, then swooped into the air.

"Look down," Kimmer called from her kayak. There was a school of bait fish moving under our boats. A pelican crashed into the surf ten feet away, then rose into the sky with its neck bulging and something jumping under the skin there.

The sea gulls on the spire were calling to one another in a voice I'd never heard before. It sounded like mad laughter, and the pelicans lifted off the rock, one after the other. On all sides they were plunging into the surf, sometimes sending up five-foot-high plumes of spray.

And then the current drove us on, toward a lonely white glittering beach on the lee side of the point. We pulled in for lunch. A trail led to the summit of Octopus Point, which looked to be about seven hundred feet high. The wind was fierce up there, and I watched a small fishing boat rounding the point. It was pitching violently and rolling from side to side. Wouldn't want to be down there in a kayak, I thought.

There were dark moving spots on the sea stacks that fronted the point, and I could hear the echoing bark of sea lions. There must have been another school of baitfish in the area because the sea lions slid off the rocks, pelicans crashed, and blue-footed boobies dived like fighter planes. I could just make out the boobies' neon-blue feet and see them as they folded in their wings, hit the water, and left a slanting trail of bubbles fifteen feet deep.

Later we paddled out to the point to meet the sea lions. Martine kept us close to the shoreline cliffs, out of the churning water to the north. The sea lions basked on the rocks and regarded us with the mild curiosity humans reserve for, oh, cows ambling across a suburban lawn: I know what that is, but what's it doing here?

There were several perfect arches jutting out from one of the sea stacks, but they were a bit north, close to the nasty water at the point of the point. Martine and Shine, in a two-man kayak, paddled near the arch, timed the rush of water through it, then paddled through. Fast.

Dave and I watched from cowardly safety. Several of the sea lions were circling our kayak. One was floating on its back, flippers in the air. Two others stared at us with dark, impenetrable eyes. They had the friendly faces of golden retrievers. Perhaps half a mile out to sea, a series of black fins rolled one after the other. Killer whales will attack sea lions, but this pod seemed to be moving south at about thirty miles an hour.

The point was the most dangerous place we would have to negotiate in the kayak. It was also a great confluence of life, and this combination of peril and substance sent the spirit spinning off into various ethereal regions, in which a man might be tempted to commit philosophy.

Oceana did indeed become my girlfriend. She sat with me at night around the fire as the adults talked. Her father, Steve, warned me never to get her excited after eight o'clock. "She'll sleep then," he said, "but if you get her going, she'll be up all night and it'll be a horror show, guaranteed."

Dave, the scientist, said that there was "a lot of geology going on" around our campsite. He could see upthrust and erosion, all of it looking as if it had just happened yesterday, by which he meant in the last 2.5 million years, in the "the Quaternary."

"What's that?" I asked.

"The most recent geological period. It includes the Pleistocene and the Holocene."

"Oh," I said, "that Quaternary."

"I used to have me one of those," Steve said. "I never could keep a clutch in it."

We played a game in which a person told two lies and one truth about himself. Kimmer said that in the sixth grade she could throw a ball farther than anyone in the school, that at age nineteen she had won an arm-wrestling contest, and that she had a twin sister who died at birth. We all nailed the twin as a lie. No one picked out Martine's lie, and she had to explain that no, the Czechoslovakian climber hadn't actually proposed to her near the summit of Mount McKinley. He had only propositioned her. Both versions were 100 percent believable.

It was getting late, and Oceana was fading, but she was so sweet lying in my arms, so fresh, that I couldn't help asking her if she remembered what it was like in the time before she was born. Oceana misinterpreted the question to mean did she remember being born. "I was borned," she proclaimed—everyone was listening intently—"and I went 'wah wah wah wah wah wah wah. . . .' "

After the twenty-fifth "wah" or so most of the adults had absorbed the point.

". . . wah wah wah . . ."

"But, Oceana," I said (here Steve caught my eye and shook his head, please no, but I was too far into my question to stop), "do you remember anything else?"

"I was borned and I went"—Oceana was enjoying this immensely—"WAH WAH WAH WAH WAH WAH WAH WAH WAH . . ."

The adults regarded me with a combination of loathing and animosity.

The next morning, as we broke camp, the wasps that had been confined inland invaded the beach. There were all over everything, like a biblical plague, and they stung the children and the adults without mercy. Dave and I jammed our gear in the rear storage compartment without regard to weight distribution. I had been stung on the right forearm and would have felt intensely sorry for myself, except that poor six-year-old Loghan had been stung twice, once on the neck.

Out on the water, a good distance from shore, we lost the last of the great horde. A few stragglers crawled over the kayaks, settling on the brightly colored spray skirts buttoned around the rim of the cockpits. We had a long paddle, four straight hours, I figured, and the exertion was pumping poison into my stung forearm. I had begun to swell, visibly. I didn't want to think about the awful . . . sensation . . . on my legs. It felt like, well, like some kind of . . . bug . . . crawling up my leg. Under the spray skirt. On my knee. Up the thigh . . .

It was all imagination, of course. I was acutely aware of wasps only because my right arm was beginning to look like Popeye's.

And now, on the way back past our first campsite, we had to round another point. It was late for paddling, about noon, and the wind had picked up to fifteen miles an hour. Large, regular waves about four and five feet high were washing in toward the beach at an oblique angle, so that the kayak wanted to take them broadside. Which was what Martine called a "capsize situation." Dave and I had to paddle fast in order to keep our poorly packed kayak maneuverable. My right forearm was bigger than my bicep. It felt like a water balloon.

And there was no stopping now, because the point was ahead of us and the water was getting choppy. Paul Dix was paddling alongside us, but I could only see him in slow-motion strobo-scopic bursts. He'd sink into the trough of a wave and disappear. And then, suddenly, the bottom would drop out from under our kayak, but there was Paul, on the crest of a booming wave, tow-ering eight feet above us.

And goddammit, if there was a wasp under my spray skirt it was crawling up my shorts, and this was intolerable, it would not happen, and in the mushy-handling kayak, between what seemed to be monumental waves, I pulled off the spray skirt, and yes, a long yellow wasp crawled out onto the deck of the boat just as a wave hit us broadside and splashed up onto the deck and washed the wasp into the Gulf of California. There was a wave of adren-aline, a shot in the belly, that sensation of falling before you actu-ally fall. . . .

We leaned over close enough to kiss the sea, but managed to right the kayak and work up enough speed to regain control. We headed in, lickety-split, toward shore and the campsite. The point had given everyone else some trouble, too, and we were all talk-ing at once on the beach.

"Dave," I informed the company, "was crying the whole way."

"Tim," Dave pointed out, "kept using his bilge pump for something."

And then people had to laugh about the wasp in my shorts for entirely too long a time. It wasn't that funny at all.

"Tim," Dave said, "knows some very colorful language."

"Latin terms for wasp," I explained.

Some time later, I opened a plastic sack containing several different kinds of cheese. A wasp staggered out onto the rock, woozy from the heat. It was so full of cheese that it couldn't fly, and I stomped it flat.

"POPEYE MY ARM, WILL YOU, YOU SON OF A BITCH!"

I jumped up and down on the wasp, and screamed at it and cursed it and stomped on it in a mad jig of murder and vengeance. It occurred to me that there might be people about, and that I could be overreacting. Indeed, Loghan and Oceana were staring up at me with large, innocent eyes.

"Wasp," I said, nodding at a yellow smear on the rock.

"It's dead," Oceana pointed out.

"It was dead a long time ago," Loghan added.

"What's a basser?" Oceana asked.

Our campsite was set on beach that fronted a bay shaped like an hourglass. The water in the inner bay was calm and blue-green, and there was a lot of geology going on everywhere. A large, sloping flat-topped rock stood in the middle of the inner bay. Grasses and shrubs and cacti grew at the summit, but the rock was crumbling away on all sides. Calm water arches under the fallen rock framed the sea beyond.

There were four Mexican fishermen camped nearby. Paul Dix and I went over to talk with them, and they offered us fresh clams with salt and lime. You dive for these brown-shelled clams at low tide, the men explained, out near the rock. One of the fishermen said that eating such clams made a man very virile. We all laughed at that, as men are supposed to do. I translated the phrase "lead in the old pencil," and we all laughed some more, in an obligatory way, though I found myself wondering what good it did to have lead in the old pencil if you had nothing to write on.

The fishermen gave us a large yellowfin tuna for our dinner, and we invited them to share it with us. Long after sunset they still hadn't come over to our camp.

"They're very shy," Paul said.

"We'll fix them," Steve said. He had brought along some bottle rockets to amuse the children this last dark night on the beach. We set them off one at a time, and called out the names of the fishermen: Jorge—boom—Mauricio—bam—René—ka-bloom—Ramón.

The fishermen could hardly refuse. After dinner Oceana abandoned me for Mauricio, a handsome, curly-haired young man. She sat on his lap, half under his jacket, and made him hold her doll. You had to be careful with a baby, Oceana explained. And sometimes they pooped. Did Mauricio know about the poop? He nodded his head gravely. Mauricio couldn't speak a word of English. Oceana prattled on for over an hour.

Jorge said he drove the catch all the way to Mexico City. It was a scary place, and he never went out after dark there.

We passed around a small bottle of tequila, but Mauricio shook his head when I offered it. He didn't want to disturb Oceana, who was asleep in his arms.

The next day, the same Mexican driver we had before pushed his van down the red rutted road, and we packed up our gear in a little less than an hour. When we hit the paved highway, I suggested we stop at the first roadside cantina for a cold beer. I wanted to say good-bye before we hit Loreto and scattered.

The cantina was a porch, open to the wind. We were sipping beers and reminiscing already, as if the trip had happened a decade ago. What about those sea lions near the arch? And the fishermen: great guys. That last sorta scary point. The wasps . . .

Oceana said she would not come back to Montana with me and be my little girl. Her parents might cry if she came with me.

"I have to go back to Alaska," she said seriously.

It felt like the last scene in *Casablanca*.

"We'll always have Paris," I said.

"I like you very much," Oceana said. Human females, I thought, it's in the genes.

"When you go back to Alaska," I said with what I thought was a good measure of nobility—Oceana nodded seriously—"don't eat the yellow snow."

"Why?" She cogitated on the matter for some moments. "Because of pee?"

"That's right," I said, and then we all had to pile into the van, go back to Loreto, fly north, and face up to the various varieties of yellow snow in our lives.

OTHER
PEOPLE'S
LIVES

▲

Speak Oz

▲

Most of us flaming septics visiting Oz either shoot through like the Bondi tram or muck about playing silly buggers and never properly apprehend the lingo. I was pondering this phenomenon one day while demolishing several dozen stubbies in the cattle-ranching country of far North Queensland, specifically at a rubbity in the town of Coen, whose quaint motto is "Eat Beef, You Bastards." Three weeks into my trip to Australia I was aware that "bastard" is a term used to describe acceptable and pleasant members of the human race. The rubbity was located in what had been the Exchange Hotel, but the new owner—in the interest of economy and typical Aussie bullsh—had altered the name with a single letter, so that the only sign of any size in this town of some forty houses now read, DRINK AT THE SEXCHANGE HOTEL.

One of the bastards doing just that was having a go at me: "Geez," he said, "there must have been fifty flaming roos out there that night." The image of fifty kangaroos leaping and lurching about in an agony of fire tugged at the mind, though I knew perfectly well that "flaming" is a universal adjective often applied to perfectly uninflammable objects, just as the word "bloody" is used to modify any noun: "I twisted me flaming ankle on a bloody rock."

Much of what is unique about Australian English derives from the flash talk of transported criminals, and rhyming slang—"I have some Gene Tunney [money] in me skyrocket [pocket], and I'm going to the rubbity [dub-pub] for a pig's ear [beer]"—is dinki-di (a dinkum Aussie term meaning genuine Oz speak.) Another ridgi-dige bit of lingo has it that Americans are "seppos" or "septics" (septic-tank Yank.)

As the only septic at the Sexchange, I had to ask directions to the snakes (rhymes with snake's hiss) so I could unbutton the mutton and wring the rattlesnake. There are dozens of phrases for this particular activity, and they range from drain the dragon to syphon the python to simply "go a snakes."

In a rubbity like the Sexchange a bastard would be a flaming galah not to demolish several dozen stubbies (small bottles of lager), and a polite bastard steps out back to have a bit of a chunder. This process of enjoying oneself in reverse may be one of Australia's most popular indoor and outdoor sports, judging by the sheer number of phrases used to describe it: "cry ruth," "hurl," "chunder," "play the whale," "do the big spit," "park the tiger," "have a nice technicolor yawn," "laugh at the ground."

Since there were no jam tarts in evidence, a bit of the talk concerned certain Sheilas with norks like Mudgee mailbags. One potato in particular was known to root like a rattlesnake, and one of my companions expressed a desire to be "at her like a rat up a drainpipe." The preferred organ in an R.U.A.D. situation is known as "the wily old snorker," or, alternately, and more graphically, "the beef bayonet," the "pork sword," or the "mutton dagger."

In all fairness I should mention that certain proper residents of Australia—wowsers of the worst ilk—object strongly to such conversation and feel that some of the words and phrases used here are "best left written on the wall in an outback dunny." This attitude, I think, does not do justice to the distinctiveness of Australian usage. All the above words and phrases may be found in the new *Macquarie Dictionary,* a dinkum Aussie dictionary published by Macquarie University, New South Wales, after eleven years of research.

Very few of the bastards at the Sexchange were concerned with verbal propriety, however, possibly because most of us were full as a bull's bum. The English language as spoken by Aussies— toilet talk and all—seemed robust and important. Several dozen stubbies'll do that to a bastard, of course, and when someone referred to the local dentist as a "fang-ferrier," I got to laughing in an entirely hysterical manner. Someone decided, quite loudly, that "the bleeding septic is as silly as a bagful of arseholes," and I couldn't stop laughing.

"He's gone troppo," they said.

"Fair dinkum."

"Meself," one bastard opined, "I blame the climate."

Sanghyang in Bali

▲

"I myself," I. Ketut Suwena explained, "have been the monkey, the pig, and even Memedi, the evil spirit."

"You acted like a pig," I asked, "in front of the whole village?"

"Yes."

"And this did not embarrass you?"

"I was in a trance. The spirit of the god had entered me. Then, later, I felt sanctified."

"But to crawl on your hands and knees in the dirt, grunting and eating discarded food, garbage. . . ."

"Sometimes," Ketut admitted, "the trance is not very deep. Sometimes, for a moment, you are aware of what you are doing, and you see the people of the village, and you are embarrassed. But they are singing for you, and the trance comes back, deeper."

"Tonight you will not go into a trance?"

"No. I will not become *sanghyang.* I will be a helper. A guard."

"You need guards?"

"Oh, yes. When the dancers become *sanghyang,* when they go into the trance, they become very strong. The fire horse, for instance, is very dangerous. We call this *sanghyang djaran gading,* and there is a time, in the fire, when he is more like a man running amok. Oh, I tell you, the man who is *sanghyang* has much strength. Sometimes it takes twenty men to hold him down and bring him out of the trance."

On the island of Bali men and women routinely fall into bizarre and sometimes violent trance states during certain carefully prescribed religious ceremonies. Bali is a small island, just one and a half kilometers east of Java, one of the over thirteen thousand islands that comprise the nation of Indonesia. The people, to Western eyes, are uncommonly attractive. They are fond of music, dancing, stage plays, and festivals. The extraordinary trance dances occur in a state of spiritual ecstasy and are religious in nature.

In the seventh century A.D. Indian traders brought the Hindu religion to Bali. When Islam triumphed over Hinduism in the sixteenth century, Bali became a refuge for Hindu intellectuals and nobles. Today it is the last bastion of Hinduism in Indonesia.

Balinese life is centered around the religion known as Agama Hindu. It is an amalgam of Tantric Buddhism, Malay ancestor worship, magical beliefs, and various animistic rituals that have survived a thousand years or more on the island. The ancient animistic faith is strong and has been incorporated into the overlying Hindu belief structures.

To an outsider it sometimes seems that the old animistic beliefs properly define the people and religion of Bali. Often the rituals of classical Hinduism seem a mere afterthought, especially in the extreme case of violent trancing ceremonies.

The animistic elements of Agama Hindu are so ingrained in the people that few can actually explain their meaning. When asked why a man goes into a trance at a certain time during a certain ceremony, people will shrug politely. It is a question that has little meaning to the Balinese. "It is the way we do things," they will tell you. In Europe there are few animistic rituals still surviving, though I suspect very few people could explain the "meaning" of the Christmas tree. "We do it because we have always done it," people will say. "We have Christmas trees because we like them." So it is with the Balinese.

* * *

As in Europe, there are some few people familiar with the origin and meaning of the ancient rituals. I. Ketut Suwena was one. He was fifty-two, the klian, or headman, of the banjar of Jangu. A banjar is an organization of households—usually several hundred of them—and is the most important social unit on the island. The banjar dispenses justice according to the traditional law called *adat*.

The banjar of Jangu is famous for its folk trances: nighttime ceremonies in which the people gather and sing while men in a state of trance perform feats of strength or dexterity that they could not do in a waking state. They climb trees like monkeys, lift heavy objects with the small finger of the right hand, or run barefoot through three-foot-high mounds of blazing coconut husks.

The trances, or *sanghyangs,* Ketut explained, were originally performed in times of trouble, especially when the banjar was threatened by disease. "You see," he said, "when Sira Mede Mecaling came to Bali from the island of Nusa Pinida, he brought with him many butas and kalas." Mecaling is considered the overlord of the evil spirits. Butas and kalas are various demons whose joy in the spirit world consists of tormenting human beings with grief and illness. The overlord went to Bali's most powerful benevolent god, Ida Batara Dalem Besakih, and asked permission to bring sickness on the land. Permission was granted, though the butas and kalas could not afflict those villages where the proper sacrifices were performed.

"But," Ketut explained, "Sira Mede Mecaling is evil and sometimes does not keep his promises." Sometimes, even after the sacrifices are performed according to ritual, the demonic followers of the evil god visit sickness upon the land. The rice crop may fail. Epidemics may occur.

"If my family is sick," Ketut said, "I am helpless. Then I may see a monkey at the door. I know this monkey is an evil spirit, and I chase it away, but I cannot catch it, because I am not strong enough or fast enough. So I go to the god of my banjar, and I make an offering of flowers and food. I ask for the strength to chase the evil spirit. And the god allows me to go into a trance and become the monkey. Then I can climb trees and am very strong. I do this in front of all the people in the banjar, and the women sing the old songs to help me chase away the spirit. Then, later, the sickness is gone."

In Jangu one night, on the hard-packed mud of the school yard, several hundred people gathered for a *sanghyang* ceremony. Men and women sat on long wooden benches while others stood five deep around a sturdy wooden corral constructed for the ceremony. In the center of the arena there was a young palm tree that had been recently cut down and propped up on the dirt with a clever arrangement of boards.

Over twenty men stood inside the corral, waiting. A man wearing a leather loincloth and a long, disheveled black wig stepped into the corral. He was led to a small bamboo mat at the corner of the arena. He knelt, looked up, and nodded to a woman holding a plate of offerings that consisted of some biscuits, many flowers, and a bottle containing a small amount of clear liquor. The woman took the offering twenty yards away to a small stone structure about five feet high. This was the "seat" of the god of the banjar. It was shaped like an elongated pedestal with an open box on top. When the offerings had been made to the god, the man in the loincloth bent his head over a small, exquisitely crafted silver dish. One of the guards lit some twigs that had been soaked in aromatic oil. The man in the wig began rocking forward and back as he breathed scented smoke. The women of the banjar sang the ancient song, begging their god to inhabit the rocking man with the spirit of the monkey.

Suddenly, he fell over onto his back and writhed about on the hard-packed dirt. He leapt to his feet and ran around the corral with a strange simian gait. His eyes were completely closed, and his front teeth were exposed. He looked very like a monkey.

The man turned for the tree and climbed it rapidly, without looking for handholds. It is fair to say that he dashed up the tree. At the top he pulled against a branch, leaning far out over the dirt, and the tree pulled loose from the wooden struts that held it. This seemed to infuriate the monkey, and he pulled and swayed in the topmost branches without regard to his own safety. The guards rushed to the tree and held it upright.

Some of the men tried to lure the monkey down with freshly dug roots. The women continued to sing. Eventually, the monkey descended a lower branch and ate the muddy roots. He seemed to notice one of the guards and began grooming him, picking imaginary lice from his hair and eating them. Some of the women laughed, and the song was briefly interrupted.

About ten minutes later, a kind of brittle tension seemed to animate the crowd. The monkey man's brow was furrowed, and his movements had slowed. There was an ancient anger in his face. He leapt at one of the guards. The crowd exploded in a single shriek that seemed composed of equal parts glee and fear.

All twenty of the guards fell on the man, but he fought them off in convulsive bursts of what seemed to be superhuman strength. It seemed as if the monkey man was suffering a kind of fit. Several guards were thrown across the corral. Others were knocked off their feet. One man suffered a bloodied nose. A minute later the guards had the man restrained: There were several men on each arm, several on each leg. The man was lifted high on many hands, and Ketut sprinkled him with water that had been blessed by a priest.

Slowly, the man came to his senses. I could see a distant bleariness in his eyes, a confusion there that you see in drunkards. He was lowered to the ground. Several of the guards spoke softly with him until he rose and walked away, stumbling slightly.

There were several other *sanghyangs* that night. A man crawled about on all fours and ate garbage like a pig; another ran through a blazing fire and stomped it out with his bare feet. And always, at the end, there was the final violent, convulsive fight.

Bali is, by and large, a peaceful island. In the mountain villages, miles away from the bustling tourist beaches, it is possible to leave a suitcase by the side of the road and return several days later to claim it. People do not fight, drink excessively, or steal. The culture is based on agriculture, and the agricultural system—one that has fed the island for uncounted centuries—requires cooperation of a very high order. Village water-control boards apportion irrigation rights to the water that flows off the slopes of the central volcanoes. The average size of a family farm is 2.5 acres, and water—hence cooperation—is essential. It is a system that works: No one goes hungry in Bali.

It is also a system that pays social dividends. Two and a half million people live closely on Bali's 5,623 square kilometers. In another culture this crush of humanity might breed crime and disorder. Not so in Bali. Infractions of the traditional law are dealt with harshly.

Every Balinese can tell of someone who was banished from his village for fighting or stealing. The banished person may stay, but he will receive no water for his crops, no one will sell him food or buy his services. No one will speak to him. Worse, he may not be cremated in his own village, where the ashes of his ancestors reside. This means there is no one to intercede for him in the afterlife and no chance for a favorable reincarnation. Banishment is a punishment that lasts for eternity.

A Balinese man told me a sad, terrifying tale one day. A young man had been banished from his village. He had gone to another place and changed his life. He married and settled down. When he tried to return to his home village, the people stood on the path with their arms folded across their chests and would not let him pass.

Adat, the traditional law, is very strong in Bali and supercedes Indonesian legality. A month before my visit, a man had been caught burglarizing a home. He was turned over to the police and released pending trial. Several days later the man was caught taking goods from another home. Drums sounded in the temple calling all the men from the banjar to a midnight meeting. It was decided that every man must strike at least one blow.

The burglar's corpse was found the next day, and the police could find no one who knew what had happened.

Adat is a stern and unforgiving law. It has formed the peaceful and honest nature of the Balinese. The corollary is that the Balinese often mask their daily disappointments and frustrations behind a smile. Sometimes, however, as in any society, people break under the weight of their responsibility. Men simply go insane. They lash out in rage; they slash their loved ones to death with long knives; they kill anyone they encounter in blind rage. When a man runs amok, he must be hunted down and killed.

Running amok is an Indonesian phrase, and the phenomenon is not uncommon in Bali.

The violent trance states—the convulsive fights and blind rage exhibited by trance dancers—are a social safety valve for the Balinese. True, the trances only occur at certain times, accompanied by certain rituals, but the violence is entirely real. Men who might be near the breaking point can vent their rage in a socially approved ritual. It was, for instance, amazing to me how many times Ketut of Jangu was injured while attempting to subdue a trance dancer. He was, of course, the headman of the banjar, and there were those who resented him. One man hit him with a piece of wood and opened up a three-inch cut on his forehead. Ketut shrugged off the injury that would leave a lifelong scar. Men in a trance state are not responsible for their actions.

So trance is a social safety valve and a way of playing out village strife. It is, I think, also a warning. In the end it is twenty of the strongest men in the village who must subdue the trance dancer. It is a reenactment of the amok scenario complete with a symbolic death at the end.

In the village of Pakse Bali, near Klung Kung, there is a ceremony known as Prang Dewa, the war of the gods. It happens on the anniversary of the local temple, an event called the Odalan. The ritual lasts three full days, and on the final afternoon, women bearing offerings lay them before the gods of their temple. Rice is brought to the temple and ritually fed to the children of the village. Then figures representing the gods—small, beautifully carved figurines—are placed in boxes about two feet square and wrapped in sacred cloth. The boxes are placed on top of two long runged poles and carried several miles down to the river, where the gods "bathe."

For most of the year the temples of Bali are empty. The gods inhabit the temples and their representative figures only when invited down from the holy mountain, as during the Odalan. In Pakse Bali people believe the gods become quite jolly during their annual bath. They are carried back to the temple but would rather stay outside for a while. They want, a temple priest told me, to *"main main,"* a Balinese term that translates to "play play."

And the gods play rough. Men carrying the gods begin to stumble. The long runged poles with the boxes atop begin to rock and sway. Not all the carriers are entranced, however, and they attempt to run the gods through the temple gates. The men who have become entranced fight back. The poles swing about. Since there are half a dozen gods and twice as many long poles swinging about, many people are injured. A food stall near the temple is destroyed every year. There is much screaming.

There are three temples in each Balinese village: the original temple, the village temple, and the temple of death. It is in the temple of death, called the Pura Dalem, that the most bizarre ceremonies are celebrated. The religion of Agama Hindu aims to achieve a balance in the spiritual world. The demons of its mythology have a power that must be honored. Offerings are made to them in the same spirit that bribes are given to corrupt officials: "Here, take this and leave me alone." Sometimes the demon gods are honored in a ceremony that takes place in the temple of death.

In the Pura Dalem known as Kestel Gumi a very dark ritual is enacted on the Odalan day.

A gamelan, the Balinese fifty-man percussion orchestra, plays all afternoon. Presently, the gamelan tune becomes less ethereal, more frenetic, obsessive in its percussion. Suddenly, eight men burst from the inner courtyard, carrying daggers and the serpentine Balinese swords called krisses. For the most part these men have their eyes closed, and they run into the inner courtyard of the temple. Local people, spectators, move back to the walls to make room for the dancers in their frenzy. The men turn on one another. One swings a kris at another and misses by an inch.

Suddenly, all the men begin fighting with krisses. If a fight seems to be moving toward the crowd, a guard—very carefully—puts a hand on one of the combatants and tries to move him toward the center of the courtyard.

The dancers form a line. A priest in white, a temple priest, a *permangku,* falls into a trance. Another priest brings out live chickens. He holds the chicken up to one man's mouth, and this man bites the head off of the living animal. The spirit of the demon has entered him, and the dancer (or the demon) delights in demonstrating his iniquity: With his bare hands he rips the chicken apart and devours parts of it, entrails and all. The white-clad priest is on the ground, on his hands and knees, doing an odd kicking motion with his back legs. There are feathers clinging to the blood on his lips, and he crawls on his hands and knees to a dismembered chicken that has been dropped. He eats it, like a dog. Then all the trance dancers begin eating chickens, tearing them apart in some strange frenzy. There is no evident revulsion on these men's faces as they eat the writhing chickens; there is, in fact, only an odd savage joy.

It is dark in the temple of death, and the gamelan is frantic. Eventually, after an hour or more, the hypnotic percussive music stops. One by one, but not in unison, the men wake from their frantic trance state and fall to the ground. They are sprinkled with holy water. Sometimes they fight as they come out of the trance, and many men hold them. The wakened trance dancers appear bleary-eyed, confused, like men in the last stages of blithering drunkenness. Their mouths and chests are covered with blood.

I met the *dalang*—the storyteller—I. Made Sija in his family compound in the village of Bona. Made Sija was fifty-six years old, and there was a bustle of activity in his courtyard. He was building a cremation tower for a client, and his sons were working hard on the project. Both of his grandmothers, one whom he said was 101 years old, were walking about bare-breasted in the old style.

I was brought hot tea in a glass. Made Sija said that "if photos are to be taken, the ceremony should be done properly. However, if we do the proper ceremony with the proper offerings, the young ladies, the *sanghyang dedari,* might actually go into trance."

Sija explained that the people of Bona hadn't done *sanghyang dedari,* the dance of the heavenly nymphs, in over forty years. The dances are performed to exorcise a sickness that lies heavy on the village. In the last forty years, Sija explained, "there have not been any contagious epidemics. This is because there are drugs to contain these diseases. The children go to school, and they are inoculated."

At the famous tourist performances in Bona, where Balinese act out the *dedari* ritual, there are no trances. "We don't make offerings," Sija said, "these are performances."

He said that the last *sanghyang dedari* done actually for the villagers was in 1945. In that year there was a *gurubug boh bedeg,* a contagious epidemic. And in his best storyteller's tradition Sija added that the dogs howled, owls hooted (owls are strong magic), and people were frightened. The village, he said, was suffering from typhus and dysentery.

The headmen of the banjars in the village became frightened and called upon the gods of the village's three temples. Young girls would dance in a trance. Sija said that the girls dance to drive away devils with their very beauty. The girls must be too young to menstruate, and they must be untrained in the classical dance called the legong. They will, in a trance state, dance the very graceful and extremely complicated legong perfectly. And if they do, it is thought that the gods may speak through them. "Someone may say to a *sanghyang* dancer, my son is sick," Sija said, "and the gods, speaking through the young girl, will tell him to get such and such an herb."

In a *sanghyang dedari,* songs are sung to entertain the heavenly nymphs and invite them to inhabit the bodies of the young girls. The songs are about flowers, especially those with a strong fragrance. "It is," Sija said, "a way to sweet-talk them." He laughed. "Evil spirits and sickness, they do not like nice songs," he said.

In the old days the people of Bona used to pinch the girls or burn them lightly. "If they have no feeling or response," Sija said, "they are in trance."

At four-thirty that afternoon I went to the temple to see a special *sanghyang dedari*. The proper offerings would be made.

The temple was the Pura Dalem in Bona. It was drizzling slightly, then the rain stopped, and a fresh wind blew in. There was to be the Odalan in three days, and dozens of women were sitting about the inner and outer courtyards making offerings. I counted fourteen young women in bright red blouses with green sashes.

Two girls, each about ten years old, wore the classical green legong costumes that did not cover their shoulders. We went into the inner courtyard, and the girls knelt on their sandals. They clasped their hands in prayer above their heads. The women in red knelt behind them. They were laughing and talking among themselves. All around, women oblivious to the *dedari* ceremony were making offerings for the Odalan. The young girls were sprinkled with holy water. A headdress of flowers and beaten gold was put on each of their heads. A stick of incense was put in the headdress.

Fourteen men, bare-chested and wearing the black-and-white skirts called kains, stood to the side. A woman fanned incense on the kneeling girls. The women in red sang for the heavenly nymphs to descend. A dog trotted by, looking for offerings on the ground. A man watching shooed it off: *"Chek, chek."*

It was a dark afternoon, heading toward dusk. The graveyard was just off the Pura Dalem, and a dark forest of palms and twisted jungle trees fringed the death temple.

At 5:50 the girls began to sway slightly. Suddenly, one fell backward into the arms of a waiting woman. It seemed to me that the other didn't fall at quite the same time and was gently pulled. She fell heavily into the arms of the woman behind her.

Two of the men lifted the girls onto their shoulders. The *dedari* did not open their eyes. They were given fans, which they swung about in sinuous, perfectly coordinated motions while they rode on the shoulders of the men.

The entire procession—the men in kains, the women in red—

moved through the Odalan preparations in the outer temple and stopped outside, before the intricately carved gate of the temple.

There was a large white canvas spread out on the gravel there. The women knelt to the left, the men sat to the right. The women sang about flowers for a time, and the little girls danced in perfect unison, although it appeared that both had their eyes closed. It was a dance where the movement of the fans and the hands and the arms meant as much as the movements of the feet. In Balinese dance there is little of the jumping of Western dance. Movements are rooted to the earth. The positioning of the feet, the sinuous movements of the arms: These are the significant gestures. It is, to my eyes, a celebration of femininity and grace.

Presently, one of the men began a wordless syncopated tune— he had a fine voice and was smiling broadly as he sang—and the rest of the men joined in, their voices sharp and percussive in the gathering gloom. It was the *chak-a-chak* sound of the kecak, the male chant of a *sanghyang dedari* ceremony. Since the orchestra, the gamelan, cannot play in times of sickness, the sound of this percussive orchestra is sung by men. As Sija had said, the kecak song has martial overtones: It sounds like people fighting, and it is unnerving. As the kecak chant increased in tempo, the girls danced faster, never losing their grace.

Behind them, carved into the stone that formed the gate of the temple of death, there were two stone demons, a little like gargoyles, that guarded each side of the entrance. Above the gate was the face of a great bulging-eyed, fanged demon.

Suddenly, the little girls fell, as if in sleep. Two women in red arose and ministered to them. The other women sang again, asking the heavenly nymphs to enter, and the little girls rose. Their dance was ethereal, floating.

Finally, after about twenty minutes, the girls danced to the last kecak chorus and fell. They were gently shaken awake and were sprinkled with holy water. The little girls seemed to come out of their trance then. There was none of the bleary, drunken expression I saw on the *sanghyang* dancers at Jangu. The girls had danced the legong perfectly.

* * *

I do not know whether the girls at Bona were in an authentic trance state or not. Western psychologists who have studied trance have been testing Balinese dancers for five decades now. The best judgment they can make seems to be this: Some of the dancers are in a genuine state of trance, and some are not.

This accords well with the Balinese attitude toward trance. Since the trances are culturally conditioned—because they happen at certain prescribed times in the ceremony—some dancers are not quite ready when the ritual begins. Nevertheless, even those who do not fall into a trance are expected to dance. The depth of the trance, or the lack of it, is always a matter of lively speculation among Balinese spectators. In one of the more famous trance dances, a young man riding a stick horse runs through several burning piles of coconut husks. It is said that if a dancer is not in a state of trance, this can be an exceedingly painful exercise. Those men who have chosen to do the fire dance and who do not fall into a trance—who show evidence of pain—are an occasion of great merriment to the Balinese. There is much laughing.

There is, in Bali, a persistent belief in *leyaks,* or witches. They haunt the graveyards at night, where they dance ecstatically and hurl curses upon innocent Balinese. The head witch is named Rangda. She is both revered and feared in Balinese culture.

Rangda may change her form at will. In the classical Balinese witch play she first appears as a bitter old woman named Calon Arang. The play concerns a prince who spurns a beautiful young woman because she is the daughter of Calon Arang. The witch, in a fury, calls her *leyaks* to dance with her in the graveyard. Sickness infects the land. The king's magical adviser discovers the cause of the disease. There is a magical fight, and just as Calon Arang is about to be vanquished, she flees, only to reappear as Rangda, the witch goddess.

The actor playing Rangda wears a carved wooden mask that features protruding bloody teeth, bulging eyeballs, and fangs. The sewn sausagelike scarves around her neck represent human intestines, and the tongue—a long strip of red cloth with one or more mirrors sewn in—represents flame. If the mask has been empowered—that is, blessed by a priest—the actor playing Rangda may fall into a trance.

This is where the tension builds, and even very young children know to move away from the stage to avoid injuries in the trances that may follow. Rangda defeats the king's adviser, and immediately the mythical beast known as the Barong makes its entrance.

The Barong is best thought of as a kind of dragon, part demon, whose mandate is to protect mankind. (The Barong is a large, furry beast with a bulging-eyed, fanged head and is usually played by two men, in the manner of a pantomime horse.) The play ends with another fight. Neither the Barong nor Rangda are finally defeated. The forces of good and evil, life and death, remain in balance.

Some witch plays may last seven or more hours and are replete with references to local gossip—which young girl was seen walking hand in hand with which boy. Vulgar jokes are spoken by clownish retainers of the nobles.

Other plays are magical and/or religious in nature. (Almost all temples on the island contain sacred Barong and Rangda masks.) In these plays the most perplexing spectacle occurs. For reasons not immediately apparent to Westerners, men in the crowd pretend to stab themselves with krisses.

At the Pura Pengerebongan, in Kesiman, the Odalan is a gigantic ceremony of offerings, music, cockfights, and an orgy of krissing. It is best described as grand pandemonium. Rangda and Barong masks from nearby temples were "invited" to the ceremony and empowered. At Pengerebongan, late in the afternoon, five men dressed in Rangda masks breathed scented smoke together. Suddenly, there was a terrific howling, and the Rangdas raised their taloned hands into the air.

The Rangdas seemed to be in a trance, and many stumbled as they were helped to the temple door. They would go outside and parade three times around the walls. In the procession there were dozens of men and women carrying high, arched curved flags, and other men carrying boxes of the sort seen at Pakse Bali. A large gamelan played so furiously that you could feel the beat of the drums in your chest.

As the Rangdas passed through the narrow path formed by thousands of spectators, various men, enraged by the very sight of the witches, took up swords, and, inexplicably, turned them on themselves. With arms extended before them, the men seemed to put the swords into their bellies. No skin was broken.

Eventually, after some minutes, helpers and guards disarmed the men in what turned out to be a typical end trance: the convulsive fight. The most entranced and violent of the men were carried up the steps of the temple. Their limbs were held by a dozen or more men, and the dancers were carried upside down, high above the helpers' heads. This was a violent and dangerous undertaking. Once inside the temple's inner courtyard, the dancers were sprinkled with holy water and brought out of the trance.

Later, after the gamelan had stopped playing and the Rangdas and Barongs were back in the temple, a small group of men stood before a raised platform and attempted to stab themselves. Priests in black or red or purple vestments sat on the platform and watched this scene of extraordinary violence with impassive, hooded eyes.

At the banjar of Penarukan, in the village of Krambitan, I was allowed to examine the ceremonial krisses. They were dull as butter knives—the Balinese keep their working knives very sharp—and were made of thin, inferior-grade metal. I thought they might have been fashioned from the leaf springs of old automobiles. They had been bent before—the rippling metal showed that clearly—and it would not take a great deal of strength to bend them again. I felt I could do it easily over one knee.

This banjar is famous for its staged version of the Calon Arang play. The performance I saw took place at sundown, on black-sand volcanic beach. The air itself seemed to sigh with the setting of the sun.

The gamelan introduced the show, the prince met the witch's daughter in a forest: all in all, a typical Calon Arang. But when the Rangda finally emerged, howling in rage, the terror was very real. Penarukan is a poor banjar—the costumes are threadbare—but the Rangda mask was among the more frightening of the hundred or so I had seen.

The witch swaggered toward the gamelan, waved a white flag, and the entire orchestra fell into a faint. At least one man lay with spittle dripping from the side of his mouth, and his eyes rolled in their sockets.

The Barong emerged, and there was another fight with the witch waving her deadly white cloth and the Barong snapping its jaws. Suddenly, the Barong fell, apparently lifeless, and various men, at least a dozen of them, took up krisses and charged Rangda in genuine fury.

Men ran fifty yards across the black beach, at top speed, and thrust their swords into the actor playing Rangda. The blades did not pierce flesh. Often the kris simply bent double. The men with the krisses, followers of the dragon, came at the witch from all sides, and she was driven back along the beach, but her magic prevented the swords from piercing her.

In one part of my mind I was able to see the play as an incredible display of athletic ability. Clearly, each time the witch sighted a man running toward him, he waited, braced, then stumbled backward several hurried steps, like a boxer "rolling with the punches." Rangda's retreat prevented the actor's death by blunting the force of the blow. Still, there were men coming from all directions, and a mistake would have been deadly.

Suddenly, Rangda's magic asserted itself and forced the men to turn the swords upon themselves. Incredibly, even though the men's arms were tightly flexed, the muscles quivering, no one drew blood.

Moving pictures, played in slow motion, show that, in the krissing ceremony, the muscles that extend the arm and the muscles that contract it are flexed in near equilibrium. The swords are placed against the belly at a slight angle, and some force is exerted inward so that often the thin swords are bent double.

Balinese are delighted to let polite outsiders examine the swords or film the krissing ceremonies. Their intent is not to deceive. The play—the krissing ceremonies—are about balance in the spiritual world. If I want to explain it in terms of athletic achievement, no Balinese would argue with me. They would just assume I'd missed the point.

It is Rangda's magic that makes the dancers attempt to stab themselves. It is the Barong's magic that protects them. It wouldn't do to have Rangda defeated, even in a play. Balinese believe she exists and her wrath is deadly. On the other hand, it wouldn't do to have the Barong defeated and risk insulting mankind's protector. The play, with the violent krissing, was a study in spiritual balance.

When the Calon Arang was over, when the last man had been disarmed and brought out of his trance, a stage manager packed up the bent swords, along with the sacred Rangda and Barong masks. The gamelan musicians carried their instruments a mile over the black beach, toward the village. The play had reaffirmed the balance of the spiritual world, and had, I thought, guaranteed the social contract in a symbolic acting out of the amok scenario. The last streaks of color were dying in the sky. Soon it would be dark. People began walking faster. There is magic in the Balinese night, and no one wanted to be left alone. In the dark.

Taquile

▲

There was a freight train highballing down a track that seemed to be situated just above my roof. I had been asleep and wasn't entirely sure where I was. The room I found myself in was brown adobe, and very small, with one window high on the opposite wall.

It was cold, near freezing, and I was lying just off the floor on a mattress made of reeds, covered over in a couple of thick woolen blankets aged to the softness of cashmere and woven in colorful designs. My queasy lethargy and dull headache felt like altitude sickness.

Someplace high, then.

And it came back, slowly, that I was in South America, out in the middle of Lake Titicaca, on the island of Taquile. The lake is 12,507 feet above sea level and is located on the Alti Plano, the high plain that runs north and south between two snowy ridges of towering Andes. The Alti Plano stretches from Peru into Bolivia.

Taquile is considered part of Peru, a tiny hummock of land only three miles long and less than one mile wide. There was, I recalled, no plumbing on the island, no electricity. Not a single car.

And no trains at all to rattle overhead in a deafening clatter.

I glanced up at the corrugated tin roof. Someone flashed an arc light in my one window, flicked it off, then blasted me with it again, full power this time. Everything in the room went blue-white, the way things look under the light of a stroboscope. Then a bomb exploded outside, and the freight train kept running over the roof, and I divined that I was sleeping through a hailstorm.

It occurred to me that some time ago, perhaps yesterday, I left the town of Puno, on the shores of the lake. The boat to Taquile was a forty-foot-long gasoline-engine affair, and fifty people sat on benches, or on the floor, or on the bow, as we coughed and spluttered through a channel cut out of a sea of golden reeds. The water, in the shallow bay, was a soupy green, and ducks by the hundreds called back and forth from the sky to the reeds: "Are you feeding? We're feeding, are you feeding? We're feeding."

As the boat cleared the reeds, the water glittered cobalt blue under cloudless skies. Ahead, still fifteen miles away, I could see the bulk of Taquile Island. It seemed to sit directly in the middle of the lake, and the sun shone upon it like a benediction.

The island was little more than a spine of mountain, a ridge knifing out of the blue water. It rose eight hundred feet above the level of the lake. The highest area was north, and the land sloped down a series of rounded vertebrae to a low-lying beach in the south.

The vertical face of the land was terraced from top to bottom, and the each of the small, flat terraces was ringed with stone piled about three feet high. Snaking here and there through the terraces were pathways that were lined by waist-high stone walls. The whole island looked as if it had been sculpted for aesthetic effect. On some of the terraces, new crops shone bright green in the sun. Sheep grazed in other terraces where the stone walls supporting the land doubled as nifty corrals. The grass there was a darker green, and very short, so that the island seemed composed of bands of alternating color.

Most of the people on the boat were Indians, people of the Alti Plano. Before about 1300 they spoke a language called Aymara, and lived in separate medieval fiefdoms. About 1400 they were conquered and absorbed into the Inca Empire. A century later these same people were conquered again, this time by the Spanish.

Other Indian people, on nearby islands, spoke the old language, Aymara, but these people spoke Quecha, the language of the Incas. They considered themselves descendants of the great Indian Empire and dressed to set themselves apart from other peoples. The women wore dark shawls over their heads and red skirts, several of them at once, so that the uppermost skirt belled out in an exuberant and festive manner. The men, all of them, wore a kind of red or white wool Santa Claus hat, wool shirts, vests, dark woolen pants, and wide woven belts.

There were some visitors among the locals: myself, a Japanese couple, two young Englishmen, and a couple from Spain.

The boat docked at a stone pier. There was a flagstone path, set with long steps, that led to the village, eight hundred feet above. I began trudging up the hill, gasping in the thin air. Barefoot Indian women carrying gooseneck pots full of water walked by me effortlessly. All wished me a good morning, but when I tried to reply, I had nothing in my lungs to propel the words from my mouth.

The men carried fresh fruit, bottles of drinking water, cans of beans, automobile batteries, cases of beer, and great slabs of lumber up the hill. Everything was wrapped in heavy wool blankets, which the men tied over their shoulders and across their chests so the weight fell at their shoulder blades, like a backpack.

They were slender men, and few of them were over five and a half feet tall. They laughed and shouted to one another as they walked effortlessly and rapidly up the impossible slope.

At the summit of the hill there was an archway where several men dressed in those odd tasseled hats asked if I wanted to spend the night. Yes? Then I could stay with Sebastian. The price amounted to seventy-five cents a night.

One of the men showed me the way, and we walked down a sloping cobblestone walk with waist-high stone fences on either side. My room was on the second story of a stone building, covered over in brown adobe. I climbed a small, rickety wooden

ladder, ducked into the door—which was about two feet high—
and collapsed on the reeds, feeling very sick indeed.

In Taquile families live in several small houses set around a central courtyard. The stones are covered over in adobe and sometimes smeared with sheep dung against the wind and cold. Each
stone house is very small, a single room. One is used for cooking,
one for sleeping, one for working. Sebastian Yurca's compound
included a larger room that he used as a restaurant to serve his
guests.

I was not, I think, good company that first night. Sebastian's
daughters seemed very shy, and when I asked them their names,
they blushed, stared at the floor, and felt obliged to cover their
faces with their shawls. *Oh, that a man could ask them such a
question.* They answered in whispers: Revecca was four; Angel-
ica, twelve; Lina, sixteen; and Juana, nineteen. All the girls spoke
fluent Spanish, a second language for them. They pumped a bit
more light out of the kerosene lamp for me and told me that I
could have pancakes, potato soup, fried potatoes, eggs, or trout.
There was never anything else to eat on the island, and the only
spices used were salt and pepper.

Juana, the oldest, noticed my condition. She'd seen it often
enough before: some gringo with a bad headache and no appe-
tite. Altitude sickness: the *sorache.* She brought a cup of hot water and set a few sprigs of mint in the cup to steep. Maté de
muña, she said, was good for pain. Women drank strong maté de
muña when they gave birth.

I sipped at the tea, had a bowl of bland but filling potato soup,
and watched the daughters of Sebastian Yurca go about their
work in the warm light of the lantern. Lina was weaving one of
the red men's belts on a wooden loom. The designs were intricate: a bird, a diamond radiating rays, a circle divided into six
parts. Lina worked the threads with a lamb bone polished sharp
and smooth. The designs, she explained, all had meaning. The
belt was a kind of agricultural calender: when the scissor-billed
bird laid its eggs, it was time to plant. The diamond was Inti, the
sun, the god of the Incas. The circle in six parts represented the

island of Taquile, which was, in turn, divided into six agricultural regions. Terraces in some regions were to remain fallow in certain years—there were dots on those areas of the belt Lina was weaving—and others could be planted.

A woman, Lina said, would make such a belt for her husband. It would represent a man's past, present, and future.

How long did it take to make a belt?

Lina paused. She had never thought about it. She guessed that if she worked five or six hours a day, it would take her less than two months.

The other girls had connected a small tape player to an auto battery. They played the music of the Alti Plano, the high, mournful sound of flutes and drums and guitar: *"El Cóndor Pasa,"* a kind of national lament of the Alti Plano. Paul Simon's version had nothing to do with words of the Peruvian song, but his interpretation caught the mood: "I'd rather be a hammer than a nail." It was the music of a conquered people, plaintive and melodic and somehow triumphant.

The two oldest girls had colorful tassels at the corners of the shawls they wore. Juana said that the tassels meant they could date boys. Single men, she said, wore hats that were white at the end.

Girls who wear the tassels, Juana told me, are said to be "in flower." A married woman cannot wear tassels.

"You mean," I said, feeling much better after my mint tea, "that when you get married, all the color goes out of your life?"

This comment was treated as the height of flirtation. Juana dissolved into giggles and felt forced, once again, to hide her face behind her shawl. My headache was now only a minor annoyance, and I sought to make the girls giggle and hide their faces.

Did Juana have a boyfriend?

Oh blush, giggle giggle, hide behind the shawl, whisper to Lina . . .

And Lina?

The girl went through an agony of exquisite embarrassment. *Such a question.* It was possible to look only at the floor. *A boy-friend! The very thought . . .*

There was a new tape on the machine now, a Peruvian version of the lambada. Juana asked if I could dance. It occurred to me that in South America, the lambada, as they say in the movies, was "forbeedin." Somehow I couldn't imagine these shy young women performing a dance that looks like something the dog does to your leg.

"Can't dance," I explained.

A chorus of disbelief for a reply. If I was going to tease, Juana said, then I had to dance. She stood with her hands on her hips, staring at me, falsely stern. I stood, took her right hand in my left, put my other hand on her back, and she brushed it away. *No, sir, please, don't: not like that.* This was, apparently, a lambada in which you only touched your partner's hands. And nothing else.

I had no idea how to proceed and spun Juana away from me in a kind of cowboy two-step. This was received with much laughter and applause. Soon Juana was whirling this way and that and would have looked right at home cutting a rug in any Montana saloon. I was very conscious of my heavy boots and Juana's bare feet.

What kind of dance did I call that?

It is, I said, a cowboy dance.

And so, every night for the next week, at least once, Juana and I danced to the music of a tape deck connected to a car battery in a brown adobe room with the high country wind booming and whistling outside in the night. We danced the cowboy lambada.

The next morning I had pancakes and coffee with the daughters of Sebastian, and started a walking tour of the island. In contrast to the freezing hail of the night before, the sun was now hot and harsh at 13,300 feet. It was, I knew, burning my face.

About an hour from the village, I heard a rhythmic tap, tap, and stumbled upon three men, all of them dressed in the men's basic costume. There were two married men and one bachelor. Alejandro Flores and his two brothers were cutting stone that would be used to build a new schoolhouse. They were donating the work to the community. Tomorrow other men would cut stone for the school.

Alejandro didn't mind talking while he worked. Everyone on the island donated a few hours of work to the community every week, he said. There were 2,000 people on the island, 318 families. Agriculture had to be very strictly controlled so that everyone could eat: The island was very small, and the weather very harsh. Each Sunday, after Catholic mass, the people met in the central courtyard, where the events of the past week were discussed and plans were made. The highest political authority was the first lieutenant governor.

Sometimes, Alejandro said, men from the outside came to Taquile to "organize" the people. These men talked about inflation, insurgency, and police corruption. What did these things have to do with Taquile? There were no police on the island. The people did not want police. Where there are police, there are thieves. Everyone knew that.

Alejandro had been tapping on a rock the size of a large footstool. He used a simple hammer and chisel, gently rapping along the grain of the rock. Suddenly, it fell apart, into two pieces, each of them almost perfectly square. He began trimming one of the pieces, and I recalled that the Incas were, perhaps, the finest stone workers in pre-Columbian America.

The sun disappeared behind a cloud, and the temperature dropped 15 degrees in a matter of minutes. I dug around in my pack for a jacket, but Alejandro and his brothers continued working, apparently quite comfortable. The weather was harsh—it might be 75 during the day and 30 at night—yet people never wore jackets, nor did they strip off a shirt or vest in the sun. Layers of heavy wool, finely made, some anthropologists suggest, create a kind of personal microclimate around the people of Taquile.

The curious uniform the islanders wore allowed a man or woman to work in the fields under all conditions. The clothes a person put on in the morning indicated his or her marital status, age group, relative wealth, and social position. The island existed on subsistence agriculture, but the textiles produced by the people represented the soul of Taquile.

Why was it, I asked Alejandro, that the people of Taquile were so honest that they didn't need police?

Alejandro said that if a man stole a sheep, he would be taken before the community at the Sunday meeting; he would be forced to carry the sheep on his back six times around the square, and the traditional twelve authorities, the men who governed the six parts of the island, would whip the man as he passed with heavy woven ropes. If a man killed another man's sheep, he made the same humiliating walk wearing the intestines of the dead sheep wrapped around his head. Then he was taken to the mainland. That man could never return.

"So you see," Alejandro said, "we have no need for police."

Alejandro himself, it seemed, was running for the position of first lieutenant governor.

What were the issues?

"Natural fibers," Alejandro said without hesitation. "Natural colors."

There were, it seemed, some people on the island who would knit hats or scarfs with synthetic material. They might even use artificial dyes to color the products and sell them to tourists like myself. Alejandro thought tourists could buy such things anywhere.

People had such short sight. There was television everywhere in the world, Alejandro said. Why would people need it here? Or loud music. It was a quiet island, very traditional, and it should be kept that way. When the political men came to organize the island, Alejandro asked them, "And where do you stand on natural color?" The men had no answer. They knew nothing of Taquile. The people asked political organizers to go away.

Alejandro, like most people I met on Taquile, was a tireless talker and storyteller.

All the young men of his island, he said, want to visit Lima, if only for a few days. For the men of Taquile, Lima is a kind of Disneyland of danger and violence, of strange, gratuitous wonders.

So when Alejandro decided it was time for him to see the great city, he approached the local shaman, called a *paq'o,* and asked advice. Was it his time?

The *paq'o,* who was very wise, sat at a wooden table and

spread out three of the leaves of the sacred plant, coca leaves. A coin was placed on the middle leaf, and this represented the all-seeing eye of God. A crucifix was placed below the coin to indicate that Alejandro and his family were Catholics. The leaf to the left was turned over so that the dull side was up: It was a sign of bad luck and trouble. The right leaf lay shiny side up. If God and the spirits willed it, the right leaf would triumph in the upcoming test, and Alejandro could go to Lima without worry.

The *paq'o* gave Alejandro five of the dull green leaves, and they fit neatly in the palm of his right hand. He closed his eyes and emptied his hand in a sweeping gesture, so that the leaves fell across the coin and the crucifix. The *paq'o* examined the way the leaves had fallen. All shiny side up, a very good sign. And the leaves traced a relatively straight line, somewhat below the crucifix. They rose from the left and pointed to the shiny leaf at the far right. Alejandro Flores would have good luck in Lima.

Lima. The air there, in that great city, was very thick and very dirty. Still, the bright-colored lights glittered at night, because there was electricity everywhere.

On Taquile, there is no electricity, and a man can see the stars.

One day, during his visit to Lima, a strange-looking foreign man stopped Alejandro on the street. He was very excited about something, and Alejandro thought perhaps this tall, thin man was crazy or drunk. No, the man said, please don't go. Please, sir, the man said, just allow me to ask a few questions. Where had Alejandro gotten the wool to weave his belt?

From sheep, of course.

His own sheep?

Yes, everyone on Taquile raised sheep.

And how did they spin the wool? Did Alejandro have a machine?

No, he spun the wool by hand. Mostly the wool is spun clockwise.

Mostly?

Sometimes, Alejandro explained, the wool was spun in the opposite direction when it was to be used to finish the edge of a garment. The backward spin created good luck and warded off nasty spirits.

The man stared at Alejandro as if he'd just said something strange and amazing; something like: I can fly like a bird when I like.

The man began to guess about the clothes Alejandro wore. They were woven on a wooden loom, he said, the kind where the four edges are pounded into the ground.

That was true.

And the colors, this golden yellow, it came from the leaf of a certain tree? Boiled for several hours?

Yes.

And the reds: Were they from the beetle of the cactus plant? Cochineal?

Yes. Alejandro grew his own cacti, and allowed the beetles to infest the plants. His wife might sometimes take one or two of the insects and press them in her hands to form a bright red juice she used to paint her lips and fingernails. It was, Alejandro thought, the fullest, most beautiful red color on earth.

And to color the wool with cochineal?

Alejandro said that he gathered the beetles, allowed them to dry in the sun, and boiled them for several hours until he had a pot of the most beautiful red dye anyone had ever seen.

And the foreign man knew about the process, which surprised Alejandro. He knew that the color was fixed—so it wouldn't bleed when washed—with salt, fermented potato water, and fermented human urine.

The man said that, with a few exceptions, Alejandro made textiles in exactly the way they had been made in the Alti Plano several thousand years ago. Those ancient textiles, the man said, were among the finest ever produced, anywhere. Perhaps Alejandro could come to his country. There were many scholars who would want to speak with him, many people who would come see him create "art."

Which is how Alejandro Flores, of Taquile Island, traveled to England, where he demonstrated pre-Columbian weaving techniques for three months. There were articles in magazines and newspapers about him, and always these articles showed pictures of Alejandro dressed the way he had always dressed. People recognized him on the street, and some of them could speak Spanish. They called him a great artist and shook his hand constantly.

It had been an interesting trip: There were huge buildings and things called escalators and automobiles and beer to drink and strange-tasting food. Alejandro was glad he went, but he was happy to come back to his quiet island where there were no police, where no one lied, and a man could see the stars every night. He was happy to come back to a place where the potatoes tasted the way potatoes should.

"England," Alejandro Flores told me without a hint of irony, "was a nice place to visit, but I wouldn't want to live there."

Still, the *paq'o* had been right: Alejandro hadn't had any real trouble on his trip to Lima.

What he had learned there, and in England, was that life on Taquile was good. It was worth preserving the traditions that made the island different from all the rest of the world. The perception was encompassed in Alejandro's single issue in his campaign for first lieutenant governor: natural color.

On my walks around the island I often met women in their seventies tending sheep. It was a matter of some comedy on Taquile: Quecha grandmothers, people said, complain all day long. The old women herding sheep down the stone paths seemed to be in on the joke and conspired to amuse everyone. They spoke Spanish with a guttural Quecha accent and protested the hardships of life in a merry singsong manner. *The village is so far away. My son has gone to Puno to work, and I have no one. The sheep know I can't see very well anymore and hide themselves from me.*

Whenever I found myself walking with a man from the village, we laughed together about the grandmothers' complaints. That was expected of me. Privately, I thought, a seventy-five-year-old woman, walking barefoot over rocky hillsides, at 13,500 feet, with the wind driving a cold rain before it? What's so funny about that?

For the most part, however, I met very young girls tending sheep and spinning wool into yarn, by hand.

Alejandra was ten years old, and I met her above the village, tending a flock of about ten sheep. Alejandra was both curious and shy, so she hid behind a stone arch and spoke to me for quite some time, peeking out every once in a while in an unconsciously flirtatious manner.

The sheep belonged to her father's brother. She was watching them in what I understood was a reciprocal work arrangement. Her uncle was helping her father prepare his land for planting. Today they were on the other side of the island, turning over the soil in four big terraces, using foot plows, planting maize and potatoes as people had planted these crops since the time of the Incas.

It would be easier, Alejandra said, to prepare the land if her family owned a cow that her father could yoke to a plow. They were saving for one even now. The wool she was spinning would be woven into belts and blankets, called *mantas*. It would be knitted into hats. Perhaps tourists would buy her work.

Alejandra wore a woven bag on one hip, and, as she spoke, she pulled newly washed black wool from the bag, stretched it out in a long cord, wrapped it around a toplike bobber in a quick, complicated maneuver, and set the bobber spinning like a top on the smooth surface of a flat rock. Her ten-year-old fingers were nimble, and she did the work automatically, as she talked.

Occasionally, a sheep tried to wander past Alejandra. She hissed at it, loudly, a horror-movie snake sound, and the animal fell all over itself getting back to its fellows.

The worst thing the sheep did, Alejandra said, they did on hot days like this. (It was about 70 degrees.) The brainless beasts would wander down to the lake, where, for whatever reason, they would hurl themselves into the cool water and sink like so many stones. Then you'd have to stand on a rock and stare into twenty feet of clear, cold water to see the sheep on the bottom, white or black against green mossy rocks, held down by all that waterlogged wool.

I thought Alejandra seemed a happy little girl. She was only ten and doing productive, responsible work for her family. I thought she must be very proud of herself.

This, Alejandra said from behind the arch, was not so. There were eight children in her family. It was hard to keep everyone fed. They needed a cow to prepare the fields, and the cow would be expensive. Last year Alejandra had been allowed to go to school. Now, because the family needed money for a cow, she had to work. Her older brothers got to go to school, but she had to spend her days with these sheep: *los estúpidos*. Her old teachers, she said, had come every week from Puno. They spoke such beautiful Spanish. She wanted to go to school and become a teacher who spoke beautiful Spanish.

I gathered Alejandra had a crush on one of her old teachers. It is possible, however, that the little girl will grow up frustrated and unfulfilled in this highly organized society. I didn't want to think about this because I found the people, in general, so happy, so handsome.

I wanted to believe that there were no problems at all on Taquile.

Don Pedro was seventy-five years old, a talkative man in vibrant good health who told me that people almost never die on Taquile. The last time a person died was two years ago, and the woman had been 105 years old. (In point of fact, I had talked to a man who had recently lost his seventy-three-year-old grandmother. I had no wish, however, to dispute this matter with Don Pedro. It seemed a pleasant fiction—this idea that people seldom die on the island—and one likely to prolong his life.)

Agriculture, Don Pedro said, was very important. Every year, in February, the people went to the highest flat spot on the island, the Mulasina Pata, and made a sacrifice to Pachamama, Mother Earth. They killed a baby llama, lamb, and alpaca. These were wrapped in serpentine paper and buried in three small holes, along with some coca leaves and corn beer.

Don Pedro said that the last time a tourist came to his remote farm—he thought that might have been 1976—there had been bad crops for a year. I said I would go, but Don Pedro was already on another subject. Hailstorms, like the one the other day, could kill crops very easily. Happily, this storm had hit during planting season, not when the crops were high in the field.

What caused the most damaging hailstorms, Don Pedro said, was when a young, unmarried girl got pregnant and aborted herself. These irresponsible girls buried the babies without a proper Catholic baptism. Then the hail came, and it would come for days until the woman confessed and showed the authorities where the baby was buried. It was then baptized, and the hail would stop. I had a vision of the men of the village digging in the wet ground, with the thunder and lightning striking all about. Holy water sprinkled on rotting flesh . . .

But Don Pedro was talking about lightning now. Once, many years ago, a woman had been struck by lightning at her wedding . . .

"On May third," I said. Everyone on Taquile, I had just learned, gets married on May 3. Don Pedro, who didn't like to be interrupted, stared at me as if I had just informed him that water is wet.

"Yes," he said, "May third." After that, there were three years of good crops. But then, several years later, lightning had killed a cow. There were three years of bad crops. Now, when a person is struck by lightning, a family will grieve, but the island is reassured. If a cow is killed by a bolt from the sky, however, there are many rituals to perform. These involved taking a cake to the spot, building a small altar there, and getting the blessing of a priest's representative.

There was no priest living on the island, and no doctor. Only a public-health nurse. But the *paq'o* was very good. Even when a man had been to the doctor in Puno and was still sick, even then the *paq'o* could help. The sick man might be given a white guinea pig, told to put the animal in a small bag and hold it to his heart for twelve hours. All the man's sickness would infect the guinea pig, and the *paq'o* could dissect the animal and find what was wrong with the man. The *paq'o* could prescribe certain herbs. No one died on Taquile.

I asked Don Pedro if he could introduce me to the *paq'o*.

"You have seen him," Don Pedro said. "You have seen his face."

I danced one last cowboy lambada with Juana and wandered back toward my room. A vicious storm had passed over the island earlier, and now it had moved far to the south. Lightning was striking along a fifty-mile front behind the snowcapped mountains of Bolivia. The storm was so far away that I couldn't hear the thunder. Every five seconds or so the sky exploded, and a mountain, blue white, shivered on the horizon.

The island, it seemed to me then, was a living, breathing thing. The stone fences were pleasant to look at, but they also kept the sheep out of the crops. And when the fields lay fallow, they would feed the sheep, and the sheep would fertilize them with their droppings. The wool provided by the sheep was woven into textiles that received a man at birth, clothed him through his life, and protected him on his journey to the next world.

At dinner, I had asked Sebastian Yurca what the island needed more than anything else.

"Natural color," he said.

Above, the night sky was clear and black, full of luminous and unfamiliar stars. At this altitude, the stars did not twinkle. They were great globules of light, and their colors were brilliant: white, blue white, red, green, gold . . .

Natural colors.

A man, I thought, could see the lights of Lima. Or he could see the stars.

The Miner's Paradox

▲

A diamond is the hardest naturally occurring substance known to
man. The only thing that can scratch it is another diamond. Diamonds are insoluble in acids and alkalies and are normally infusi-
ble. If you are unsure whether a certain stone may be a diamond,
one test is to suspend the stone in a jar of oxygen and raise the
temperature to about 875 degrees. If the stone burns with a blue
light, you used to have a diamond.

The first diamond miners in South America employed a similarly destructive and certainly less scientific test, one that probably demolished thousands of priceless gems. In the Brazilian
district now known as Diamantina, gold miners had long noticed
small, shining crystals of some weight in their gold pans. These
stones were kept to be used as counters in card games until a
diamond dealer named Bernardo de Fonseca Lobo examined a
few of them in 1725. De Fonseca Lobo informed the miners of
Diamantina that they had been playing penny-ante games with
fortunes in gems. The dealer explained that these card counters
were, in fact, diamonds, gemstones so hard, so impervious to
wear and scratch, that the name itself, derived from the Greek
adamas, means "unconquerable."

What de Fonseca Lobo failed to mention, or what the miners failed to understand, is that while diamonds are hard, they are also brittle, and may be broken along four major cleavage planes and several secondary ones. The hardest naturally occurring substance known to man may be damaged, even shattered, by a fall or a sharp knock.

Early Brazilian miners fully understood that diamonds were hard, but it took them almost four years to realize that they were also brittle. The Brazilian test for a diamond between 1725 and 1729 was to place the suspected stone on an anvil and give it a crack with a heavy hammer.

"Tough luck there, Francesco — one hundred twenty-seven big stones and not one of them a diamond."

For 150 years Brazil supplied the bulk of the world's diamonds. But in 1866 diamonds were discovered along the Orange River in South Africa, diamonds that could be mined efficiently by machines, that did not have to be panned out of some steaming jungle river. These days Africa supplies all but a fraction of the world's diamonds.

In Africa diamond mining is a big business, requiring big machines and big investments. In South America diamonds are still mined by gamblers who may own little more than a pick, a shovel, and the clothes on their backs. In Brazil, Guyana, and Venezuela diamond mining is still a gambler's game.

The French journalist Lucien Bodard, writing about Brazilian miners, called *garimpeiros,* caught the flavor of their lives when he wrote, "Sometimes they stumble across a real treasure." Miners by the thousands flock to the find. "Then, even in the most forbidding swamps, they create . . . a shantytown. There are stores, cabarets, brothels and inns; every kind of woman and every sort of trade. Not just cheap hardware items, but luxury items to gratify the big winner, the finder of the big diamond."

Soon enough a bit of the jungle will be burned away beside the river, and a mud runway will be constructed. Planes, hired at one hundred dollars an hour, serve the big winners. Bodard heard of a *garimpeiro* who "had a Cadillac brought over in pieces into the heart of the virgin forest, which he put together again and used over the 100 yards of pavement in the place, until it rusted away."

Sometimes a *garimpeiro,* a big winner, may hire a plane to ferry him out of the disease-ridden shantytown. Then it's time for a binge in Rio or São Paulo until the money's gone. As far as Bodard could see, "No *garimpeiro* has ever made his fortune and none ever can. . . . The *garimpeiros* know this so well that when they finally find their hands full of wads of notes, they go on a binge to beat all binges." Then it's back to the jungle and an existence that verges on mere survival.

Diamond miners I met in Venezuela, near the place where the borders of Guyana, Brazil, and Venezuela meet, lived lives full of squalor, misery, and sudden incredible wealth inevitably followed by more squalor and misery.

The camp I visited was near Santa Elena, a prospecting venture. No large strike had been made. Half a dozen men—blacks, whites, Venezuelans, Brazilians, Guyanese—lived in lean-tos where they dug in the earth and battled tiny, stinging gnats that hatch off the river in millions, gnats even local Indians call "the plague."

The land near Santa Elena is a riverine oasis, a bit of low-lying jungle in the high, cold, wind-whipped flats known as the Gran Sabana. Standing like so many coffins throughout the Sabana are strange flat-topped mountains with walls that rise like cliffs, sheer and perpendicular to high prairie all around. These mountains— the Indians call them *tepuis*—catch most of the rain on the Gran Sabana, and, on their flat tops, rivers form and flow to the cliffs where they fall forever into the cold world below. Angel Falls, the world's highest waterfall, drops down the side of a mountain known as Ayun-tepui.

Millions of years ago, at a depth of about seventy-five miles below the surface of the earth, heat and pressure and an unknown catalyst tortured carbon deposits in some mysterious manner and formed diamonds. These gemstones rose to the surface of the earth along with water and carbon dioxide, rose to the top of the *tepuis,* where the rivers caught them and sent them cascading over the cliffs, a literal waterfall of diamonds.

The diamond mine I visited was under a particularly rich mountain called Parai-tepui. The men had set up camp near a small river fed by the falls of Parai-tepui. They had dug a pit on the banks of the river. One man was blasting the sides of the pit with a fire hose. Another held a suction hose to the resultant water and mud at the bottom of the pit, and this muck was carried to a large, vibrating machine called a lavador, which separated sand from heavier minerals. The next day all six men would sift through the heavy stuff with gold pans.

A large, heavily muscled black man who spoke that peculiar stately brand of Guyanese English—nineteenth-century British colonial with a Caribbean lilt—told me the mining equipment cost twenty thousand dollars. The crew had been working the area for six months but had found nothing.

"Nothing at all?"

"Oh no, we are very poor here and shall leave soon."

When word of a big strike leaks out, men come on foot from Canaima, from Ciudad Bolívar, from the depths of the jungle. They come by boat, by chartered plane; they come, and the law is of no avail because the only law is the law of the jungle. Claims are jumped; men are injured; men die. When the army finally arrives to restore order, claims are apportioned among those who are there whether they were one of the original miners or not.

"We have absolutely found nothing here," the man said.

Later, in Santa Elena, I talked with a diamond buyer who knew the miners and who had invested in and worked the mines himself. His name was Floyd, and he was originally from Texas. Floyd's comment about the situation was "Oh God, I hate the taste of anteater."

Miners will spend months prospecting in the bush, and if they are finding anything, they will stay even after their food runs out. No one can be trusted to leave, stock up, and keep his mouth shut. "So each crew has a hunter," Floyd said. "I've eaten every kind of animal there is in the jungle. The deer is good. Sometimes I've been out so long our hunter ran out of bullets. But you don't want to leave, and any river that is coughing up diamonds will spit up a few gold nuggets too. So what we've done—and more than once—we've made bullets out of the gold nuggets. Keeps us there another few weeks. And then the son-of-a-bitch hunter goes out and shoots an anteater, which is the most rancid-tasting damn meat on the face of the earth."

Floyd had taken a suction hose to the bottom of the rivers on free dives, with scuba gear, and with a compression rig. "The piranha don't bother you when the water's running fast, but in the dry season, the river will leave isolated holes they call *posos,* and the piranha in them are hungry little devils." He claimed to have seen an anaconda "thirty feet long and big around as a fifty-five-gallon oil drum. Why, I saw one of those snakes sunning itself on the banks of a river, and it had the horns of a buck deer sticking out of its mouth. That big fellow was just going to have to wait awhile until the deer's head rotted away and he could spit those horns out."

Most of the diamond miners Floyd knew lived like the *garimpeiros* of Brazil. "Some of these guys, they'll hit a strike, get them some diamonds, and maybe they'll try to save a few of them. Some of them, they get back to Ciudad Bolívar, load up a shotgun, and fire six or seven dozen of them into their ceilings. Doesn't help, of course. Pretty soon they're standing on a chair, digging in their ceilings with pocketknives. They got to be poor before they come back to the jungle, and sooner or later every single one of them is poor again. Being poor is part of being a diamond miner. You can't be a diamond miner—your mind just won't let you go humping through the jungle looking for diamonds—if you own any of the suckers."

Floyd talked a little about a town I had passed on the rutted dirt road into the Gran Sabana, a place so nondescript that it had no name. The settlement was called Kilometer 88 simply because it was 88 kilometers from someplace that did have a name. "You see those scales on the bar there?" Floyd asked. "Those are for measuring out gold or diamonds. Bartender's seen so much gold, so many diamonds, he could be a master jeweler. Anyway, fellow I know, he hit it big, had a bag full of diamonds, and he was up at Kilometer 88 waiting for a ride. Probably figured he'd go to

Caracas, meet some woman, buy her a mink coat straight from New York City, something like that, and the two of them would go riding around in a limousine for a month. . . ."

What actually happened, Floyd said, is that the lucky miner dropped a stone on the scale and bought drinks for everyone in the house while waiting for his ride. There were the usual four or five patrons, but within an hour there seemed to be hundreds. The miner bought more drinks, and everyone, one after the other, proposed toasts to his good fortune. The fellow said he was honored to have such friends, and, as diamond miners will do, he began giving away stones to those colleagues who were less fortunate. The patrons there at the bar in Kilometer 88 stood patiently in line to receive their gift, then scuttled out the back door, and got in line again, so that by the time the Land Cruiser arrived for the Benefactor of Kilometer 88, he had nothing left. Several of the patrons saw that the miner got a meal—it was the least they could do—and then they rented his Land Cruiser, with his diamonds, and took off for Caracas looking for women who might need mink coats for cool tropical evenings.

"That miner was back in the jungle within twenty-four hours," Floyd said, "and it didn't take his pals much longer."

"Well," I said, "somehow that story reminds me of the way they used to test stones to see if they were diamonds down in Brazil. They used to put them on an anvil and whack 'em with a big hammer."

"Figures," Floyd said. "Diamond miners got traditions too."

Chiloé:
An Island Out of Time

▲

Umiliana Saldivia never knew exactly what she had done to get herself in trouble with the witches and wizards of Chiloé, this large, verdant, heavily forested island off southern Chile. Umiliana was a tiny, ebullient woman who appeared to be in her early sixties. She looked a bit like Dr. Ruth, the television sex therapist, and she was a fixture on the docks of the capital city of Castro, where she sold copies of a paperback book she had written entitled *Casos de Brujos de Chiloé*, cases of witches in Chiloé.

Some of the cases in the book had to do with *brujos* at play: how one of them had made a large pot walk about on its iron legs, how one unfortunate individual came home to find a large bear in his bed (this on an island bereft of bears).

Umiliana's words twanged at some of my own childhood memories. Witches and woods? A bear in the bed?

The *brujos* could, however, be vengeful, and somehow—Umiliana never knew why—she had fallen afoul of one of them. Maybe several. *"Brujos,"* she said in Spanish, "can be very evil. They cause death and illness."

We were sitting in a waterfront restaurant on Castro, a town set high on a hill overlooking the ocean. Paved streets plummeted down the hill to the line of restaurants that faced the water. This was not the most elegant of establishments—it was something of a dive—and there were rough-looking men, fishermen and day laborers, drinking heavily at the bar at ten in the morning. They were big men, descendants of the Spanish conquerors, of Italian and German immigrants who came later, and there was little or no visible evidence that any of their people had intermarried with the local Indians.

The men were drinking pisco, a fiery pale brandy made from the first pressing of grapes. The most popular brand was Pisco Control, and the most popular drink was the pisco sour, a blend of two thirds pisco, one third lemon juice, a bit of sugar, and egg white shaken with crushed ice. Five or six of these can drop an untrained drinker to his knees (take my word for it), and, in Castro, should one see a man walking down the street naked, with an ax in his hand, it is a good bet that he is under pisco control. (I never saw such a scene, or anything like it, and was not entirely disappointed that I never had occasion to utter this rather anemic witticism.)

Meanwhile, a waiter wearing a red vest and black bow tie placed my breakfast on the table: grilled sea bass, baked bread still warm from the oven, and freshly squeezed orange juice. I considered the hardworking, hard-drinking men combined with the civilized service and great food and caught the vague odor of San Francisco at the turn of the century.

But there was something else here as well, and I tried to put my finger on it. Umiliana was telling me about her problems with the *brujos*. In 1956, when her first daughter was born, she had trouble breastfeeding, and the doctors found slivers of wood under her skin. Umiliana pounded her chest to show where they found the wood. And then, every morning, she began finding dogs and cats in the house, though she locked all the doors at night. For nine years she never felt entirely well.

These manifestations suggested magical interference in her life: *brujos*. Umiliana investigated and discovered that there was, in fact, an association of *brujos*. There were, she said, initiation rites: ceremonies in which men and women went to outlying uninhabited islands and walked naked in the frosty cold of winter. Umiliana raised her eyebrows to indicate the supernatural strangeness of the act. The would-be *brujos* walked three times around the high-tide line as a way of making deals with the Devil in exchange for power.

Umiliana had stumbled onto a woman who was head of the association of *brujos*. She was, Umiliana said, a good woman, an atypical *brujo,* one who wanted to help people. For a certain sum of money Umiliana was given a document insuring her health and that of her family. Neither Umiliana nor anyone in her family had had a single sick day since that document had been signed in 1965.

And yet, Umiliana said, there were still *brujos* everywhere on the island, in every small village, and sometimes, at night, in the deep, fog-shrouded forests, they danced their ecstatic *brujo* dances, reconfirming their pacts with the Devil. God help anyone who stumbled onto such a gathering.

And it came to me, then, the odd sense of *déjà vu* these stories of witches and woods and bears in the bed engendered. The Germans had come around the turn of the century, farmers looking for land in the dense forests of Chiloé, men and women familiar with the work of the brothers Grimm, who had collected folktales of the forests of Germany, Scandinavia, and the Netherlands nearly a century earlier. Here, on Chiloé, people still believed those tales or tales very like them, and they told the stories at night, sometimes by the light of kerosene lamps.

Chiloé: the last fairy-tale island in the world.

Chiloé, 157 miles long and 32 miles wide, is the second-largest island in South America (only Tierra del Fuego is bigger). It is separated from the mainland by the narrow Chacao Channel, which is served by a regular and efficient ferry service. When I crossed over on the ferry, dolphins raced the boat, and small penguins porpoised alongside, flying through the cold water with a grace they would never exhibit on land. A cold gray jet of steam rose in the distance: a whale blowing.

Located on the Pacific coast of Chile, the island lies at the 42nd degree of south latitude, about the same position south as Coos Bay, Oregon, is north. The weather is also about the same in both places: cool, damp summers; biting cold, sometimes snowy winters moderated by the marine environment.

At 42 degrees south and 42 degrees north, the sea is provident, often shrouded in fog, and the locals take great pride in their rock-ribbed independence. They are fishermen, timber workers, farmers, and shopkeepers. In both places there is a small tourism industry that caters to those looking for solitude and seafood rather than luxury resorts and sophisticated entertainment.

With a population of about 120,000 people spread out in two main towns and dozens of small villages, Chiloé is lightly populated, though Ancud and Castro (the two main towns) are crowded in the summer tourist season (December, January, and February).

Visitors are almost always from mainland Chile, and generally from the capital city of Santiago. Renato Arancibia and his wife, Isobel, for instance, once worked as travel agents in Santiago. After the birth of their two boys, the couple took stock of their situation. It was a two-hour commute to and from work every day. What was the purpose of having children if you had no time to enjoy them?

A few years ago the family visited Chiloé. Recent development had ended the island's endemic power and water shortages. Telephones—in the main cities—worked just fine. The people were, in Renato's words, "simple," by which he meant they were men and women of the land and sea, upright, honest folk, and very shy. The island was "tranquil"—it was a word every Chilean tourist used at least once to describe Chiloé—and a good place to raise children.

Renato and Isobel set up a travel-oriented business across from the market on the waterfront at Castro. His business, Pehuen Expeditions, rents mountain bikes and runs party boats to the small outlying islands where the last vestiges of "old Chiloé" are to be found.

It's a hand-to-mouth business. Tourists, especially foreign tourists, haven't quite caught on yet.

*　*　*

I pedaled my rented bike past the Castro market, where colorful hand-knitted wool sweaters sold for about seven dollars. The road wound down the waterfront, and past the *palafitos:* homes of fishermen that extend out over the sea on great stilts made of hard local wood. The houses were shingled in weatherbeaten wood and were very picturesque. Indeed, they are best enjoyed in pictures, because it is clear that garbage and perhaps sewage are dumped into the sea from these homes, which are considered one of the tourist attractions of Chiloé.

The homes are a holdover from the old days, when there were no roads on Chiloé, and merchants sold the fishermen of the *palafitos* sugar and salt through open windows, from boats. Today, there is a paved road bisecting the island from Ancud in the north all the way to Quellon in the south. (Okay, the last ten miles or so aren't paved, but they are negotiable by rental car.) Still, near the historic and photogenic *palafitos,* there are signs warning that it is unsafe to swim.

The road I was riding cut across a bridge and rose into the steep farmland across from Castro. The sky was several different shades of gray, and a light breeze set numerous brands of wildflowers swaying in the fields. Pastures, apple orchards, wheat land, and potato fields were set out in square patches. The farmers had left the forest intact at the periphery of their fields, and the undulating, alternating patterns of agriculture—the dark green of the potato fields, the gold of the wheat, the verdant greenery surrounding them—made the island seem softly sculpted.

There were robust dairy cattle in the fields, and they shared the pastures with small island horses. At the fences, on my side of the dirt path, where the animals couldn't get at it, the land literally erupted in vegetation. There were blackberry bushes, bright red drooping flowers that looked a bit like Indian paintbrush, yellow snapdragons, and a kind of purple flowering clover. For a moment the sun bullied its way through the clouds, and several shafts of purely celestial light fell across the landscape so that Chiloé seemed a kind of Eden, complete with birdsong.

Seven hundred feet below, I could see the ocean inlet in front of

Castro. It was shaped like a piece in a particularly baroque jigsaw puzzle. Tiny figures were digging for clams directly in front of the Castro market. The Catholic cathedral stood on a rise and fronted the town square. It dominated the town, a huge rococo affair paneled in tin and painted a strange, almost iridescent, orange. The roof was bright blue.

The intricate shingled houses of Chiloé, with their gables and ornate battlements, are often painted in such fever-bright colors. One theory has it that the odd bright colors help fishermen at sea locate their homes in the fog.

I scanned the water for a home traversing the sea and was disappointed. For reasons that have remained impervious to investigative reporting, people on Chiloé, or one of the nearby outlying islands, sometimes need to move their homes. The house is rolled down to the sea on logs, with dozens of men singing and whistling and pulling at ropes.

The house—and I've seen many pictures of this: It happens—is floated on the sea and dragged, by boat, six or ten or even fifteen miles to another island. Only the roof protrudes above the waterline.

When the house has been resituated on another island—"Honey, don't you think it would look better over here?"—there is generally a *curanto,* the seafood equivalent of an American barbecue. I intended to treat myself to a *curanto*—the dish was advertised outside most of the waterfront restaurants of Castro—but first I wanted to visit the soul of the island, the impenetrable interior forest, the damp and mysterious land of witches and sorcerers.

Tiny Cucao, the only village on the west coast of the island, is set along an immense curving gray gravel beach, ten miles long, that is guarded by rock spires on either end. The Pacific Ocean thunders into shore in huge breakers. Men on horseback—they wear panchos and wide-brimmed black hats—carry nets that they use to snare a kind of sea bass that proliferates in the surf. Women, bundled up in multiple skirts against the chill of the water, stand knee-deep in the breakers, looking for all the world as if they are dancing to music of the ocean. In point of fact they are digging in the sand, feeling with their bare feet for a kind of shellfish called *macha*.

Other men spur their horses into a top-speed gallop down the beach. The horses cut sharp left, then right, agile as cats. They rear up on their hind legs, holding the pose, with their forelegs pawing the air.

The men are practicing for the local rodeo, always held in January or February. Most of the villages have a small stadium that looks a bit like a bull ring, but there is only one event, and a bloodless one at that, at a Chiloé rodeo. A bull is released. It is pursued by a man on horseback and driven against the high wooden circular ring. When the bull tires, the horse rears up and pins it to the ring for ten full seconds. During that time the forelegs of neither the horse nor the bull should touch the ground.

Rising above the beach at Cucao are the impossible emerald mountains of Chiloé National Park (established in 1982). These coastal mountains—protected now from lumbering interests—are a chaos of erupting vegetation, so thick that the government has established a wooden walkway through the woods. The forest is particularly dark: a twilight gloom at high noon on a hot, sunny day. The trees are covered with moss and lichen. There is an odor of rotting organic matter that mingles very closely with the fragrance of living things—parasitic flowers—and the marshy land is veined with small tea-colored streams.

In any clearing there will be ferns and large elephant-ear plants called *malca* that look fragile but feel like rough leather. A tree will grow in a twisting, slow-motion lunge, looking for the best place to steal the sun from its nearest competitors. The losers in this agonizing game of life and death fall, but they seldom reach the ground, such is the sheer proliferation of living things. Dead trees, held aloft by others, rot in midair.

Walking through the forest, I heard the warbling, junglelike call of a bird called the *chucao*, and it was coming from my right side. This, I had been told, is good luck. Strange sound though: half loon, half meadowlark.

I decided to experience, to the degree that I was able, the forest primeval, and left the boardwalk. The marshy ground took my boot to the ankle for the first two steps, then I crawled, creepy damp, through the choked underbrush until I was out of sight of the wooden walkway. There was a tree that dominated this section of forest, a great straight-trunked monster that rose above all the others like a monstrous stalk of broccoli. A kind of warm, organic fog steamed up off the dark brown stream to my left, and the forest was thick with the odors of birth and decay.

It occurred to me that this was the kind of forest that gave rise to the grim tales of *brujos*, to a mythology that included many half-human creatures I had heard about: Trauco, Machuco . . . all of them dangerous and sinister characters, like the talking wolves and witches of my own childhood. I am a man unmoved by superstition, but when the *chucao* called on my left side—bad luck for sure, Chiloétes say—I decided to make my way back to the walkway. I did this in some haste and managed to scratch both my arms crawling through the thorny vegetation, all the while assuring myself that I am a man unmoved by superstition.

Maybe, after my *curanto*, someone would tell me about Trauco and Machuco, these supposedly mythological creatures indigenous to Chiloé.

Octavio was a plump, jolly man, the proprietor of a Castro waterfront restaurant called, not surprisingly, Octavio. He wore one of those thin door-to-door salesman's mustaches, and his establishment was a dark, bare wood, windowless cavern that you entered through a long, unlit hallway.

It was a friendly, family-run operation, obscenely inexpensive, and Octavio joined my table for a glass of good Chilean wine. A waiter brought fresh-baked bread and a bottle of the best local cabernet, which was excellent and cost all of six dollars.

Octavio said that there wasn't much of a café society on Chiloé, not during the winter months, anyway. He had to make his money during the season. His restaurant wasn't as fancy as some, and there was no view, so he had to depend on the quality of his food to draw customers. Every year, he said, the same tourists came back for more of his grilled conger eel (it tastes a bit like halibut), or his salmon, his oysters, or the seafood stew called *pilas marinas*.

Some repeat customers, Octavio swore, came every year from

Europe just to sit at one of his tables and eat the *curanto* he served.

Originally, *curanto* had been a kind of Chiloé survival dish. At the end of the summer, in March, when the water is getting too cold for diving, fishermen go out and collect great quantities of shellfish. A hole is dug in the ground, and a fire is started. After a time the fire is covered with rocks, and they, in turn, are covered with thick leathery *malco* leaves, which hold moisture. The fruits of the sea are piled onto the leaves, and, over the course of hours, a thick, fragrant soup develops, while the shellfish are smoked for future use.

The *curanto,* like a barbecue, is a social affair, and herdsmen might add mutton or beef or sausages to the portion of the stew to be eaten on the spot.

The waiter placed an enormous bowl on the table in front of me: *curanto.*

"Where do they have the best food in the world?" Octavio asked me.

"Right here," I said, ever the diplomat.

"No. Tell me the place where everyone says the food is the best."

"Well, France, I suppose."

Octavio smiled brilliantly. "There are many people," he said, "who come from France. Every year. To eat my *curanto.*"

I tasted Octavio's famous *curanto,* and it confirmed every word he said.

Renato Arancibia thought I should see the real Chiloé, which was not Chiloé itself but the outlying islands where there were no roads, few visitors, and no telephones. Every hour, local radio stations broadcast messages from one family to another; from a merchant with a load of goods; from a man in love to a woman waiting by her portable Panasonic.

The sea was glassy calm, tranquil, and it took on the color of the sky, which was to say, it changed throughout the day. One moment the vast expanse of water seemed lifeless and forlorn, cold and gray as iron. And then the sun burst through the clouds for an hour, and the water was cobalt blue, clear as crystal, and I could see clouds of baitfish going about their single-minded business fifteen feet under the surface.

The largest settlement anywhere on the outlying islands was always the port. The village might consist of ten or twelve houses, and an enormous church bigger than all the habitations combined. On Quehui, the sound of mournful singing wafted out of the church—a funeral perhaps—and I walked up to the cemetery set on a hillock above the village. The graves were contained in small wooden houses, about eight feet long by five wide. Some of the houses were paneled with shingles, and inside there were rusting paint pots containing fresh daisies, and crosses above small altars where pictures of the deceased had been placed.

OUR DEAR MOTHER, CATALINA SANTANA, REST IN PEACE.

The graveyard itself was overgrown with ferns and grasses and wildflowers. One or two of the small houses had fallen into disrepair: They were filled with a riot of wildflowers and ferns. The trunks of small trees snaked out of broken windows.

On the island of Mechuque, a man was building a forty-five-foot fishing boat. He was working without a plan, hammering out the graceful swooping lines of the craft that would identify it as his work. The man's family had been the boat builders of Mechuque for generations.

There were *palafitos* built along a riverbed that drained and filled with the tide. A man stumbled out of the forest with a load of firewood on his back while children whooped and squealed at play on the beach.

I stopped to talk with Don Paulino, a gentlemen of eighty-six years, who lived alone in an old wooden house with great high ceilings and dull green walls. There were several hard-backed chairs in the parlor and a photo of his long-dead wife on the wall. Some artist had colored in the old black-and-white photo so that a golden light haloed the face of the determined-looking young woman who had been Don Paulino's wife. A large horsefly buzzed loudly in the silence.

Don Paulino had been born on Chiloé, but he left at the age of fourteen. In those days there was no school for the children of these islands. In 1826 Chiloé had been the last refuge of the Spanish, the last royal foothold in Chile. Its history was a festering sore when Don Paulino was young. The island was remote, and the government ignored its needs.

Don Paulino had traveled to Argentina, to work the sheep ranches, and he noticed that rich men owned land. When he returned to Chiloé, he bought land, then worked at sea to earn more money. Eventually, he owned two cargo boats—there were framed black-and-white photos of both on the walls—and he put the money from those ships back into the land.

Now, Don Paulino said, he was a very rich man. But it was all on paper, in deeds. He needed cash. This man—who never went to school, who taught himself to read and write—had many grandsons and granddaughters he wanted to send to college. He was selling his land and timber to the Japanese, he said, for the sake of his grandchildren.

There were no restaurants on Mechuque, but a woman named Dina Paillocar was said to provide a good lunch at low cost. Her simple wooden house was clean and bright. There was an unframed picture on the wall. It had been torn neatly from a magazine and tacked up at eye level: a drawing of a friendly-looking lion with large blue eyes labeled, in Spanish, "Today is a marvelous day."

Dina served raw, marinated clams, a soup of rice and smoked fish, followed by fried clam cakes. Everything was delicious, and Dina was effervescent, indomitable. She talked about her husband, who had gone to work in Punta Arenas. He had been gone a long time when she heard that he had been seen with another woman. Dina went to Punta Arenas, confronted her husband, and told him that he could have one more night with the hussy he'd taken up with. In the morning he'd come back to Mechuque and help her raise their son.

She never saw him again.

"The one more night," Dina said, "it wasn't a good idea, I guess."

"Probably not," I said, and Dina's quiet laughter flowed like a stream in summer.

She was, she said, better off without her husband. She loved to cook and earned some money doing it. Her son was fourteen, very smart, and would earn a scholarship.

And she herself had survived many harrowing experiences in the forest that rose behind her house. Once, she even saw Trauco.

"Oh?"

"Yes." He was a little man, perhaps three feet tall: he wore a cloak of moss and a pointed hat made of lichen.

She had been out with her cousin cutting wood in the forest—stakes for the sheep pen—when she heard the sound of an ax. One single whack, and then the sound of a falling tree. Trauco: the man who could fell a tree in one stroke. Dina turned and fled. Trauco can kill with a look; he can bring sickness on a bad wind; he often makes young girls pregnant.

I wasn't sure if Dina was telling me about the folklore of Chiloé or if she was relating what she believed to be the truth of her own experiences.

"Trauco makes young girls pregnant?" I asked.

"Oh, yes," Dina said brightly. "Many parents have sued Trauco. In court. Because he made their daughters pregnant."

I asked Dina if she'd like to drink some wine I had with me. I had the afternoon free and loved stories.

Dina told me about *Caleuche,* a ghost ship that appears in the fog. There is always loud music and laughter on board this ship—sometimes you can hear the supernatural hilarity echo off the water—and when fishermen fail to return from the sea, it is assumed they have joined the party on *Caleuche.*

The wine was a Rhine from a vineyard outside of Santiago. Dina told me about Machucho, the man with three legs, who can jump fifty feet at a bound, and whose step sounds like the booming of a great cannon. Sun poured in through the window, the wine was tartly crisp, and today was just as advertised: a marvelous day on a fairy-tale island.

Moonwalk Serenade [1978]

▲

The chassis of Pepe's long, low, customized, flame-crimson Chevy nearly scraped the pavement, and it cruised like a great hungry shark. Pepe, a muscular fireplug of a fellow with a Zapata mustache, is a nark, and he was pointing out drug abusers abusing drugs on the streets of East San Jose, in the populous barrio Chicanos call Tropicana.

"When you're making a heroin buy," Pepe said, "there are always guns around. With KJ, you don't see guns, but you got to watch they don't get combative on you." By KJ, Pepe meant PCP (Phencyclicline), which is most often smoked in joints, kristal joints, and the street name most often heard is KJ. Pepe said users were frequently violent.

This pretty much coincided with information I had from the Santa Clara Valley Medical Center, which handles area KJ problems. "The PCP-ingested patient" was described as sometimes "zombielike," but quite often "combative and hostile." Doug Potter, an orderly, said that a lot of patients came in after they punched out a window or something and that they liked to make animal sounds: He heard a lot of barking, growling, and gorilla-like snorting. They tended to stutter and sweat and drool and had very poor coordination.

"Even so," Potter said, "they seem to gain enormous strength, crazy strength. It takes a lot of people to hold them down." The drug acts as an anesthetic, and on it, you feel only deep physical pain. "You can hit them in the face," Potter said, "break their noses, and that would stop anyone. On PCP it might just agitate them."

Pepe and I were cruising the corner of Story and King Road, in the heart of the heart of the barrio. The corner was a maze of parking lots, gas stations, and fast-food franchises: Jack-in-the-Box, Shakey's Pizza, Taco Bell, and a huge building labeled "the World's Largest Indoor Flea Market." In the parking lot outside the flea market, Pepe said, thousands of young people, mostly Chicanos in tricked-out cars—lowriders—gather in the late hours of a weekend night, and there KJ is openly smoked and sold.

I saw it all in my mind's eye: thousands of chronic PCP users stumbling and lurching through the parking lot, all of them sweating and drooling, growling and barking, attacking anything that moved in their delirium, stumbling after their prey with glazed, marble eyes. And you couldn't hurt them, these zombie assassins. They'd just keep coming for you, like creatures out of the *Night of the Living Dead*.

The place, I figured, had to be a real goon show.

PCP has had a history of near-universal rejection. It was developed by Parke, Davis in the late fifties and used as an experimental surgical anesthetic, a potent painkiller that worked without depressing respiration. Unfortunately, the side effects—agitation, disorientation, delirium, and frightening hallucinations—were so terrifying that human use was discontinued. In 1967 PCP was sold to veterinarians as an anesthetic for lower primates. Drug lore has it that one of the first shipments of this monkey tranquilizer was hijacked, and that it hit Haight-Ashbury in 1967 as "the peace pill."

PCP quickly acquired a reputation as a bummer drug. People named Strawberry were going around punching people named Wildflower. Others were seized by a terror so complete that they were afraid to move, or even speak. There were convulsions too: an electroshock snapping of the spine, followed by the shaking sweats. And, especially in cases of multidrug use, coma was common. So, while PCP was sometimes a good high, one that made you feel in tune with the music of the spheres, you had to watch those four ugly C's: combat, catatonia, convulsions, and coma.

In the early seventies PCP skulked back onto the drug scene. Certain scumbag dealers peddled it as "organic" mescaline or psilocybin. Even today there is a 90 percent chance that that stuff you thought was THC or cannabinol was actually PCP.

By 1972 people never much interested in psychedelics were getting into PCP and, indeed, accepting it as the drug of choice. The government was cracking down on reds (Seconals), but people who wanted to achieve that truly helpless, irresponsible, wall-banging euphoria—people who wanted to get *all* fucked up—could take a couple of tokes on a KJ and get there in about five minutes and stay kristalized, ozoned, for four to six hours.

There are times, in the ozone, when movement is difficult without sustained, even heroic concentration. "Let's see, lean forward, move the right leg . . . bend the knee and, uh, right, lift the toes so the foot doesn't drag. . . . This is taking *forever*. . . . Holy Christ, stiffen the knee or we all go down. . . ." In East San Jose this mode of stoned locomotion is known as the moonwalk.

The problem is that the line between moonwalking and serious trouble is very thin. You can get off on three milligrams of PCP; ten can make your stomach feel like it's full of dirty socks, and you may end up doing pull-ups on the toilet bowl; 200 milligrams is a suicide attempt. By sprinkling the drug on parsley and smoking it (rather than eating, snorting, or shooting it) you can more easily control your intake. This is why your chronic user is almost always a smoker.

Investigators have found that PCP aggravates preexisting psychosis. It also mimics the primary symptoms of schizophrenia, and it does this much more accurately than mescaline or LSD. By late '76 you could read about these effects in the paper—a guy broke a big chunk of glass off his shower door and ate it. Cut his insides up pretty good. Another fellow was using PCP pretty heavy, and one night, swimming around in the ozone, it occurred to him that since his wife was exactly nine months pregnant, it would be a good idea to use a big butcher knife and "hatch" the kid. Luckily, his wife talked him out of it. She had to tell him about it the next day. Amnesia is a frequent side effect.

In Los Angeles an unemployed actor who wasn't the Hillside Strangler told police that he was. Another man found himself in a jail cell and put his eyes out with his own hands. (This is a hard one not to have nightmares about. Scientists believe PCP disrupts or distorts the way the brain receives stimuli from within the body. This is what frightens people and freezes them into catatonia. "It just seems," one chronic user told me, "like your brain cells can't hack it.") Treatment for a PCP bummer involves removing as much external stimuli as possible. No excitement.

There are other horror stories: One man murdered his parents; another stabbed a tiny baby to death. Users themselves die, not only from massive overdoses, but from what is called "behavioral toxicity." People fall from great heights, burn to death, drive their cars into large stationary objects, or drown in a few inches of water because they didn't recognize the danger, or couldn't cope with it, or simply because they were too fried to do anything about it, even move.

People of all ages, races, and social station are using PCP, but experts give San Jose, California, the nod as the epicenter of the epidemic. And in San Jose the focus of public use and sale was the parking lot at Story and King Road.

There were, at a guess, some seven hundred cars in the lot, and, aside from the lights of a club called Disco East on one side and those of Story and King Liquors on the other, it was very dark. At least four thousand people were standing around in the lot. Young men in groups of four or five leaned up against cars. Young women roamed the lot in groups of two or three, stopping now and again to talk with guys, have a beer, or share a joint, or just comment on the music blasting out of the car stereo. There were more people by the liquor store, more in the club, and cars were coming and going at all times. Most everyone was Chicano.

It was, in fact, rather like being in Mexico, where every town has a plaza where people gather on weekends and feast days. In

America the tradition has taken wheels, and the plaza has become a parking lot.

People were there to enjoy themselves, and they refused to lurch, sweat, drool, vomit, curse, murder, die, or flop around in convulsions on the pavement. Socially, the place was like a huge stand-up cocktail party. I'd introduce myself to a group, exchange pleasantries, and stroll on. No one—not even those who thought I was the world's most inept Anglo nark—had a nasty word. I saw some people smoking KJ—it has a distinct, fishlike chemical odor—but they mostly did it in their cars in a secret, masturbatory fashion.

I stopped to talk to one group primarily because one of them was just finishing up a KJ roach. The fellow wore sharply creased black slacks, a patterned Qiana shirt, and stacked heels. I never did get his name—he may not have known it—and so I will call him Party Boy. No one really talked to Party Boy. He just moonwalked around for a time, and his eyes seemed to roll around in his head without regard to focus.

Just as I finished my second beer, Party Boy noticed me for the first time. It was as if some hideous extraterrestrial had materialized before his flaming eyes. "What?" he asked and grabbed my arm urgently, nodding for me to complete the sentence. I must have looked blank.

"What religion?" He was clearly annoyed at having to elaborate.

"Raised Catholic," I said, and nodded for him so he would understand that this was a good thing. Party Boy threw back his head and screamed, "I want to be free." He glared at me. His face was fierce. "Me too," I offered lamely. He grabbed the beer can from my hand—I had been using it as an ashtray—and downed the dregs, ashes and all. "You want to be free," I reminded him in the hope that this would take his mind off the ashes.

Party Boy pondered the familiarity of the phrase for some time, then asked me what religion I was. "Raised Catholic," I said.

"Uh . . . good." He tried to show me a swirling red-and-black tattoo on his chest that apparently had religious significance, but his shirt was in the way. It took him a long time to get it off, and he fought with it, as if the shirt were a sentient thing.

Bernardo, a tall fellow with a goatee, pulled me behind some cars, out of Party Boy's sight. "The *vato*'s [The word *"vato"* corresponds pretty much to the word "dude." It is good to be a *vato loco*, a crazy dude. It is not so good to be "a *vato* who's all fucked up."] all fucked up," Bernardo said. We watched Party Boy lurching around, trying to get his shirt back on. It took him most of ten minutes, primarily because one arm was inside out, and whichever way he put the damn thing on, there was always something wrong with it.

It was about this time, 2:00 A.M., that the fights started. There was one every half hour or so, but Bernardo didn't want me to watch. Instead he told me about the cars: *hours* of information about cars. "A lowrider," Bernardo said, "buys his car stock. Never customized. An artist doesn't display someone else's work." A hundred feet away I could catch the action in stroboscopic bursts: arms whipping like hummingbirds' wings, thumps, whumps, smacks, and groans, fists thudding into flesh with the sound of a tenderizing hammer pounding into a two-inch beefsteak.

"The first thing you want to do," Bernardo said, "is mold the make and model name off your car." Your ride, he explained, is your pride, and to have a big chrome advertisement for Buick Riviera on it is tantamount to having Buick Riviera tattooed on your chest.

Party Boy, his shirt buttoned in an exceedingly strange fashion, wandered over and tried to say something, but there was no sense in him. "Man," Bernardo said in exasperation, "tomorrow I'll wake up with a hangover, but you're going to wake up as a tomato, man, a vegetable."

"Fuck . . . vegetables," Party Boy said, and Bernardo was off again about the cars. You want true spoke wheels ($600), and little tiny, thin tires with about half an inch of whitewall on them, the 560s or 520s ($150). And you'll need to get rid of your twenty-inch stock steering wheel and replace it with an eight-inch chain, welded into a circle and chromed ($20). Then there's your stereo and tapes ($200) and when you have $1,000 together, you'll want your ride painted to your design. A diamond-tuck crushed-velvet interior job goes for about $500 in town, half that in Tijuana. Of course, you'll lower your car, but that causes problems on sloping driveways and over speed bumps, so when you have about $800, you can put in hydraulics—lifts, juice—and make your car do push-ups.

Engines are not modified for speed. That's for the Anglo kids who run the other side of town in cars that say Trans-Am on the side with the back end all jacked up. "Roadsniffers," Bernardo called them.

"Lowriders," he said solemnly, "are slow riders."

Bernardo saw the scene in the parking lot as a gigantic party for mechanical artists, a place where lowriders could display their work. The key word, he said, was unity, Chicano unity.

"Unity," I said, "Jesus, what about *that?*"

There was another fight in progress not forty yards away. "Hey," Bernardo said, "if a *vato* gets bad with you, you don't want to turn away with your tail between your legs." A couple of police materialized out of nowhere—they were bareheaded, no provocative riot gear—and the fight disintegrated. Party Boy was stumbling around in the vicinity, and I wondered if he had enough sense not to ask them if they were Catholic.

Okay, Bernardo said, I was here on a bad night. Sometimes there are no fights at all. But even when there are, they are one-on-one, no organized shit like East L.A. where the car clubs are sometimes more like war clubs. Their operations are planned with maps and CBs and walkie-talkies—the whole enchilada. The object is to take a tire iron to some car belonging to a rival club and make off with the plaque in the back window. Then you fly the plaque with the vanquished club's name on it in your back window. Upside down. Then someone burns down the president's house. Then the guns come out. It's *West Side Story* on wheels.

In San Jose car clubs have gotten big again in the last few years, and there is a central council designed to keep them at peace. On weekend nights there may be thirty-some clubs represented in this parking lot, perhaps the world's largest regular gathering of lowriders.

"And you want to write about KJ," Bernardo snorted. "Okay, some *vatos* deal to get money to cherry out their ride. But how many dealers can there be? Most lowriders I know have jobs. A lot are married, with kids. And they're not going to go getting all kristalized, man. One KJ costs twenty-five dollars. You do four a week, that's a hundred dollars you can be putting into your ride.

"*Mira,* I'm no hypocrite. I smoked KJ, everybody has. It's a good high. But everybody knows that it burns your brain cells. I don't like to be around people who smoke KJ, man. One *vato* poked me in the back with a knife behind KJ, man, I went to the hospital. And you know what else? People who smoke KJ all the time are ashamed, man. You talk to them when they're straight, they're ashamed. They don't want anyone to know that they're burning up their brains."

The two cops came by again, hurrying a guy in handcuffs toward the squad cars parked on the periphery of the lot. The guy was dressed like Party Boy, but you couldn't tell from the distance.

Bernardo said that what I ought to do is find someone who had his ride together—anyone, my choice—and cruise around with him for a day. "See if he talks about KJ or cars. Give the lowriders a chance."

"Yeah," I said, "maybe I'll do that."

"Make me a promise," Bernardo said, and he kept at me until I finally did.

I was cruising on Saturday afternoon with Huero when he decided to show me some placas, those walls of stylized graffiti you see around Tropicana. Huero's personal favorite was several feet high, written in spray paint on the back of the McDonald's near Welch Park, a prime cruising spot. The script had that peculiar Aztec-style Chicano graffiti artists strive for, and it read "Huero of Sa Jo." For good measure he had added a "14," which means northern California, as opposed to southern California, which is "13."

Huero got arrested because of that particular *placa*. The police took him off to court. They argued that Huero was something of a flamboyant and well-known character in the barrio, that everyone knew him as Huero, and that he had even modified the grillwork of his extremely noticeable car to read "Huero."

Huero, for his part, said that many people in the barrio share his street name, which refers to lightly complected Chicanos or Mexicans. Literally, the name means white man, and for all Huero knew, maybe some white guy came down to the McDonald's near Welch Park and wrote "Huero" on the wall in Aztec script.

Perhaps the judge agreed. Maybe he took note of Huero's wounds. He had been hit fifteen times in Vietnam. One of his legs and one of his arms don't work so well, and just at the outside corner of one eye there is a bullet-sized groove that runs back to an ear pretty much chewed away. Huero earned a Congressional Medal of Honor in 1969, and the judge might have taken this into account before deciding whether he was going to put a thirty-one-year-old man in the slammer for writing on some wall with spray paint.

Then again, Huero's luck may have had something to do with the *rifa*. It is sometimes written, sometimes it appears like this: = r=. The word means quarrel, and a *rifa* on a *placa* means "Don't mess with this, because anything you write on my *placa* reflects back on you." The *rifa* is a spell, a little bit of magic, and as much as anything, it might have been the *rifa* that brought Huero through his big graffiti bust.

Cruising with Huero on a warm afternoon is a little like being handed the key to the barrio. First of all, he has sunk over six thousand dollars into his '75 Chevy Monte Carlo, jacking it up to the really florid heights of the baroque lowrider style. From the chrome grillwork, reading "Huero," back, the car is all color and splash. The basic color is star-burst bronze, and brown and amber tendrils snake through the long, off-white side panels. These tendrils are interspersed with vertical blue and light blue flames that look a bit like desert plants in some lights. Indeed, the trunk sports a representational desert scene with cacti and an otherwise naked girl wearing a sombrero. Under that scene are the words

"*Mi Vida Loca*,"—my crazy life. On both rear fender wells are the words "Lowrider's Dream," and on both opera windows, painted in white, is the suggestion "Let's fall in love."

We were cruising through Tropicana—down Havana and around Florida and through Sumatra—and people on their lawns would shout, "Hey, Huero, man," and Huero would pull over. People stepped to the car, alert for any new changes.

"Hey, Huero, man, when did you throw crush into your ride?"

Just last week as a matter of fact. The light blue diamond-tuck crushed-velvet interior covers the doors, the rear seat bench, and extends into the rear window well. The front buckets have been replaced with padded swivel seats, and they are covered in shiny bright blue vinyl with silver metal flake, and that same material covers the ceiling. The little glass sunroof Huero installed is tinted a gentle purple, and the sun streaming through on the crush and the metal flake, on the silver brocade scarf hanging from the rearview mirror, gives the interior the stained-glass atmosphere of a Mexican church. The hood ornament is a very substantial swooping silver eagle.

Still, the most important thing about Huero's ride is his wife, Babe. She rides to his right, and on the dash, just in front of her, are four golden letters reading BABE. She is a good deal darker than Huero, and they laugh about this a lot. They laugh about everything. They are so much in love it is simultaneously delightful and embarrassing; always stealing quick kisses, always tickling and touching one another.

Babe works as a counselor in the high schools. She reads Margaret Mead and uses words like "ethnocentricity," words that send poor Huero into paroxysms of laughter.

For Huero, everything and everyone is wonderful. I was wonderful because I was in San Jose spending my own money to find out about lowriders. Well, not exactly. I explained that I was getting expenses and being paid on top of it. No matter, Huero was happy to have me with him.

And it is at this point that many a lowrider might fire up a joint of Columbo and just cruise at fifteen, twenty miles an hour with the purple streaming through the roof onto the silver brocade scarf and the willow trees swaying in the breeze outside—watch it here, the intersection, you have to take them at a diagonal so you don't bottom out—and El Chicano or Malo blasting out of the stereo, all horns and drums, or maybe that all-time lowrider slow dance classic, Santo and Johnny's "Sleepwalk," and here comes another lowrider, fifteen, twenty miles an hour, taking the intersection on the diagonal and you should shift into neutral and blast the pipes in greeting and maybe, while the road ahead is clear, give Babe a kiss.

On any given Saturday afternoon about half the car clubs will be meeting. Members drive to the president's house, and if a car is dirty, or dented, or riding on a spare wheel, fines will be given out. I was not really sure of Huero's position. He said that he was a member of the National Lowriders, but he'd dropped out. Now, for photos of his ride, he'd like to be flying a plaque. We stopped at the president's house. He was a bright young guy named Jesse, and I overheard him tell Huero that "you got a dent man, I can't let you fly our plaque." Time passed, and more cars arrived, but we didn't seem to be invited to the meeting.

We cruised over to Disco East where some of the Street Escorts were hanging out. The Escorts have thirty-six cars, while the National Lowriders have fourteen. They seemed to be a better disciplined, more organized club. A few of them commented favorably on Huero's ride, and somewhere along the line there was a misunderstanding. We got the impression that just for today we might be able to fly the Escort's plaque in Huero's ride. Following the Escorts to their president's house, Huero commented on what a bunch of good *vatos* they all were. We socialized on the front lawn for a time, and someone asked Huero to please move his ride. It was parked in the middle of a long line of Escort cars, and it stood out like a giant ink stain on the flag. The Escorts favor solid-color paint jobs—they like 1963 Chevy Impalas with skirts. Their interiors are stark, dark leather. No Escort would even think of installing a hood ornament.

So they wanted Huero's car out of the way, and he moved it, still smiling but clearly hurt. The meeting started, and we were told that it was private. We stood for a time on the front lawn with maybe half a dozen other hopefuls. Huero went back to sit in his ride. His limp seemed more pronounced, and Babe talked softly to him all during the long shuffle back to the Lowrider's Dream.

"Why did they have to be so hostile?" Babe said. There was a quaver in her voice. "The vibes were so bad."

"What did you say, Honita?" Huero asked. She was speaking on the grooved side of his face where he had no hearing at all.

"Shh, baby," she said, "you're not supposed to hear." Then, softly, to me, she said, "He was hurt in the war. He shouldn't have to conform."

And maybe Babe meant the car with its splashy paint job and the silver eagle on the hood. Maybe she meant Huero himself, all the time displaying his embarrassing love for her, for all lowriders, for people in general. Maybe she meant that great, happy, goofy smile he usually wore, and maybe she meant his desire to help, his sincerity, his need to be loved in return.

"He shouldn't have to conform," Babe said. Her eyes glistened. "It isn't fair, is it?"

"No," I said, "it isn't."

"He deserves better, doesn't he?"

"Yes," I said, "he does."

In mid-'77, in the midst of San Jose's PCP blizzard, Project DARE, a private, nonprofit drug-education and rehabilitation program, introduced a PCP treatment center, and in the spring of this year I spoke with some clients there, chronic KJ smokers trying to dump the habit. Sitting to my immediate left was a twenty-one-year-old woman with small black tear-shaped tattoos falling from the corner of her left eye. This is a style sometimes seen in the barrio, and it is called "Sad Eyes." Originally, each black teardrop was supposed to represent a year spent in jail, and quite often the tattoos were self-inflicted with a ballpoint pen during a bad downtime in some cell. Less frequently, you may see men wearing sad eyes. In some cases the teardrop has nothing to do with prison, but is, instead, something of a statement about the condition of the soul.

And my friend to the left had them, for whatever reason. Her hair was dyed a darkish blond and teased into an elaborate bouffant. She wore high-heeled boots, very tight bell-bottoms, and a tight, dark, knit halter top: all very much of one particular lowrider style. Women who adopt this style often have street names: Spider Woman, Dancing Lady, Sad Eyes. The woman to my left did not call herself Sad Eyes, but since I have changed names and places and descriptions of many of the people and cars throughout and because my friend seemed so bewildered, because her large brown eyes echoed such pain, because one agency or another took her child from her after she fell into a serious KJ habit, I have decided to call her Sad Eyes.

She was trying to quit. All the Project DARE clients were. During the first few weeks they come into this large, comfortable room every day. Depression, sometimes suicidal depression, follows withdrawal from a chronic habit, and the temptation is very great to spark up a KJ and kick back. So they come in for moral support, to be reminded of how clearheaded, how fresh and alive, they feel without KJ.

Most of the clients I talked to had been clean for days, even weeks, and they were clear-eyed and articulate. Except for Sad Eyes. It took her nearly half an hour to complete the simple form —name, address, signature—giving me permission to talk to her. Her soft eyes refused to focus, and they moved in slow, short arcs, like a trapped nocturnal animal staring into a light.

She tended to stutter, to lose her train of thought, to repeat herself. When she spoke of the things that had happened to her— about how they took her baby from her—the temptation was very great to hold her. Men, she said, would give young girls KJ and encourage them to smoke great amounts until their senses shattered and their brains burst, and then the men would have them, one after the other, all night long, and the next day that girl would wake up, and the long bad night would come back to her only in vague shadows, like the dimly recalled meat of last year's nightmare.

Another client, Mike, said he supported his habit with a little low-level dealing to friends. A gram of KJ goes for about $140.

Out of that you can make eight heavy joints at $30 a pop for a profit of $100, or twenty-four street joints at $20 for $340.

Guys deal on this level from their houses or apartments. They deal on the street and at the parks and at the parking lot at Story and King. I know of one woman who turns her welfare check into grams and deals out of her house. That's why it's so hard to quit, Mike said. There's someone dealing on most every block.

Eve Torres, a senior counselor at Project DARE, told me that they separate the heroin therapeutic group from the PCP group because the addicts think the KJ freaks are "punks."

Eve said that since the PCP treatment program started in July of '77, a number of distinct groups had come through, and that, currently, she was seeing chronically unemployed young people with serious emotional problems.

And that was where it lay these days in Tropicana, or so it seemed to me after six weeks of poking around. The epidemic was at its periphery, and about to collapse on itself. In the beginning Project DARE's PCP section couldn't even get a group together. Now, people were volunteering for the program.

In the barrio, this most mannered of all American communities, things that fall from style fall fast. And when even the junkies finger you for a punk, it becomes very apparent that you ain't got no style at all.

We are hunched in this sweat lodge, which is about three feet high and six in diameter, cramped quarters, dark as the womb of the earth itself, and in a pit at the center of the lodge are a dozen or so rocks, hot from the fire outside, and they are glowing malevolently. In a few seconds the medicine man, who is a Chicano named Sal Candelaria, will pour water on the rocks, and a scalding steam will rise, burning our chests and faces, which are already rolling with sweat. To cope with the pain of this strong ceremony, we will chant an old Indian song that sounds to me like "hi how are ya, hi how are ya," and it will feel good to chant in this manner, much better than screaming in pain, which is in very bad taste because this is, after all, a religious ceremony, and we are singing the old song in prayer. The prayer is for all the Chicano brothers and sisters in the parking lot at Story and King. We are praying for these young brothers and sisters because some of them have burned their brains on PCP. We are sweating in prayer for these burned-out brothers and sisters.

Sal pours the water. Steam fills the lodge. Candelaria has been a community organizer for over half of his thirty-four years, first with the Black Berets, then in the mid-seventies with the Monitors, a street-level group funded by the Campaign for Human Development and formed for the express purpose of preventing trouble in the parks and parking lots.

Early on, Sal and the Monitors discovered that a lot of the problems at the local parks—fights, rapes, serious beatings—had to do with the use and sale of KJ. The Monitors launched an anti-KJ campaign complete with bumper stickers, posters, rap sessions in the parks and schools, and a sophisticated "boycott the pusher" campaign.

It was tough to get people to listen in those days. The pushers responded by circulating rumors in the barrio: The Monitors were raiding houses, flushing the KJ, and ripping the dealers for their cash. The Monitors were in league with the police and accepting kickbacks from certain dealers.

On August 31, 1974, a shotgun blast shattered a window, and Sal caught seven buckshot pellets in the head. Then came the anonymous death threats: rasping voices on the telephone. Sal was arrested for possession of stolen guns, and later for inciting a riot during a march protesting the death of a Chicano shot by the police under suspicious circumstances.

It seemed to Sal, in those days, that he was caught between the dealers and the police. "I didn't know who to trust," he says now, and felt as if . . . as if he were going crazy. He fled "up north," where he lived with "some Indians" which is how the Sundance religion came to heal his mind. Sal thought I might find similar solace in Sundance.

The rocks in the pit are glowing like meteors, and in a minute Sal will pour more water on them, and the steam will rise, scalding us for the fourth time. This has been going on for two hours.

When I close my eyes, I see little dancing colored lights. Sal says they are spirits.

Having already prayed for the people at Story and King, Sal says, we may pray for anything we like. He pours the water, and the steam comes hissing up off the rocks. I pray for Huero and Babe in the lowrider's dream. I pray that I don't have a heart attack. I pray that I am right about KJ's imminent fall from grace in Tropicana. I pray that my teeth won't melt. I pray that Bernardo knows I kept my promise.

It occurs to me, in the middle of this last, strong sweat, that I am really praying—actually praying—for the first time since being "raised Catholic." I am not praying to our Grandfather, which is Sal's vision. Or, at least, I don't think I am. My mind doesn't work that way. I imagine I am praying to something in the spirit of all the people I've talked to in the last six weeks.

And I'm thankful. I'm thankful I wasn't devoured by zombies, and that Bernardo was right, and that I can walk into the goon show any time and spot ten cars I know and see the owners' personalities in them. I'm thankful for my big moment in the club called Disco East when the disk jockey introduced me and the people cheered.

I feel clean, sanctified, goofy as a god. I am not used to this sort of thing, and so I close my eyes to see how the spirits are taking it all. They are still dancing, madly.

Calving Season

▲

I wanted to see how cowboys lived in Montana circa 1890, and they gave me Goofy Dick. Dick has soft brown eyes with the veiled and distant tint of a man dreaming of rifles and rooftops. This is a horse with a dark strain of the misanthrope. Such an animal is described, in these parts, as being "about half-broke," is praised for his stamina, his "cow sense," and is said to be "a helluva cow pony."

The moment I put my foot in the stirrup, Dick whirled, bucked, threw his head, snorted, kicked, lurched, and stumbled. It was sort of like rock climbing during an earthquake. Somehow Dick and I collided, head to head. There was a muffled thonk, and little colored stars exploded in my field of vision.

The two cowboys, Leo Cremer, twenty, and Edd Enders, nineteen, watched the complicated mounting procedure with deep concern. Now that I was relatively safe in the saddle, swaying woozily, they turned to their own horses, their shoulders shaking with emotion.

Native Montanans, I've discovered in my years here, find any horse-related injury short of a fatality a cause for great hilarity. "Yeah," you'll hear someone say, "the horse bucked him off and dragged him a couple of miles. When we finally got to him, he looked like he'd been scrubbed with a wire brush. Funniest damn thing I ever saw." You see some of the same attitude in a few of Charlie Russell's turn-of-the-century western paintings: the humor of mishaps on horseback.

We rode through foot-deep snow, down toward the banks of the Sweetgrass River, where the cows were. They were all black Angus, a hardy breed, and Edd spotted one off by herself, half hidden in the willows along the banks of the river. It was, he said, "suspicious." We rode across the river, dismounted, tethered our horses, and walked through the thick willows. There was some blood on the snow, some frozen water, and a small trail where something wet, about the size of a full-grown bird dog, had been rolled over and over. The cow was still licking her newborn calf when she saw us.

Leo Cremer moved in close, checking the mother's udders. Sometimes the bag is so tight and the teats are swollen so large that the calf can't suck. "She looks okay," Leo called back to us. The mother shied and waddled off a few feet into the willows. Her calf chose that moment to rise on its spindly legs. It swayed, stumbled, kept its feet. Its front legs bent in toward one another in a knock-kneed fashion, and it looked about with a kind of deep bovine wonder.

The calf hadn't had a lot of time to figure things out, and it stumbled toward Leo, taking him for Mother. Leo felt the calf's muzzle. It was warm, a good sign. A "cold calf"—one that is likely to freeze to death—generally has a cold muzzle. If the calf had been cold, Leo would have taken it back to the forty-year-old trailer where he was living and warmed it up by the wood stove.

The mother was watching through the willows about ten feet away. Leo spoke for the calf. "Bok," he said. It was a pathetic little bleat. The mother responded in the manner of full-grown cows. "Bok," Leo bleated again, moving away from the calf as the mother edged toward it.

We walked to the horses and mounted—more Comedy Horsemanship on my part—and rode to the top of a low ridge nearby.

Leo and Edd wanted to make sure the mother came back. "They're like birds," Leo said. "You disturb the nest too much and the mother won't come back." Below, in the willows, the mother nuzzled her calf, which stumbled a bit, said "bok," and eventually found a teat. "Once they're up and sucking," Leo said, "you almost never lose a calf."

We walked the horses farther up the ridge, watching the cows below. The ranch belongs to Leo's parents, George and Helen Cremer. It is a good-sized spread—about 156 square miles—and the Cremers run two thousand head of cattle on it. Cremer cows calve in April. The timing, of course, is a simple matter of when you let the bulls in with the cows. Most of the smaller operations hereabouts calve in February, hoping for the fabled thaw. If it doesn't come, a fellow who is only running a hundred or two hundred head can get his calves into a barn or shed. The advantage of early calving is that when the buyers come around in November, the calves will be heavier.

But with two thousand head spread out over 156 square miles, the Cremers calve in spring. That's the way the big ranchers did it in 1890, and the methods of a century past are still the most efficient. We might have herded the cows on snowmobiles—later, mud bikes would be in order—but it is impossible to rope a sick calf from either of those vehicles and equally impossible to catch even a week-old calf on foot. Horseback is the only way to go.

Leo and Edd live in a trailer, twenty miles from the main ranch house—one of three cow camps on the ranch—and they have managed to get the six hundred cows they are responsible for into about two square miles. They rise at first light, and one of them goes out to catch the horses and saddle them up. The other makes the coffee. (A recipe for cowboy coffee à la Edd and Leo: Fill pot with one quart of water from river, add an equal amount of coffee, boil fifteen to twenty minutes.)

The bridles are brought in and set beside the wood stove while Edd and Leo wince down their coffee. The bridles are warmed so the bits don't stick to the horses' tongues. In Montana blizzard conditions are not unusual in April.

The first morning I rode with Leo and Edd, a foot and a half of snow fell in the three hours it took us to check the cows. Leo held an incredible amount of information in his head: There was a "suspicious" cow—one he thought was ready to calve—hanging out too near the high bank of the river. He didn't want her accidentally rolling a newborn calf into the frigid waters below. There was another cow off by herself on top of the ridge, but her bag wasn't tight with milk—a sign that she would be about ready to calve—and he wanted to check her out. There was a mother and calf in the trees by an abandoned homestead, and Leo thought the mother's teats might be too big. If they were, he'd get the calf mothered up with an old cow who had lost her calf. Leo marked down the new calves in a notebook he had back at the trailer, but I believe he knew, without thinking about it, where each individual was and how many there were.

That knowledge is important, because just as it was in the 1890s, rustling can be a problem. The calves aren't branded yet, and a fellow could drive down the poorly maintained county road, hop the fence into Cremer's land, and steal a calf. A strange vehicle will make its way down the road about once a week, and Leo will mark it in his mind. If a calf is missing, there is a two-way radio in the trailer. A fellow with a calf lying beside him in the cab of his pickup might find a few vehicles waiting for him at the end of the road.

After making the rounds, Leo and Edd came back to the trailer for breakfast. Later they moved cows from one pasture to another and mended fence. Late in the afternoon they made another round, checking the cows. I calculate they spent an average of ten hours a day on horseback. They slept in their long underwear and went to the main ranch for a shower about once a week.

One afternoon I went out to check on the cows with Leo. I lurched onto Dick's back, and we rode out to a desolate stretch of windblown prairie where an old cow had dropped a stillborn calf. She had stayed with it more than a week, licking it mournfully during the day, sleeping with it at night. "Usually," Leo said, "they give up after a couple of days." The mother had finally left her calf. Now there were coyote tracks near the body, which had been ripped open.

We came up over a ridge, and a huge golden eagle rose soundlessly no more than ten feet from us. It had left behind a bit of blood and one hind leg from a jackrabbit. I thought, This is the way it was for the people who worked this land a hundred years ago.

Goofy Dick, as if in agreement, jumped three feet straight into the air, for no discernible reason. Funniest damn thing you ever saw.

Tracking 'Em Down

▲

I would have preferred a lost child, but instead we drew a homicide.

Jim Grasky, a Border Patrol agent and man-tracking expert who might have been the Marlboro Man in another life, laid out the hypothetical problem. The body had been found out by the old gravel pit. It was discovered last night, he explained, at a low point in the southeast corner of the pit, along the fence. A bullet had passed through the heart, on a downward angle.

The twelve of us, all in our first tracking class, began looking high, along the dusty ridges that ringed the pit to the north and west. It was late afternoon, and the sun was low in the west, a fine time to track. We found a muddle of bootprints near the highest promontory. They were hard to miss: The ground was covered with a thin layer of black grainy dust made for tracking. We positioned the prints between the sun and ourselves. The shine—the reflection of light off a flattened area, in this case made by a pair of boots and the weight of a man—showed a definite line of travel. You could see it from twenty yards away.

On a good day, with the sun hanging low, Jim Grasky has used shine to track men for miles. In an airplane.

With the sun behind us, however, the tracks were not visible at all. Grasky told us to always keep the tracks between you and the sun. If possible, track early or late in the day to get the best angle.

We wanted to see where the tracks started, so we followed them backward for one hundred yards. Just under the ridge the tracks ended in an area of elaborate compression. Then hoofprints led away to the west. Someone had ridden a horse to the area under the ridge. When he knew he wouldn't be visible from below, he dismounted. It looked as if he had tethered the horse to a stout bit of sage—the sage was surrounded by a circle of shine.

"What can you tell me about this horse?" Grasky asked us. Someone who knew a lot more about horses than I did noted that the animal was shod front and back. Judging by the size and depth of the hoofprint, it was decided that the horse must have weighed about a thousand pounds and stood perhaps fifteen hands high: a medium-size saddle horse.

We followed the shine forward this time. The prints were definitely those of a western boot. There was a pattern of thirteen forward-facing chevrons on the sole, and five reverse-facing chevrons on the heel. We got out our tape measures and took some notes. This very distinctive boot measured twelve and a half inches long and four and a half inches across at its widest point: Judging by the size, this was a man's track. The stride length was thirty-three inches, which seemed to indicate a relatively long-legged man. The straddle, the distance between the inner side of one shoe and the inner side of the other, was about six inches. A fat person will tend to walk with a wide straddle of, say, ten or twelve inches. As a person becomes fatigued, his straddle increases. This was a fair-sized fellow in decent shape. Maybe six feet tall, 180 pounds.

The body by the fence had been found the previous evening. How old were these tracks? We got down on our hands and knees, eyed the prints from the side, and compared them with our own fresh ones. There was a bit of loose, unflattened dust in the depressions made by the Western boots. Our own tracks were clean. There had been no rain in the past twenty-four hours, but it had been a windy night. It was a fair guess that the wind had blown loose dust into these tracks.

Indeed, the western boot tracks were not quite as distinct as our own. The ridges around our heels were, at eye level, as distinct as vertical cliffs. But the chevron tracks had collapsed slightly, much the way a cliff wall will collapse over the centuries. There were tiny scree slopes below the heel ridges.

I moved along the shine and found a place where our man had stepped on a small, scrubby bit of living sage. There was a distinctive five-chevron heel print, but where the sole must have landed, I could see only a few flattened branches. Their bark, however, was abraded. The inner flesh of the plant was white, but the wound was brown around the edges. I stepped on another branch. The bark came off in the same way, but the inner flesh was entirely white. It would take a full day before the wound I had created would brown up around the edges.

All of us felt pretty confident that the tracks were about a day old, that they dated almost precisely to the time the person had been shot down by the fence.

"All right," said Grasky, "line him out and send a team on a box cut." We could pretty much see our man's line of travel by the shine. A three-man team walked perpendicular to this line, then turned and walked forward, parallel to the direction of travel. At about three hundred yards, they cut back and looked for tracks. Frequently used by search-and-rescue teams, this leapfrog approach to tracking is a fast way to find a lost hunter, a wandering child.

Law-enforcement personnel, on the other hand, are in the business of collecting evidence. They must track step by step. Otherwise, they may find themselves in some courtroom telling a clever defense attorney that, yes, the defendant might have made a sharp right-hand turn, and that, yes, someone else with a thirty-three-inch stride wearing twelve-inch-long boots with thirteen chevrons on the sole and five reversed on the heel might have walked to the scene and committed the crime. It was possible, the officer would have to admit, because he didn't track his man step by step.

In 1981 the Supreme Court explicitly okayed tracking as an investigative technique. The facts, in *U.S.* v. *Cortez,* were these: In Arizona, along the Mexican border, Border Patrol agents kept finding the prints of anywhere from twelve to twenty people on weekend nights when the moon was full. Finding the prints wasn't difficult: The Border Patrol maintains a dirt drag-trail along the border fence. A dusty lane just ten feet wide, it is smoothed twice a day by dragging tires behind a couple of cars.

The prints on the drag road were almost all made by tire-tread sandals, bare feet, or a kind of inexpensive Mexican-made shoe that leaves a print that Border Patrol officers call an Aztec. Each crossing incident left a different mix of prints, though one set of tracks was always the same, made by a more expensive boot with a distinctive chevron design. On different occasions the tracks came through the fence in different places. They always moved north about thirty-eight miles, and ended at different places along a paved road leading into Tucson.

The Border Patrol deduced that a guide wearing the chevron-design boots was bringing illegal aliens across the border and taking them overland. Once he got to the road, he probably piled them into a van or a pickup with a shell, then drove them into the city. Because the tracks were generally found at the border fence just after midnight, the officers inferred that the guide and his charges would spend the next day traveling overland and hiding, getting to the road just before dawn.

The next time the guide's tracks were found at the fence, the Border Patrol set up a trap. Just after dawn on a weekend morning, along the guide's customary road, they stopped a pickup with a shell. Inside was a Mr. Cortez in his chevron boots, along with about a dozen illegal aliens.

Cortez maintained that there had been no probable cause to stop him, and that the Border Patrol was therefore guilty of illegal search and seizure. The Supreme Court, however, decided that "inference and deduction," which "may elude an untrained person," constituted sufficient probable cause.

Grasky himself once worked the Mexican border, where the tracking is heaviest and where he developed "a lot of respect" for the illegal aliens. In contrast to the local bandits who preyed on the illegals, and the drug smugglers who might shoot an officer just for the prestige, they were brave, even admirable, people. "We had a saying," said Grasky. "The illegal alien is your only friend."

These days Grasky is stationed near the Canadian border in Havre, Montana, where the investigative pace is different. But he is often called in by local sheriffs to track bad guys, and he and the other Border Patrol officers often give classes in the discipline to other enforcement agencies, and to search-and-rescue teams. Which is why Grasky was teaching this course in Livingston, Montana. About half the students were police officers. The rest of us were search-and-rescue volunteers.

Another Border Patrol officer, Dave Walker from Twin Falls, Idaho, was watching Grasky teach. They had been screaming for man-tracking classes down in Idaho, said Walker, ever since they'd lost the deaf-mute child several years ago. He had wandered away from a picnic, and searchers had a line of travel on him. It should have been easy. Ordinarily, you take the position last seen and draw a circle around it, enlarging that circle for every day the person has been missing.

The search area is like a big pie. If you have a line of travel, you can cut that pie down to a slice. With enough people working a grid search, you'll find the lost person. But because this child could neither hear the searchers nor call out to them, they found him, days later, dead of exposure. One search team had passed within a few hundred yards of him. If they had been better versed in tracking, the boy might be alive today.

That was the kind of work I wanted to do—finding lost children—but there was something about Grasky's crime scene that kept tugging at my mind. Something vaguely familiar.

"Hey!" It was the team that had leapfrogged ahead. "We got tracks, but they're different. Flats. Almost like bare feet."

My team stayed on the original line, tracking step by step. It went over a sloping area of small stones. We could see the dirt that our man had tracked onto the stones. It gave us a line of travel, but after four or five steps, he'd walked the dirt off his boots. The line stretched out over the bare rocks. We'd need our sign-cutting sticks for this part.

Mine was a ski pole with no basket and a rubber band wrapped around it thirty-three inches back from the point. It measured the length of the stride. We knelt on the rocks where the dirt ended and measured off where the next step might have fallen. And there it was, just ahead of the point of the pole: a dark rock lying bottom side up. It must have been kicked over with the toe of the boot. Measuring the stride from there turned up a rock that had been imbedded along the same line of travel. You couldn't just see these small clues because, as Grasky put it, the eye tends to "flock shoot." You see too much, which, in the end, means you lose the track. The sign-cutting stick had pinpointed the footfall.

It took us a long time to follow the tracks, step by step, but when our man moved back out into the dirt, we could fairly run along the shine until we came upon a large, inexplicably compressed area. New prints led away from it. They were flat, almost like barefoot tracks. It took us a minute to realize that the killer had sat down to take off his boots. He had known the victim was down near the fence, and didn't want to make any noise. He had gone the rest of the way in his socks.

The scenario was becoming very familiar. The sock prints led to a promontory that overlooked the gravel pit. There was a long flattened area there, and up front were two small cuplike depressions in the dirt. Behind them and to the right lay a spent rifle cartridge. At the end of the flattened area were two shallow trenches in the mud.

Our man had laid out full length. He'd dug his toes into the dirt behind him, and leaned on his elbows as he sighted the rifle.

The compressed area—from toe line to just above the elbows—measured six feet. Someone who knew about rifles studied the shell. It was a thirty-thirty. I looked down at the fence, where the hypothetical victim had been found. It was at least 250 yards away; Grasky said 238. Anyone who could shoot a man through the heart with a thirty-thirty at that range was an incredible marksman, whatever else he was.

Our rifle expert noted that the shell had been found to the right and behind the elbows. The only thirty-thirty he knew that ejected shells over the shoulder and to the right would be a Winchester model 94.

"Okay," said Grasky, "what do we know about this guy?"

We knew that last night, before dark, a man about six feet tall, riding a medium-size saddle horse, had dismounted not far away. He probably weighed somewhere between 170 and 190 pounds, was in good shape, and was a hell of a shot. He used a thirty-thirty, a Winchester 94.

"Iron Mountain, Wyoming, mean anything to you folks?" asked Grasky. "Think July 1901." It's a famous story in Montana and Wyoming: In that year a fourteen-year-old boy was shot with a Winchester 94 from 238 yards. The cattle regulator, Tom Horn, was eventually convicted of the murder, mostly on the kind of evidence we had discovered. Horn rode a medium-size saddle horse, shod front and back, was six feet tall, and known to be a hell of a shot. He owned one of only two known Winchester 94s in the territory. He was hanged for the murder in 1903.

It was a moment in western history, no doubt about it, and a lot of people still think the evidence was manufactured or falsified and that Horn was innocent. Either way, however, I was more interested in finding lost people and bringing them back alive. I found myself thinking of some of the classroom work we had done earlier in the course. With the help of some slides, Grasky had discussed techniques for tracking at night, with flashlights; he'd told us how to track people through streams, over ice, and through tall grass. There was one shot I particularly liked in Grasky's slide show. It was taken in the brown October grass of northern Montana. The sun was low, the angle was right, and you could see that the grass was covered with a fine layer of dust. In the center of the frame was a straight line where the dust had been kicked off the grass—a grass trail.

"You search-and-rescue folks," Grasky said, "I can't tell you how this feels." He pointed up the trail in the slide to a small boy huddled under a tree. The boy stared at the camera, clearly alive.

"That's your reward," he said.

Missing

▲

It's snowing today and cold. I would like to believe that Peter McGee is sitting by a fire somewhere in the mountains of southern Montana, comfortable and happy. The truth, I'm afraid, is harder than that. I don't think Peter McGee's luck held.

Peter McGee was reported missing by a Yellowstone Park ranger named Joe Fowler. The deputy who filled out the proper forms appended a handwritten note to Park County sheriff Charley Johnson. "Fowler says he doesn't like the looks of this one. When Joe tells me that, I don't like it either: He usually knows what he is talking about."

This is not a story with a happy ending, and I have decided to change a few details. The young man was not named Peter McGee, and, although he lived east of the Mississippi, he did not come from New Jersey.

The body of the police report read: "The person is [Peter McGee], 22 years old, a (summer) employee from Old Faithful, 6', 165#, w/m, brown shoulder length hair. Was to report back to work Friday at 1500 hours and didn't show. Acquaintances describe McGee as an aggressive hiker, but not knowledgeable. McGee is reported to be a reliable employee, and would not have skipped work. Was supposed to hike with a friend, but apparently went alone. Possible areas are Granite Peak [in Park County] or the Amphitheater area [in Yellowstone Park]. The Park Service did not have much information at this time, but are in the process of tracking down a few leads, one of which is a person named 'Mike' from the same [New Jersey] town as McGee. 'Mike' works for the Park Service in Mammoth and was supposed to be the person that was hiking with McGee. Joe Fowler told me that he would try to check the Amphitheater area out by helicopter on July 31st, in the morning. Park Service will call with any new information as they receive it. Al Jenkins advised at 2140 hours."

Al Jenkins heads up the search-and-rescue team in Park County, Montana, where I live. Early the next morning, a Sunday, he was on the phone, contacting members of the team. I was still asleep when he called. How soon I could get down to the sheriff's department with gear enough for an overnight run into the Beartooth Mountains?

Jenkins said the situation was urgent. The missing hiker was supposed to be back at work on Friday afternoon. It was now Sunday morning. Fortunately, it had been unusually warm in the mountains the last few nights. The guy had a good chance if we got out there quick. I'm not a skilled searcher, not really the guy you'd pick first for your team, but the search-and-rescue crew needed as many bodies as possible, and they needed them right away. The little bit I know about search-and-rescue work indicates that the first forty-eight hours are the most important.

Our team of about ten men studied the maps: Yellowstone rangers were combing the Amphitheater area by helicopter. We would work Granite Peak, and our headquarters would be a Ranger station called Colter Camp, just outside Cooke City.

I had never participated in a search before and was becoming impatient. I wanted to get out into the mountains, start walking, get to it right away, but cooler heads prevailed. Where was I going to go? Which trail? The entire greater Yellowstone system of National Park and wilderness areas encompasses literally millions of acres.

No, the first order of business was not to run off in all directions at once. What we needed was a better fix on McGee's hiking plans.

Early that afternoon, the reports began filtering in from investigating rangers and sheriff's deputies. McGee had hitchhiked through the Lamar Valley in Yellowstone Park, which meant that he had passed by the Amphitheater area. He had last been seen in Cooke City, buying a small amount of food for his trek. The shop owner couldn't recall what McGee had purchased. A motorist said he thought he'd seen someone answering McGee's description walking east, out of Cooke City, away from the park.

We knew now that he was wearing a blue-and-red plaid shirt, green wool pants, and was carrying a sky-blue pack. His only shelter was a light blue tarp. The Park Service had contacted "Mike," who said that he and McGee had purchased identical pairs of boots. There was a very distinctive nine-lug pattern on the heel of the boot. If we knew which trail he had taken, McGee would be easy to track.

According to people who knew McGee, the young man admired mountaineers in general and rock climbers in particular. It seemed, from what little we knew, that McGee, an "aggressive" hiker, might have tried for Granite Peak precisely because, at 12,351 feet, it is the highest point in Montana.

There are three likely trails out of Cooke City that would take a trekker to the base of the mountain. Granite Peak is pretty much of a walk up if approached from the north. McGee, however, would be coming at it from the south: a treacherous route, without much in the way of a trail. The southern face of the mountain is mostly flaky rock, prone to come away in the hand.

Late that afternoon, three search teams waited at the three likely trail heads. Dozens of people were walking out of the Beartooths after a summer weekend in the mountains, but no one had seen anyone fitting McGee's description. (In another search, later in the year, a lost hiker was located by this very simple procedure.)

The first night of the search, we bedded down on the ground, outside Colter Camp, with the stars swirling above. Peter McGee was the sole subject of conversation. Dumb kid. Out there alone. Didn't tell anyone where he was going. There was a long and, I think, finally embarrassed silence.

McGee had made some mistakes, but they weren't worth his life. We had been trying to think like the missing man for over a dozen hours—where would I go, what would I do if I were hurt —and that exercise in understanding had drawn out a measure of compassion.

There was a time when each of us could have been described as "aggressive but not knowledgeable." Most of us had ten, even twenty years on Peter McGee, and if we were smarter in the wilderness, it was a matter of experience. The wilderness had blessed us with blind luck.

Everyone on the team, without exception, had done something stupid, something life-threatening, in the wilderness at one time. One man had miscalculated the time his trip would take, had tried to walk out of the mountains in the dark without a light and fallen off the side of a two-hundred-foot cliff. Fortunately, he had landed on a ledge ten feet below.

I have made more than my share of blunders, one of which—I was twenty-four at the time—involved climbing bad rock, alone, at Pyramid Lake outside of Sparks, Nevada. No one knew where I was. Couple this with a broken handhold and an hour frozen on the cliff face, and you learn something. You make some promises to yourself. You hope your luck holds.

"Luck's a chance, but trouble's sure," the poet A. E. Housman wrote, "I'd face it as a wise man would, / And train for ill and not for good." It's not a line I would have savored at twenty-two, but one that made sense post–Pyramid Lake.

The next morning I was sent up one of the three likely trails in company with another volunteer searcher, a local rancher named Larry Lovely. Incident commander for the search Park County sheriff's deputy Brad Wilson had given me a roll of yellow duct tape. If the man was found, and he was dead, I was to tape off the area and touch nothing. What Wilson didn't say, but what every search-and-rescue volunteer knows, is that sometimes hikers are found injured and in a state of shock. Often they are irrational, and sometimes violent. Occasionally, a hypothermic hiker has to be subdued, and duct tape works almost as well as handcuffs.

There was no sign of McGee up at Lady of the Lake, or at Lower Aero Lake or along the Broadwater River trail.

Over the next few days, fifty searchers combed the trails east of Cooke City. A helicopter and a fixed-wing aircraft joined the search. Pictures of McGee were posted at trailheads.

One of the aircraft spotted McGee's backpack and sleeping bag about five miles west of the area I had searched, at the north end of Goose Lake. There the land rises to rocky slopes and plateaus, all above the timberline. The trail, however, was a week old, cold, and the dogs couldn't find McGee's scent.

I suspect the man tried for Granite Peak. He left his pack and bag—another mistake—expecting to make a high-speed run up the bad south face of the mountain. He was alone, climbing on bad rock, in the wilderness, where something as simple as a badly sprained ankle is deadly. On Thursday, August 4, the search was suspended. A light snow was falling at eleven thousand feet, and the nighttime temperature at that altitude was expected to drop below freezing.

Some of Peter McGee's friends like to think that he is still out there, that his luck held. Some think that, for totally inexplicable reasons, he decided to disappear into the mountains. He had left his bag and pack to confuse the issue. It's a comforting fiction, especially today, when the temperature is well below freezing and the snow is falling.

Author's Note:
"Peter McGee's" body was found a year later, near the summit of Fox Peak, a mountain he may have mistaken for Granite Peak. It appears as if a rock ledge collapsed under him and that he suffered massive head injuries.

RISK

▲

On Risk

▲

So there I was, hurtling through the air at a high rate of speed and entirely certain, in a preliterate and visceral manner, that this unfortunate accidental enterprise would only serve to prove what I already knew, namely, that I couldn't fly. Not even a little bit. The immediate future, which I had compressed down to a matter of seconds, seemed, quite accountably, dismal. Gravity issues laws not lightly challenged, and the rules of physics, in such a situation, become a calculus of pain.

I was probably ten years old. In America ten-year-olds are taught to perceive pain—and the fear of pain—as an educational tool. "I'll teach you," adults promise. They'll teach us to throw snowballs at cars, to let the bathtub overflow, to tease our younger brothers, to bring our live spider collection into the house, to giggle in church. The adults mean that these transgressions are going to cost us physical pain, and the lesson is a negative one. And so, in an effort to avoid pain, we stop giggling in church. This is called character building.

Sometimes the physical world acts *in loco parentis* and teaches us wordless lessons. At the age of ten, with the ground expanding massively in my field of vision—with the solidity of the earth seeming to accelerate in my direction—I was on the verge of one of these character-shaping disasters.

It had started innocently enough. I was pedaling my old coaster-brake Schwinn bike around Waukesha, Wisconsin, when I met up with a gaggle of unimaginably sophisticated older boys, thirteen-year-olds so "cool," some of them called their parents by their first names. We stopped for a chat at the top of the steepest hill in town: a paved one-block-long clifflike drop-off on Hartwell Street. Kids called the run "steep Hartwell," as in, "Wouldn't it be neat to roll a tire down steep Hartwell?"

In point of fact, I had seen this done. The tire worked up incredible speed. At the bottom of the run, where the land flattened out into swamp, there was a wooden guardrail, four feet high, consisting of three stout boards. The tire hit the curb, bounced up, and went through the boards like a mule through October cornstalks. It sailed through the air, trailing bits of broken two-by-fours, and hit the swamp water in a huge, viscous explosion of green algae.

So I had some idea of the velocity an unbraked rolling missile could achieve on steep Hartwell. Still, the cool thirteen-year-olds insisted that a brave individual who knew how to handle a bike could hurtle down the plunge without ever once using his brakes and still make the ninety-degree righthand turn at the bottom. I argued that reason, history, and experience would suggest that such an experiment was doomed to punishing failure. Or words to that effect. I had little faith.

My ineffably cool pals, however, demonstrated that the deed could be done. One by one they set off down steep Hartwell. I watched, but none of them used their brakes. No one pedaled backward at all. Indeed, they all seemed to be pedaling forward, fast, in a manner movie cowboys might describe as "hell-bent for leather." The faster they pedaled, the slower their bikes seemed to go. I imagined there might be some sort of gyroscopic aberration in the works, a quirky law of relativity that might be expressed: The faster cool persons can get a bicycle to move, the slower it will go.

Convinced by the evidence of my own eyes and seduced by my

own theory, I pushed off the pavement—"Here goes nothing!"—and began pedaling hell-bent for leather, lickety-split, down steep Hartwell. Soon enough, the iron laws of physics informed me that my theory was completely defective. I stopped pedaling because the bike had begun to buffet. I had seen a movie about the first guy to break the sound barrier. His plane had buffeted like my bike. It was all I could do to hold on, to keep the old Schwinn upright.

My choices at this point were limited to varying degrees of disaster. The bike was shuttering in such a way that braking would upset my equilibrium. I saw myself sliding one hundred feet or more along the pavement, contemplated the nature of the subsequent road rash, and discarded that option. I could try to make the righthand turn, but inertia, in the form of acceleration times velocity, said, "No way." In the end I opted to do nothing. Fear, my copilot, made that decision for me.

I hit the curb at the bottom of steep Hartwell and vaulted skyward while assuming a somewhat more horizontal position in regard to the ground. I didn't seem to be astride my bike any longer. "Woof" . . . through the top board of the fence with my chest and ribs. The collision had a kind of three-dimensional pinball effect, so that for a moment I was looking at the sky through my legs. Above and somewhat behind, I could see the Schwinn pinwheeling along a similar arc. All this seemed to be taking an incredibly long time to happen. Presently, I found myself oriented toward the green muck of the swamp, and it rushed up to meet me—face dive, face dive—with indifferent vehemence.

My forehead hit something sharp and rocky below the surface of the muck. Something else, a submerged and muddy hillock, loosened my teeth, cut my lips. The Schwinn landed on the back of my head. For the nonce life did not seem to be a bowl of cherries.

But, strangely, neither was it a bed of pain. I was dazed, certainly, but getting my head out of the water and mud seemed to be a wise move. I came up bleeding from the mouth, from a cut on the front of my head and one on the back. Both bled profusely, as even the most superficial head wounds are wont to do.

Long strands of mossy green algae hung from my face. I suppose I looked like an explosion in a spinach factory, something alien and terrifying and inexplicably undead. The thirteen-year-olds had gathered by the break in the fence, and I lurched toward them, green and bleeding.

"Let's get out of here," one of the boys shouted, and off they pedaled, bang-flash-zoom, with terror howling after them and nipping at their back wheels. Cool guys, indeed. Ho, ho, it was to laugh. I managed to limp five blocks home. Hours later, after a visit to the hospital and a number of stitches, just as the pain finally arrived, my father saw fit to explain that some people liked to play practical jokes and that some bikes were equipped with hand brakes.

One learns from errors in judgment, especially those that result in stitches and defunct bicycles. Even infants, who have not yet learned the nature of pain, know something of fear. In an elegant experiment conducted with children barely able to crawl, psychologists have shown that falling may be our first and most primal fear. The scientists constructed a glass surface about the size of a tabletop. Just under the glass, clearly visible, was a wooden surface, but halfway across the glass apparent solidity gave way to a yawning abyss of some four feet. Infants were placed on the glass and encouraged to crawl toward their mothers. None of them would venture out into the void.

So if children know fear, why is it that most are inveterate climbers? A few years ago I was having dinner with Yvon Chouinard and Rick Ridgeway, two of America's finest mountaineers. Rick's daughter, Carissa, a toddler, was scaling the heights of the coffee table. Bang splat. Tears. A bit of fatherly comfort. Soon enough, there she was, attempting to conquer the great looming arm of Chouinard's sofa.

We discussed Carissa's efforts and mountaineering altogether. One day she could climb Everest; either that or become a buyer for Bloomingdale's. The conversation that night centered around the question of why some of us abandon a universal early urge to pit our skills and knowledge against fear.

I suppose one answer is that pain teaches lessons in the synapses and that different people seem to interpret the lesson differently. The Debacle of Steep Hartwell is a good example. Perfectly reasonable people might conclude that riding a bicycle down a very steep hill is stupid. This is the "never do that again" approach. ("I'll teach you!") And yet . . . as I examine the event, the light that shines through the core of it, for me, is this: Know the secret, and you can ride fear right up to the edge of pain and never fall. Never. Not if you are prepared, physically and mentally. Not if you understand how to apply the hand brakes.

So why do people put themselves at risk? Isn't the experience stressful and frightening? Some people don't understand. The urge annoys them beyond all tolerance.

I know. Over the past dozen years various publications have paid me to dive with sharks, jump out of airplanes, climb mountains in Africa and South America, trek through equatorial jungles, plumb the deepest caves in America, and generally scare myself silly.

I found it was always a good idea to find a mentor, some man or woman expert in the endeavor I had chosen. If you are going shark diving, for instance, you want a dive master possessed of a complete set of arms and legs. It is best to put the mentor's professional reputation on the line: "If I get hurt, you look bad." That way you tend to hear about the various hand brakes you need up front.

So you prepare. You learn. You train. And there comes a time when your heart is beating fast, when flight is battling with fight, when the scream-and-gibber mechanism wants to engage itself. Then you take steep Hartwell, apply your hand brakes, and make the turn, just so.

There is a kind of euphoria here, a biochemical reward edge workers of my acquaintance strive to achieve. Some of them call themselves adrenaline junkies. The adrenal glands—little triangular meatballs located on the north pole of each kidney—secrete two hormones, adrenaline and noradrenaline. In the blood these substances prepare a person for emergency action: Respiration increases, the heart beats faster, the central nervous system is stimulated. The effects can be felt subjectively as fear or anxiety combined with increased mental alertness.

Now the problem here is separating anxiety and fear from euphoria and alertness. Scientists studying anxiety subjected monkeys to stress at odd intervals, and these monkeys behaved like basket cases. They were drenched in adrenaline. A second group, however, suffered the same stress, except they were given a brief warning signal before the stress was applied. These monkeys easily adjusted. It was found that the monkeys in the second group had greater concentrations of noradrenaline in the blood.

Noradrenaline affects those systems in the brain that are concerned with emotions: especially euphoria, well-being, and alertness. In situations of self-imposed stress, feeling good means minimizing adrenaline and maximizing noradrenaline. A period of training helps; a thorough study of the dangers helps. Knowing where the hand brakes are gets the good stuff pumping.

In many cases the biochemical rewards of informed risk taking can, in the words of one psychologist, take the "individual . . . beyond the apparent limitations of the self." Mihaly Csikszentmihalyi of the University of Chicago has been studying "exceptional people," risk takers of all varieties, including rock climbers, artists, dancers, and surgeons. All, he noticed, describe a euphoric feeling, a clarity of purpose combined with an ability to make time work for them. Neurosurgeons experienced three-hour operations as matters of minutes while ballerinas felt the exhilaration of performing a pirouette in what felt like extreme slow motion. Additionally, irrelevant stimuli were rejected: composers at work, for instance, didn't hear the doorbell ring. Csikszentmihalyi calls this state of mind "the flow." Children, he says, are eager to match their skills against new challenges and "have flow states all the time."

Adults seek out risk and challenge, Csikszentmihalyi believes, "because the pleasure deriving from the flow state has an autonomous reality that has to be understood on its own terms."

So why isn't everyone out jumping out of airplanes or climbing

El Cap every day? Ralph Keyes, in his book *Chancing It: Why We Take Risks,* explains that recent research has shown that "high sensation seekers seem to produce less of the mood-regulating opiates released by stress than do low sensation seekers. This could explain the frequently noted anti-depressant quality of thrill seeking." In a way this sounds very much like the Scottish proverb that states "Some men are born two drinks short of par." As children, we learn the pleasure and pain of risk: We know in some cobwebby corner of the mind whether we are the ones who need physical challenges to find the flow, whether we can be content as a buyer for Bloomingdale's or whether we will have to climb Mount Everest.

Risk, and the flow state it stimulates, can be understood in terms that become almost mystical. Measurements of brain activity taken during flow states actually show a decrease in cortical activity. Csikszentmihalyi thinks we might "get into the flow not by exerting more effort but rather by screening out distortions. That would mean flow resembles Oriental meditation practices—the notion of learning to stop the world."

Some people can sit-cross legged in a room and stop the world. Others of us need a little biochemical cocktail to enter into the flow: We need to take steep Hartwell without brakes.

Rope Tricks

▲

My climbing partner, Berkeley photographer Michael (Nick) Nichols, said, "I'm sorry, but my bladder is going to bust. I mean it. I have to." And that was the first time I thought, What am I doing here? I mean, really, what's wrong with me?

We were both hooked into a rope that dangled from the highest point on the cliff wall known as El Capitan, in Yosemite National Park. By some accounts, El Cap is the longest unbroken cliff in the world. The drop is said to be 3,000 feet, though there is a scree slope at the bottom that juts out some so the rope dropped free for only 2,650 feet, a tad more than half a mile.

Nick and I had started at the bottom, on the scree, and had hooked into the rope using special gear that allowed us literally to walk up the rope. Nick was leading. He'd climb thirty to forty steps, straight up, while I rested. Then I'd climb up to him, while he rested. Now, we had both stopped for a break. Various contraptions allowed us to literally sit, suspended, and feel the painful pins-and-needles sensation called "sleep" seep down from our thighs to our ankles. The rope, fastened as it was from an overhang, did not fall against the cliff wall. We were hanging about forty feet from the rock, and though we were not precisely twisting in the wind, we were taking occasional air rides: fifty- and sixty-foot pendulum swings fueled by gusting winds.

At this point, in this exceedingly inconvenient situation, six hundred feet above the rocks (and two feet above me), Nick needed a men's room.

He's a clever man, Nick, and he had had persuasive reasons for wanting to climb first. On the scree he had pointed out that if I led, his photos, taken from below, would feature my back end silhouetted against the clear blue Yosemite sky. "No one would look at a picture like that," he reasoned cogently. "See," Nick said, "if I lead and shoot down on you, we'll get your face and the drop below." It made good sense, but now I saw, in his demand to lead, motives that had to do with his own personal convenience; sinister motives that lay in a realm entirely beyond photographic professionalism.

We had expected the climb to take perhaps six hours, and we each carried a mere quart and a half of water. Dehydration could be a problem. Nick had drunk a half gallon standing on the scree slope waiting to hook into the rope. It had been a bit too much for his body to process all at once. "This is almost painful," he whined.

"You should have thought of that before we started," I said, sounding precisely the way my father had when one of the kids had to "go" one hour into an all-day car trip. My father grumbled, but he always stopped at some gas station, and I realized, on the rope, that no matter how much I protested, Nick was going to stop at his personal gas station.

"There are people watching us from the road," I argued. "People with binoculars." It was a feeble effort. "Cops," I said. "You could be arrested for indecent exposure. I can see the headlines now: 'Disgraced Photographer Commits Bizarre Sex Crime Involving World's Longest Rope!' Is that what you want? Can you imagine trying to tell your mother?"

But Nick was fumbling about near his seat harness. "Wait," I screamed. And then, with iron calm: "There's a way to do this."

The plan was simple enough. I would climb up so that my head was just under Nick's right foot, then unhook my top Jumar, one of three devices that held me into the rope. This I would position above the rope-holding devices hooked to Nick's feet and, with a few more technical moves, climb to a point at which my feet were just below his. Thus, at the crucial moment, I would be hanging behind Nick and holding him in a kind of bear hug.

We would both be indicted, of course, but the alternative was unthinkable.

I hadn't done any rope work in almost two years. It had been some relatively hairy stuff then: dropping five hundred feet into the deepest cave pits in America, in total darkness. I got reasonably good at it, so when the folks I worked with in those Alabama and Georgia and Tennessee pits asked if I wanted to join them in Yosemite for a little rope sport, I jumped at the chance.

The men and women who "yo-yo" those southern pits are all cavers, and their passion is called vertical caving. There are limestone outcroppings in the southeast corner of America, great prehistoric ocean beds that rose out of the sea and wrinkled into a rough hill country. In this thickly vegetated land, surface water picks up carbon dioxide from the atmosphere, creating weakly acidic rivers that dissolve limestone and form caves. There are subterranean tubes, slanting slightly downward, shaped by these rivers. Occasionally, underground water finds a fault in the limestone, or it breaks through from one series of horizontal tunnels to a lower series. A waterfall is formed. Over the millennia such a falls will form a pit. The deepest of these, Fantastic Pit in Georgia, is over six hundred feet deep.

Imagine: Here you are, half a mile below the surface of the earth, crawling merrily along, and you come on a hole into which you could fit the entire Bank of America building.

Some few adventurous folk found these pits to be a challenge, or more properly, the challenge of a lifetime. In the last thirty years rope work in these pits has been refined to an amazing degree. And the technique of vertical caving—vertical cavers call it SRT, single rope technique—has become a sport in and of itself, a not-so-simple matter of sliding down (rappelling) and climbing back up a rope.

Yo-yoing the pits has always been a dirty underground endeavor. In the past few years, however, vertical cavers have
emerged into the light of day. They have begun practicing SRT
out in the open.

In 1980 a caver named Dan Twilley organized an SRT trip to
Yosemite with the aim of yo-yoing El Cap, then thought to be the
longest unbroken cliff in the world. Before the ascent, in talking
with the climbers who hang out at Camp Four on the valley floor,
Twilley and the SRT team discovered that there was some controversy as to the longest free-vertical drop. A rough consensus had
it that Mount Thor, on Baffin Island off the eastern Canadian
coast, could drop as far as one mile.

In 1981 a team led by Twilley (and including Nick Nichols)
hiked into Mount Thor and, after a month's worth of hard trekking and careful rigging, managed to yo-yo the cliff. The free-fall
section was 3,200 feet—indeed, arguably the longest such drop in
the world. The rope itself, for symbolic purposes, was precisely
one mile long.

Photographic evidence of the SRT work on Thor was submit-
ted to the *Guinness Book of World Records,* but, after consulta-
tion, the editors decided not to include the Thor drop. They
feared that others might lose their lives trying to set a new record.
SRT was simply too dangerous for the *Guinness Book of World
Records.*

"Can you believe that," raged Kent Ballew, who was on the SRT
team at Thor. "In this book they got guys who jump off cliffs in
parachutes, bungee cord jumpers, they got guys who eat entire
Chevrolets, but SRT is too dangerous?"

Kent was here at Yosemite for his first crack at the second-
longest free drop in the world. He was sensitive about the issue of
danger because he is employed by Pigeon Mountain Industries
(PMI), the LaFayette, Georgia, company that makes the rope we
would be using, the company that made the milelong rope used at
Thor.

"Look at this," Ballew said. He was standing on the scree
slope, grabbing the rope, which was just under half an inch in

diameter. "Static kernmantle construction," he said, which means that the load-carrying part of the rope, the core, is protected by a tight sheath. "The core consists of twenty-three and two thirds strands of nylon with a breaking strength of seventy-one-hundred pounds."

PMI is the rope preferred by most vertical cavers, but since there are probably fewer than a thousand such people in America, PMI sells its ropes primarily to search-and-rescue teams. Big-city fire departments are practicing with SRT (which they sometimes call high-line work) in hopes of rescuing people from high-rise fires.

"You know what we did with this very rope?" Ballew asked. In a demonstration of the efficacy of high-line rescue techniques, PMI employees had gone to Toronto at the invitation of the Canadian government. They tied the rope off 1,250 feet up the CN broadcast tower and ran the line 3,800 feet to a traffic bridge. There, for the edification of crowds gathered for Canada Day, they slid volunteers from the tower to the safety of the bridge.

"You know why the Guinness people think it's dangerous?" Ballew asked. "Because they asked some Royal Mountaineering Club about it. Most climbers don't know anything about SRT. So they just assume it's dangerous."

Indeed, the climbers at Camp Four regarded the cavers with amused tolerance. When a few of us slung a rope over a high tree branch and did a little climbing to test our gear, a small crowd gathered to watch. There was some laughter. It must have seemed to them that we carried a lot of gear for so simple a task.

I was using Gibbs ascenders, small mechanical devices that slide easily up a rope but bite down hard, without damaging the rope, when they feel downward pressure. There was one on my right foot and another positioned near my left knee. This second Gibbs was connected by a loop to my left foot. An elastic cord ran from that Gibbs to a harness I wore on my chest. I could step on the loop—the Gibbs would bite, allowing me to take a step—then step and climb on the right Gibbs. As I raised my left knee, the elastic cord would pull the left Gibbs up the rope. The rope itself passed through a wheeled roller attached to the harness on my chest. This held my upper body close to the rope. Above the roller was a Jumar, a rope-biting device like the Gibbs. This was my safety line: It was connected to my seat harness. In order to rest, I simply slid the Jumar up and sat in the seat sling.

It was, I admit, a fairly laughable rig. The climbers also found the rope itself strange: It was heavier than climbing rope, and there was very little stretch to it. Climbing rope carries a lot of stretch; it is designed to stop a fall. A climber may move above his point of protection, make a bad move, and plummet thirty feet or more before the slack is out of the rope. If the rope were not dynamic, if it did not stretch, the climber could suffer a broken back, internal injuries.

In SRT work you are never off the rope. There is no need for stretch. The PMI rope we used on El Capitan had a stretch factor of only 1.7 at 200 pounds. Even this small amount was something of a pain: It meant that when you hooked in on the scree slope, the rope was going to stretch 1.7 percent of 2,650 feet, or 45 feet. In practice, this meant that you got absolutely nowhere in the first forty-five steps. You just stood there on the scree slope, climbing the stretch out of the rope.

Another property of the long rope was its lack of spin. On an ordinary climbing rope there is a bit of twist. On the PMI rope, if you started climbing looking at the face of the cliff, you might make one revolution in a half-mile climb. This is as it should be. Dervish dances on a long rope are a prelude to projectile vomiting.

So here we were, Nick and I, a quarter of the way up a half-mile climb deemed too dangerous to even mention in a book full of dangerous exploits. We could have walked up the back of El Cap and just done the rappel, but that would have been cheating. Nick and I were both aware of a strong Calvinistic streak in our caving friends. You had to earn the rappel. Cavers call this being "stout," and it is a high accolade. So we were climbing the rope, and we were arguing absurdly about his bodily functions.

As it happened, Nick's bladder was the least of our problems. The fact was, neither of us should have been on the rope. We were out of shape, I was using borrowed gear, and Nick's gear had been damaged during his last outing. We made some repairs on it at Camp Four using channel lock pliers and an ax head. These facts began eating away at our confidence two hours into the climb.

We were climbing fast—hadn't paced ourselves well—and soon we were doing thirty steps at a crack rather than forty. Then we were doing twenty steps, fifteen, ten. Halfway up the rope, a quarter of a mile above the surface of the valley floor, a stiff wind sprang up. It sounded like every documentary you've ever seen about Antarctica up there. We were taking long, disconcerting air rides, swaying one hundred feet one way, then one hundred the other. It was unpleasantly difficult to climb the swinging rope. Worse, these jolly little swings seemed to emphasize the uncomfortable fact that we had several more hours until the summit. The phrase "lives hanging by a thread" kept ringing through my mind. It was like some idiot TV jingle you can't shake: How do you spell relief, lives hanging by a thread, what am I doing here?

On the rope sometimes, impossibly, the wind seemed to come directly off the cliff face itself. Then we'd take air rides of sixty or seventy feet directly away from the rock out into the indifferent sky. Since I had started on the scree facing out, toward the valley, and since the rope didn't twist at all, I couldn't see the rock. It was possible, however, on these swings into space, that the gusting wind would suddenly stop and that I'd come crashing into the cliff wall like some ridiculous comic-strip character trying to emulate Tarzan: splat, then the slow slide down the rock. Consequently, I stopped climbing at these points and turned to face the wall. This was accomplished by a silly swimming sort of motion.

"God, this is fun," I told Nick. I like to think I'm a master of ironic understatement.

At this point there was a snap from above, from Nick's hastily repaired gear, and a jolting vibration ran down the rope. "I'm in trouble," he said.

I had a vision of Nick falling past me—flash certain death—then another of him just sliding twenty feet down the rope and landing on my head. Certain death or a broken neck. It felt as if something inside my belly wanted to get out through the navel;

something in there was punching at me, and I began frantically climbing the twenty feet to Nick.

It was his chest roller. Thankfully, the chest roller is not extremely important: It is a matter of comfort rather than safety. Nick would have to climb using hands to hold him into the rope. If he let go, however, he would fall over backward and end up hanging by his feet, upside down, unable to climb. He would become a tourist attraction: the body hanging from the rope on El Cap.

"I'm getting a real bad attitude about this," Nick said.

I felt I should say something to buck him up. Get his mind off our problems. "Gee, what a view! Look at that. Wow. Pretty soon we're going to see the sunset of our lives. . . ."

And then I stopped talking because we didn't want to see the sunset at all. It was a glorious mid-October day, 70 degrees or so, but when the sun went down, the temperature would drop to about 30 degrees. We were wearing T-shirts and carrying light windbreakers. A man who didn't reach the summit by nightfall could easily freeze to death. We'd be a pair of popsicles on a rope.

We set about racing the sun, wearing ourselves stupid with fatigue. Nearly a dozen cavers had already climbed the rope, and the slowest of them had taken six hours. We hit the summit at twilight, seven hours after we started—the new record, and one that lives in infamy.

It really doesn't seem fair, but there is a pretty tricky move to be made in order to climb over the lip onto the safety of horizontal rock. The rope is anchored in several places far back from the lip. To keep it from abrading on the rough granite of the lip itself, the SRT group had fashioned a roller at the very curve of the cliff. The rope passed over a large soft plastic wheel set in a metal frame, and the whole affair rested at the very edge of El Cap.

The problem has to do with the weight of the rope. At a little less than six pounds per hundred feet, the rope below weighed about 150 pounds. Wind drag along its half-mile length probably doubled that figure. In order to reach the summit, you had to lift your upper body over the lip, do a push-up capable of lifting three hundred pounds to get the rope-holding devices over the roller, and walk forward two feet, on your hands. The better solution is simply to change ropes. A short rope hangs next to a long one, and with a good deal of caution, you can snap the rope-holding devices off one rope and onto another, then cruise up over the lip.

Except that on the scree slope below I had fastened myself into the long rope with extra care. Extra knots. Extra carabiners. It was only smart. Now, I found that I couldn't change ropes. The only way to move from one rope to another—given the idiot rig I'd tied—was to take off my seat harness. Which was the most essential safety device I wore. To make matters more irritating, it had gotten dark. And cold.

Now, at times like this, a fellow ought to be able to say, "Okay, time out, I quit." Unfortunately, you can't quit without getting in trouble with the law: the laws of physics, the law of gravity. A caver named Jim Youmans, a high-rise contractor from Atlanta, had been camping on the summit, watching the rope, and he hooked himself into a short rope, sat at the lip, and tried to help. We were using headlamps in the darkness, trying out different ideas. About an hour later I was still hanging there, shivering, half on one rope, half on another, with all our failed efforts at rescue—a confusing maze of new knots and ropes— bulging at the front of my seat harness.

And I thought, not for the first time, Why am I doing this?

After two hours of infuriating and terrifying nonsense involv-ing spare ropes and carabiners, Youmans came up with an idea. I'd hook into the short rope with my left foot and put my right into a loop of rope Youmans had made and hung just under the roller. I should, Youmans felt, be able to lift three hundred pounds with my legs. I had some mental reservations about this after seven hours of climbing. "Give me a chance to rest before I try," I said.

Two British climbers, Rob and Brian, had walked up the back way and were sitting close to the lip, discussing rescue tech-niques. "This is dead serious," one of them said.

"Dead is the operative word," the other replied.

I kind of wanted to get over the lip and physically discuss matters with them. Turning fear and fatigue into bright, hot anger did the trick. I came surging up over the roller in a burst of sheer fury that lasted perhaps five seconds. Then I lay there, flopped over on my back with the stars whirling overhead. A small crowd had gathered around me, and no one spoke at all. It was a time for some somber reflection on the meaning of life. That sort of thing. I was thinking about perceived mortality and the last time I had been to church, when someone in the crowd passed wind in the silence. Rob held a hand to his ear. "Ah," he said, "the shouting of distant Frenchmen," and we all laughed at that. There were tears in my eyes, I was laughing so hard and for so little reason.

Getting back on the rope the next day was like getting back on the horse that threw you. It had to be done. If I didn't rappel off El Cap, I felt I might never do any more rope work ever. "What a good idea," a small silent voice suggested.

Still, the alternative was to walk eight miles down to camp. And rappelling, after all, is the entire point of this kind of climbing. It's supposed to be fun. There's no effort involved: Just sit in the seat harness and slide down the rope. It's so much fun that every other recruitment ad you see for the armed forces has guys sliding down ropes. We'll make a man out of you, boy. Teach you to slide down ropes.

On the other hand, if you've recently spent over two hours trying to get over the lip of a cliff with a half-mile drop below you, the idea of voluntarily hooking your life onto a thread loses some of its appeal. Making the first move—backing over the lip of the cliff—becomes an ordeal of indecision.

I put on my seat harness and clipped my rappel bar into it. An ordinary SRT rappel rack is a narrow horseshoe-shaped affair. Steel bars slide back and forth on the horseshoe frame. The rope is threaded over one bar and under the next. Your rate of descent is controlled by sliding the bars. Separate the bars and pick up some speed. Close them to create more friction and slow down.

The rack I would have to use was almost two feet long and had been specially designed for the descent of Mount Thor. It was huge, and it was called a Thor rack. I geared up, then walked around for a full four hours. I was working up my nerve and contemplating both the nature of fear and the iron laws of physics when a female trekker who had hiked up the back way made some remarks of a Freudian nature concerning the Thor rack dangling from my belt.

And I thought, No, you're wrong. That's not why I do it. I spent nine and a half hours on the rope yesterday thinking about it, and there's more to it than that. I thought, I hate this fear and I love this fear, and I'm tired of apologizing to myself or anyone else for the impulse.

And then there I was, hooking into the short rope at the lip. I backed out into space, thinking: If I fell here, I'd have nearly fifteen seconds to think about it, before . . .

But there was work to do. I had to switch from the short rope to the long one. And then I was sliding slowly down the rope, feeling like a scuba diver descending against a coral wall. The granite face of the cliff glittered pink in the sunlight. There was a sensation of dream flight. The valley floor seemed somehow brighter, harder-edged, and the colors vibrated as in a vision. There was something otherworldly and wondrous and innately spiritual about the experience. There are folks who can tune in the sensation sitting cross-legged on a pillow in an empty room, or so they say. Others of us need a little harder bump. That is what I thought sliding down the rope.

In thirty minutes, I knew, I'd be down on the valley floor. And when people asked me about El Cap, I'd tell them it was a thing that had to be done, this second-longest rappel in the history of mankind. "Did it 'cause it's there," I'd tell folks. Make it all *muy macho*. That's another thing you have to do. Otherwise you sound like an evangelical sap.

Paraglider

▲

Ere man walked, he yearned to soar, as if on feathered wings.
Ever has he sought, in supreme affirmation and ignoble pride, to
float upon the wind, high above the mute and pitiless clay. In
periodic excesses of shrieking ambition man has produced one
antic apparatus after another. Icarus lives in archetype: Children,
convinced that a red cape will enable them to fly like Superman,
leap from the garage roof and limp around for days, lying to their
parents about gravity-induced injuries. "A bunch of men," I explained to my mother, "hit me with sticks."

"What men?"

"Communists."

"Communists?"

"Big, mean ones."

You'd think man would learn. But history is a chronicle of
continued folly, and this thing I'm strapped into well over thirty
years later, this entirely moronic foot-launched parachute that's
supposed to fly like a hang glider, this airbag, this idiotic paraglider designed to send man soaring to the base of the clouds and
engineered to drift slowly back to the warm bosom of earth, this
flimsy gossamer wing, is the stuff of communist beatings. Twenty-

seven feet of bright green parachute material was laid out behind me, and I was connected to the preposterous device by a demented proliferation of ropes. The paraglider, in flight, looked rather like a larger version of a standard rectangular parachute. It was nothing more than my old red cape writ large; the ancient fancy expressed, once again, as laundry.

Or so I thought, standing atop a steeply sloping hill twenty-five hundred feet above the Salmon River about eighteen miles south of the town of Salmon, Idaho. The wind was blowing uphill, coming in irregular cycles, sometimes blowing ten miles an hour, sometimes hissing down to a stage whisper of two or three miles an hour. Just above me, the hill rose to a summit ringed by a fifteen-foot-high brim of rim rock. Water flowing down into the Salmon took its name from this formation: Hat Creek.

"This," it occurred to me standing below the brim, "is about fifteen hundred more vertical feet worth of adventure than I currently crave."

Launch, for instance, is always an opportunity for disaster. The pilot grabs the ropes in a prescribed manner, runs forward, throws his hands high over his head, and, if God is merciful, the glider inflates—*floopf*. A brief downhill run and the pilot feels the earth dropping away under him. He is flying. Unless, of course, he crashes and burns.

Mark Chirico, my instructor, was a tough, compact man who owned and operated a paragliding school—Ecole Parapente Annecy—in France. The sport, in Mark's opinion, has some exciting possibilities. In contrast to hang gliding, paragliding is relatively easy to learn. A complete novice, trained by experts, can expect his or her first flight on the first or second day of training. The gliders can be stuffed into a day pack and weigh less than fifteen pounds.

Paragliding is booming in Europe. Mark believes that America is in for a similar boom and has established an American school, Parapente USA, out of Seattle. Andy Long, a hang glider with over a thousand hours in the air, has been working with Mark for several months. In general, Andy would launch from some steep hillside, land, pack up his glider, and flip on his radio transmitter. Mark, at the launch site, would prepare a student, check the harness, the rigging, the radio receiver inside the student's helmet, and then—as Mark put it—he would "hurl" the unfortunate student "off the mountain."

"Three, two one, GO, run, run runrunrun," Mark's voice commanded inside the helmet. And then you'd fall down and go scraping through the sagebrush and bouncing off rocks.

Since the launch site is not a cliff, but a steeply sloping hillside, a blown launch results not in instant death but merely excruciating scrapes and bruises, the kind of injuries skateboarders call "a road rash." "Pick up that wreckage," Mark would say, "and get ready for another try." And you'd do it, muttering and cursing and bleeding out of spite.

Frankly, the landing zone had not been entirely kind to me either. I had, on my five previous flights, been so concerned with my launch that I had failed to consider the vicissitudes of touchdown. I had suffered, to date, four crash landings out of five flights. There were half a dozen of us learning the art of paragliding, and we videotaped several launches and landings for instructional purposes.

In the evening, after the flights, we'd watch videotapes of the day. A particular favorite was a calamitous landing by a woman who became known as Crash 'N Splash. The video showed her screaming down to the ground and failing completely to engage the brakes, a pair of ropes, one held in each hand, that pull down the back edge of the chute and stall the glider. In a proper landing the pilot turns into the wind and lifts the ropes, disengaging the brakes to gain speed. At about six feet the ropes are pulled down past the knees, the glider stalls, and the pilot steps to the ground as from a stair step.

Crash 'N Splash had gotten it into her mind that she could shoot along the ground and simply begin to run when the first foot touched the earth. Look, Ma, no brakes.

But the parasail moves faster than you can run. Just so. The video clearly shows that Crash took a step, hit to her knees, flopped onto her chest, and slid facefirst into a marsh. Crash 'N Splash.

On the other hand, I had developed a landing technique that

the others found at least equally amusing. Somehow, the anxiety of the launch combined with the exhilaration of flight conspired to produce a sort of lazy complacency on touchdown so that I neglected to get out of my seat. The seat harness comes complete with a hammocky seat, a plywood board the pilot sits on. I'd brake perfectly, but for some reason I consistently failed to get out of the seat. My feet would be out ahead of me (both of them together), they'd slide along the ground, and I'd land precisely on my tailbone.

This was a matter for continuous hooting and laughter during evening videos. The landing zone for these first practice flights was a cow pasture, and I earned a nickname both for the seat-of-my-pants touchdowns and their unerring accuracy in finding certain squishy elements the cows had left behind.

It strengthens your resolve, a nickname like that. Made you want to touch down perfectly. Who wants to spend five days as the man known as "Cow Pie"?

The first few launches are usually an occasion of minor bloodletting and curses. Soon enough—maybe on the fourth or fifth or tenth attempt—all goes well, and the student pilot lifts off without incident. Steering is fairly straightforward: Pull the right hand brake, the right side of the glider stalls, and the whole affair turns right. The student is never alone in the air. The radio receiver inside his helmet spits out Mark's informed commands—"turn right away from the cliff face, good, good, good, relax, okay, enjoy the flight, that's our best glider you're flying there, you're bulletprooof"—and about halfway through the flight, Andy Long would take over and direct the student into the landing zone.

The first flights from any deadly height were an experiment in terror, and Mark was, by his own admission, "a little hyper." That is, he tended to get excited about conditions and the proper time to launch. With over twelve hundred hours of hang-gliding and paragliding experience, Mark wanted everyone to experience the best flight possible, but the problem was that novices, like myself, often wanted to study the conditions for themselves, which is a way of saying that we were terrified and endeavored to put off the moment of the launch as long as possible. Having some nervous fellow hurrying you through your preparations caused a bit of high-altitude resentment. Mark was aware of this. That is why he found it necessary to "hurl people off the mountain." There were some complaints about this.

On touchdown, invariably, the resentment was replaced by gratitude. Chirico purely loved teaching this sport and was one of those instructors who derived intense pleasure from his students' accomplishments. No one minded his effusive and entirely sincere compliments on our flights. Hyper is just fine in the landing zone.

Indeed, Mark had endearing qualities. He runs adventure-travel hang-gliding and paragliding tours in New Zealand, Europe, Australia, and Mexico. He was scouting the possibility of running another such tour in Idaho, out of the Twin Peaks guest ranch, south of Salmon. His vision of the tour combined a horseback ride to a suitable launch site, a glide down to the river, and a raft trip back to the ranch. But Mark was raised in Massachusetts, and for all of his world travels, the West was something of a mystery to him.

Once stopping to give the horses a breather, we all heard a familiar and ominous whirring sound. Mark declared that there was something wrong with his camera. He held it to his ear and looked puzzled.

"I don't know why it's on auto rewind," Mark complained, "I still should have ten shots left." The rattlesnake was coiled about four feet from Mark's horse, with the wedge-shaped head up and the tail vibrating rapidly. It was a prairie rattler, about three feet long.

Any other horse of my acquaintance would have been off at a gallop, bucking and kicking on a kamikaze downhill run through the trees. Frank Valbo's horses, trained for dudes who ride them at the Twin Peaks Ranch, do not spook so easily.

"Uh, Mark," another rider said.

We were putting our lives into the hands of a man who couldn't tell a rattlesnake from a Nikon.

* * *

Half a mile below the summit of Hat Creek, the Salmon River, swollen and brown with runoff, wound its way through a canyon bracketed on both sides by mountains. On the other side of the river, just past Highway 93 and beyond a lush, irrigated alfalfa field, there were rounded hills, brown buttes, and rocky rims that rose to the jagged, knife-edged snowy peaks of the Lemhi Mountains.

A pair of eighteen-wheelers were barreling south down 93. Having driven that highway, I knew they were doing seventy miles an hour, at a minimum. From where I stood, they seemed to be crawling. It was the first time I ever found slow semis scary: They looked like trucks on tranks.

Our landing zone was a broad, flat field on the west side of the river. I resolved not to overshoot the LZ. There were dangers in that.

Poles carrying high-tension electrical wires lined the highway down there, and it would be best to avoid them. Who wants to get tangled up in the wires and hang there, sparking and flashing for a few hours?

It seemed wise to avoid landing in the river as well. And, let's see, what else to worry about at the moment? I was staring into an empty space hundreds of feet above the valley floor, studying imponderable menace. I was looking for invisible teeth, for cannonballs, for that darn old deflationary t-t-t-turbulence.

In the history of the world, to date, only one person had ever launched a paraglider off the Hat Creek hill. Andy Long was in position down beside the river, in the exact center of the landing zone, waiting for the second person ever to launch from this site.

The Iceman was up, standing there, sweating in his crash helmet, studying the wind with mortal intensity. If there were big teeth out there, the Iceman would abort.

The Iceman, in fact, was a friend of mine, Tom Berrum, a Montana neighbor who was new to paragliding but had plenty of experience with hang gliders. Tom knew about the hot air that rises from a valley floor in columns hang gliders call thermals. He knew about the areas of turbulence and downdrafts that surround the rising thermals. Before launch he invariably spent at least half an hour wordlessly studying conditions, and the rest of us found his self-possession admirable. He was the Iceman.

It was Tom who impressed on me the importance of launching into a wind that blew directly uphill. "If it's not blowing up, blow it off," quoth the Iceman.

And then he was off, launched, and I could see little whirlwinds kicking up dust devils on the slopes below, but the conditions were good—right now they were still good—and I wasn't quite ready, so of course I heard Mark's radio-amplified voice in my ear telling me to run run run. I was standing there with my arms stretched out, cruciform, the back risers in the crook of my arm, the front ones in my hand, the canopy spread out behind in the approved horseshoe shape, the open leading edge up, the lines untangled, the brakes clear of knots, and then I felt my legs pumping and the chute was up over my head and the ground was beginning to drop away under me but something was dreadfully wrong. Perhaps the wind had shifted. It is possible that I was inept.

The chute listed off to the right, dragging me willy-nilly along the ground until I found myself scraping along the rocks with my right forearm.

I believe at this point I voiced some crude malediction. But no, wait. Hey. I was sitting on the ground under a fully inflated sail, which was listing only slightly to the right. I should have pulled the right brake to my hip. The sail would have folded itself into the ground on my right side. Instead, I pulled the left brake to my shoulder and felt the sail lift me a bit to the left. I raised both my hands. The sail was steady, and what the hell, brake to your shoulders, Tim, and hot damn, I'm in the air. Not the world's most perfect launch, but a nice recovery. Cow Pie rising like the phoenix from his own wreckage.

Below, I could see the Iceman under his bright red sail. The gliders themselves are so large that a man in harness seems like an inanimate toy, one of those Masters of the Universe action figures designed for preschool children. The Iceman's canopy shivered slightly, and he was kicked out to the side a bit. The ride was getting a tad bumpy down there. Then, predictably, he hit it, a rising column of warm air that sent him straight up at about four hundred feet per minute.

It was a pretty good thermal: not one of those uncontrollable cannonballs that can send you screaming into the sky at over a thousand feet per second.

Mark's voice crackled over the radio. "Tim! You see Tom. Wiggle your legs if you see him."

I wiggled my legs.

"Follow the Iceman, catch that lift."

The landing zone was too far away for our chutes to reach on the glide. We needed to catch a thermal, get some lift. That meant penetrating the turbulence that surrounded the Iceman's thermal. I'd be flying directly into a condition Mark called "teeth": the chomping ups and downs involved in the penetration of a rising column of air. I had assiduously avoided turbulence in my previous five flights precisely because I had seen chutes partially deflate in the teeth of turbulence. But the paragliders, Mark insisted, were designed for this problem. There was an open leading edge with ten ports that simply caught the air and automatically reinflated the chute. The deflated chutes I had seen popped back full of air in a second or so, but I wasn't sure my heart was up to even one second of sure terror half a mile above the surface of the earth.

And then I was in the downdraft and a mass of messy air. I pulled the brakes to my shoulders for some stability, and then I was through it. The lift hit, and it was roller-coaster time. I gained six-hundred feet in just over a minute and saw that I had the landing zone well within range. An experienced pilot could spiral around inside that rising column of hot air and ride it right to the base of the small puffy cloud overhead. As it was, I simply burst through into a bit of mild turbulence on the other side of the thermal where I took a reading on the LZ and dived for safety.

On the radio receiver inside my helmet I could hear Mark turning me over to Andy and Andy telling me to "do a couple of 360s" to lose altitude. And when I came around for the second time, I saw the Iceman was down safely. I saw Andy. I saw the video camera, and I thought, No more cow pie.

Put the brake up for speed—there's the camera, do this right, edge out of the seat, legs down, okay, okay, okay—there's the ground ten feet below whipping by at about twenty-five miles an hour, and now, slowly, bring the brakes down to the neck, wait a beat, brakes to the chest, wait a beat, now all the way to the knees. I stepped down out of the sky, took two steps, turned to the camera, and declared in all modesty, and with great dignity, that I was the Master of the Universe. Icarus. Superman.

"It was a lot funnier the old way," quoth the Iceman.

Fly Away

▲

They give you a large, baggy clown suit, earplugs, a crash helmet, a pair of heavy boots, and drop you over a whirling airplane propeller embedded in the ground. The building itself is columnular, like a silo, and a glance or two at the spinning blades below make you feel a bit like a radish dropped in the Cuisinart. There is, of course, a heavy metal screen between you and the prop.

Now, stand for a moment on the padded bench, just out of the howling column of wind. Take a deep breath and fall face-first out into the current. You should be spread-eagled, like a frog that has unaccountably learned to arch its back. If you've got the position right, the clown suit expands until you look like the Michelin tire man. The vertical prop wash lifts you up, and the sensation is that of flight rather than falling. Bend your knees a bit—lose a little surface area—and you'll drop slowly toward the wire screen. With practice, a novice flyer can learn loops and barrel rolls, can drop like a rock, then frog out to a stop a foot or two above the screen.

The idea of swooping around in a controlled prop wash is such a strangely appealing concept that a rash of newspaper articles and TV "magazine" stories have appeared on Fly Away, a Las Vegas "recreation center." I wanted to try this glorified amusement-park attraction the first time I heard about it over a year ago. Go to Las Vegas, lose a couple months' worth of work at the blackjack table, and fly like a bird.

Perhaps one of my reasons for driving 869 miles to try Fly Away was subconscious. As I frogged out over the blades and felt myself being slowly lifted five, six, seven, and ten feet off the metal screen, the odd floating sensation began to feel eerily familiar: It was, in fact, the way I fly in my dreams.

Now night soaring is not the norm for me: I get into it perhaps once every six months, generally following a particularly good day. Most often, I am in a large, sunny room when it occurs to me that I can fly. I rise slowly up off the ground—just testing my wings—and tip forward until I am looking down toward the ground in a horizontal position. In dreams, I never arch my back or frog out. I fly more like Superman than Kermit.

After hovering near the ceiling for a while, I like to swoop slowly down through the open window and glide majestically over the endless rolling green pastures that surround the house. This flight is perfectly silent, and I am Hawk.

Fly Away feels like the first stages of dream flight, but it is noisy, and the prop wash, filtered through a screen, is pretty turbulent, so that stability requires certain small adjustments in position. First-time fliers often don't get the hang of frogging out properly. They end up spinning out of the column of air and plopping down on the thickly cushioned bench that circles the silo.

I had something of an advantage over the other novices in that I've done a bit of skydiving. Unlike Fly Away, which isn't terribly frightening, the first jump from an airplane is a jittery nightmare of fear. More than likely, the act of jumping out of a perfectly good airplane with a sack of laundry on one's back generates more real fear than anything short of armed combat.

The teaching method in vogue when I made my first jump, almost ten years ago, involved crawling out an open cargo door and hanging from the wingstrut of a Cessna 185. The jump-master calibrated the wind against an airspeed of about seventy miles an hour, figured in a three-thousand-foot drop, and shouted at the student to let go of the strut at the point where all these variables might combine to deposit him or her in the center of the drop zone.

On that first jump I was the second student out of the plane. A young woman went first, and when she let go of the strut, I saw her body simply hurtle down through empty space like a sack of cement. The static line, attached to the plane, was supposed to pull the parachute open for her, but she was almost gone, a tiny speck in the process of disappearing—like the last little spot of light in the center of the TV when you turn it off—before her chute opened like one of those flowers blooming in time-lapse photography on some nature documentary.

The plane circled around, and it was my turn to confront the fear of falling. The jumpmaster had stressed the importance of holding the proper position, which is very much like the Fly Away frog. One hangs on to the strut with the back arched. Let go of the strut and gravity tilts you over into an exaggerated belly flop—arms straight out and slightly above the head, legs held slightly above the butt—a position in which one falls stable. Think of a badminton birdie: Drop a shuttlecock feathers down, and it'll spin stupidly. Drop it feathers up, and the birdie falls along a perfectly straight, gravity-drawn line. In skydiving, and at Fly Away, you want to arch your back, keep your feathers up.

When the jumpmaster ascertained that I was in proper position —back arched hard—he shouted "Go," a command I obeyed with extreme reluctance. The plane disappeared overhead. I held position from the waist up, but everything below was moving at a ten flat hundred pace. I think, looking back on it, that fear, ignoring the hard facts of physics, was screaming, "Run or you'll die!"

Nevertheless, I didn't go into much of a spin, the chute opened splendidly, and I floated slowly to earth in an utter silence punctuated only by the bass drumbeat of my heart.

No matter that I'd failed to hold position. The point of the first jump is simply doing it. The niceties come later, if the student decides there is going to be a later. Jumping once is about fear rather than skill.

Some of my classmates who went on to further jumps might have been looking to recapture that first incredible adrenaline rush—as I know I was—but this is a process of diminishing returns. As the novice becomes habituated to the fear—as the student learns by doing that death is only a remote possibility—the thought process mutates. First-jump thinking—"I know thousands have done it before, but this time it's me, and I'm going to die"—gives way to a more casual attitude. "Okay, some folks have been injured, some have been killed, but I'm careful, and that'll never happen to me."

My experience suggests that the novice skydiver discovers, over the next few jumps, that one can never feel again that first thrill of pure and primal fear. He or she also learns to appreciate the skill involved in skydiving, and begins to understand that the mechanics of flying are pleasurable in themselves. Which is the reason some people become hooked on the sport. The woman I watched fall off the strut that day nearly a decade ago has now logged over a thousand jumps.

I wondered about the addictive qualities of dream flight during my standard five-minute session at Fly Away. Afterward, the people who flew with me inside the silo were pleasantly high, in the manner of children getting off the roller coaster. In contrast, my skydiving classmates, after the first jump, were positively giddy, ecstatic. Everyone mentioned "the sense of accomplishment."

I think the accomplishment had to do with terror. Those who went on with the sport started with fear and graduated to skill. At Fly Away you do it once, for the sensation, and you know right away whether you want to spend a couple hundred bucks getting good at prop-wash swooping. I'm not sure many do. Dream flight is fun once every six months or so, but the narcotic ecstasy of pure fear is missing here.

With that in mind I offer this modest, uh, proposition. In order to maximize profits by getting more folks hooked on silo soaring, the Fly Away people might consider getting rid of the metal screen between the propeller and the flier. This is a bold idea whose time has come. And no sick jokes about opening up a hamburger stand next door. Let's be serious here. I'm going to call my Fly Away franchise "Blenderama."

Is It Fun Yet?
A Saga of Sorority Women
on Crampons

▲

"They want us to rent crampons," Stephanie Safford said, and she shrugged helplessly. "What are crampons?"

Deb Williams didn't know. "Maybe they meant croutons."

"What would you do with croutons up on top of the mountain, in all that snow?"

"Maybe you feed the birds," Stephanie said. "Save their lives because they starve in the winter or something."

"What if they meant crayons?"

"You think so? I dunno. A box of crayons on a backpack?"

Steph and Deb were sitting in the Phi Mu sorority house. They were both students at the University of New Hampshire, in Durham, and they had won an all-expense-paid winter camping trip to the nearby Presidential Mountains. *America* magazine wanted to see how complete novices would react to a winter mountaineering trip. Could just anyone do it? The magazine was providing a writer, photographer, and guide. The guide, a woman named Teresa Sims, had written Steph and Deb with a long list of mate-

rials they would require. Besides the backpack, the tent, the layers of wool clothes, the spare gloves and socks, besides the
snowshoes, the sleeping bag, ensolite pad, camp stove, and the
mysterious crampons, the women had been told to rent ice axes,
which could be used for "self-arrests." The axes were about a
yard long, with a spike at the bottom and a kind of pick at the
top.

"Self-arrests," Steph muttered. Did you slip handcuffs on your
wrists, march yourself right down to the jail, violate your own
rights? It was snowing out, the last winter storm of the season,
and the winds were howling outside at seventy miles an hour.
Airports were closed from Boston to Philadelphia. Power was out
in parts of Boston, and the next day Steph and Deb were sched-
uled to climb some damn mountain in the middle of nowhere
where they would be expected to feed crayons to birds and arrest
themselves with axes.

The writer picked them up at the Phi Mu house. He was a big
bearded guy— over six feet tall, about two hundred pounds—and
he said, "The whole point is that the two of you have fun. *America* magazine wants you to have fun. If you don't have fun, I look
bad."

The writer had a huge backpack that looked as if it had suffered some pretty tough use. He seemed to know a little about
winter camping and was full of advice about how to stay warm
and various dangers they would encounter. Listening to the
writer as he drove them up into the mountains, Deb and Steph
began to see the expedition as a choice between certain death—
freezing stiff as a board, sliding down an ice field and plunging
over a cliff, being buried in an avalanche—and some nebulous
concept he called "fun." Nothing the guy had to say sounded like
all that many giggles. "We're not going to put ourselves in any
avalanche situation," he said, "but, you know, just for future
reference, if you should get caught in one, you want to keep on
top of the moving snow. Sort of swim with it, then angle out at
about forty-five degrees . . . if you can."

The writer was trying to be nice, but he seemed overly polite, in an unnatural sort of way, like a wino meeting the queen of England, and his idea of fun apparently had a lot to do with danger and discomfort. He outweighed each of the women by eighty or ninety pounds, and they began to feel that if they didn't have "fun," this big, shaggy guy was going to be plenty pissed off.

They met the photographer and guide at the Appalachian Mountain Club camp at Pinkham's Notch. The photographer was a good-looking red-haired guy, and his pack looked also looked banged up and well used. He and the writer had never met before, but they began talking about a place called Batangas, in the Philippines, where they had both been on separate assignments. There was a sense that these fellows had spent a lot of time outdoors, in difficult circumstances. A couple of guys, Steph and Deb decided, who knew a little bit about having fun in places where there was no fun to be had. The expedition was shaping up as an exercise in masochism.

And worse, worst of all, was the guide. Teresa Sims was almost as tall as the writer: a strong, broad-shouldered woman. She wore her mountain woolens as if she belonged in them, and she exuded an aura of self-sufficient competence. Steph and Deb just felt "cute" in full-cut wool pants and shirts, the way a woman feels cute wearing a man's shirt. The two women sensed the enormous gulf between cute and competent.

The guide didn't talk much, but she tore apart the backpacks and examined all of Steph and Deb's gear, clucking sadly at their boots and criticizing the crampons they had finally rented: little spiked gadgets they could strap onto their boots for some unknown reason.

"Instep crampons like these are useless," Teresa said. "You should have gotten the full-foot models." Steph and Deb felt as if they had sinned. The guide stared at them—one of those appraising up-and-down looks—and Deb felt that she was being "sized up."

The women of Phi Mu were now very tense about all the fun that lay ahead of them.

* * *

The writer parked the van at the trailhead, and everyone hoisted the heavy packs onto their backs. Skies were icy blue after the fury of the storm. Steph had done some bicycle camping, Deb was a downhill-ski instructor, but neither of them had ever carried a fifty-pound pack before. The things were impossibly heavy, and the trail that wound through the trees seemed to rise almost vertically in front of them.

The group walked across the road, to the trailhead. There was a small four-foot-high ridge of hard-packed snow the plows had deposited on the shoulder of the highway, and everyone chugged right on up and over it, leaving Steph and Deb floundering there. The snow was steep and icy. You couldn't just walk up it, not with a heavy pack on your back. Deb gave it a try—the others had walked up without thinking about it—and she slipped, falling facedown into the snow. The weight of her pack drove the breath out of her lungs. She thought, How am I going to climb a mountain when I can't even make it to the trail?

The others came back and told Deb to "kick steps." They were sorry, they said, but "kicking steps" was a trick so elemental to winter camping, they had simply forgotten to mention it. What you do on steep snow, Deb learned, is to attack the mountain as if kicking it in the shins. The boot slides into the snow, forming a little platform that is used for kicking the next step.

Five kicked steps and Deb was up and over the little ridge, where she and Steph were presented with a yellow Forest Service sign that read: "Attention. Try this trail only if you are in top physical condition, well clothed, carrying extra clothing and food. Many have died above timberline from exposure. Turn back at the first sign of bad weather."

"We're going to have lots and lots of fun up there," the writer threatened.

Four hours later, Deb was plodding along in a misery of fatigue. She just couldn't keep up with the others, not even Steph, and she wondered if she was in the kind of "top physical condition" the trail demanded. The party had been moving up the steep trail, occasionally kicking steps. They had walked up through stands of hardwoods, with an open stream rushing on below them, and everyone talked about how beautiful it was, but Deb was exhausted and couldn't catch her breath. Now, they were up near the ridge line, and the hardwoods had given way to spruce trees. Deb was forcing the party to stop every fifteen minutes. She didn't want to hold them back— she had plodded on for an hour past the time she felt she couldn't take another step—but now her legs were giving way on her, and she had no choice. She felt like a leper. A leper with emphysema.

Deb understood that everyone was getting chilled now. Walking straight uphill with a heavy pack, kicking steps, was incredibly hard work, and everyone was sweating profusely, even though the temperature was well below freezing, and a thirty-mile-an-hour wind was whipping along the ridge. Unfortunately, when you stopped, sweat froze to your skin. You had to keep moving to keep warm.

Steph was particularly cold. She had been told to wear wool next to her skin, but wool was scratchy, and she had cheated a little—fooled everyone—by wearing a cotton shirt that looked like wool. Now, she realized that she had only fooled herself.

Proper women, Steph had heard, didn't sweat, they glowed. She had been glowing all the way up the mountain, glowing to such a degree that her cotton shirt was sopping and could actually be wrung out. Wool, Teresa Sims had said, wicks moisture away from the skin, and often dries itself out from the heat of the body alone. Cotton retains moisture against the skin. Stopping every fifteen minutes for Deb, Steph began to understand why the writer had said, "Cotton can kill you." She could almost feel the wet shirt freezing against her skin, sucking away her body's heat dozens of times faster than low temperatures or wind alone. Still, she wasn't going to say anything: She didn't want to be a complainer, didn't want to put Deb on the spot for having to rest.

So the party was standing in the snow, with the wind cranking up a little more every minute. It was getting late, toward dark, the temperature was dropping, and they were still an hour and a half from a decent campsite, according to Teresa. It seemed as if there was no warmth or comfort left in the world, and when Deb caught her breath, she asked the writer: "Is it fun, yet?" Deb making a little joke that wrapped itself around a hard core of bitter truth, like a snowball with a stone inside.

It was the photographer who spotted Deb's problem when everyone put their packs back on: "Have you adjusted your straps at all?" he asked, and Deb said she didn't know you could. She had been buckling the pack's belt around her waist, and although everyone ends up finding what suits him or her best, the photographer thought Deb would be more comfortable with the belt fastened just above the point of her hips. She had been letting the full fifty pounds dangle from her shoulders, but the new arrangement would shift the weight to the stronger muscles of her hips and legs.

It was a revelation. Deb wasn't out of shape at all, and she was never again the first to call a rest. You could just shift the weight from hips to shoulders, or balance it out between them, and walk all day. It amazed her to realize that she'd been so down on herself, that she had felt so unworthy. There were tricks—call them techniques—involved here, and proper technique had an effect on one's emotional outlook. It made you think about yourself, winter camping.

Get the snowshoes off the pack and stomp around in the snow to form a solid platform. Set up the tent and remember to bury the pegs under wet, heavy snow so the shelter will be stable in case a heavy wind springs up. Sit in the snow on the ensolite pads and try to get the camp stove going. It took almost fifteen minutes to melt enough snow to make a quart of water, and the women needed water to rehydrate the dried macaroni-and-cheese they carried for that night's dinner. They needed water to fill their canteens. They had been told to drink plenty of fluids, and that water could help keep them warm. The blood, it seemed, could thicken—like oil in a car on a subzero morning—without enough water to thin it out and get it to the hands and feet. It took an hour to make enough water for dinner and drinking.

The temperature was dropping in the absence of the sun, and it was cold, bitterly cold out in the snow. Deb's boots had gotten wet, and there was a thick glaze of ice on them. "Keep your boots on the pad," Teresa said. "It'll keep your feet warmer."

While the macaroni was cooking, Teresa talked about walking the entire length of the Appalachian Trail, 2,126.5 miles. She had done it two years ago, at the age of twenty-four. Now, she was planning another half-year hike, from Montana to Mexico along the line of the Continental Divide. "Winter camping is a natural thing to do if you want to understand the whole wilderness," Teresa said. She thought that putting up with bad weather, with being cold, provided a sort of camaraderie between people on a long trek. "What I like," Teresa said, "is that hard-core trekking comes down to what I can do and what I can't do. There are no fantasies anymore."

The writer and photographer were listening. Whenever Teresa talked, they shut up. The men weren't at all reluctant to learn from Teresa, who, clearly, knew more than they did about the mountains of New Hampshire. The two guys, you could see it on their faces, had a lot of respect for Teresa Sims, who was talking about how she quit a good job managing real estate properties to work for the Appalachian Mountain Club. She had been on half a dozen rescue missions up in the mountains. One stormy night, wearing a headlamp, she had helped carry an unconscious woman across an ice field. "My parents don't understand why I do this sort of thing," Teresa said.

Eight PM. Sixteen degrees. Too cold to do anything but climb into the tent and try to sleep. Steph had secretly changed out of her cotton shirt, but she couldn't shake the chill it had given her. She woke around two, freezing to death.

"Deb," she said, "I'm just so cold."

"You have your hat on?"

"Yes."

"Is the bag tight around you?"

"Yes."

"What else did they say? If you wake up cold? Didn't they say to eat something?"

"I'll try."

Deb felt her friend was very low, and she tried to help her through the worst of the night with talk. "Teresa's amazing," Deb said.

"Superhuman," Steph agreed.

"Absolutely," Deb said in Teresa's soft Virginia accent, and they both laughed because that was the word the guide used instead of "yes."

"Ahm on the loading dock," Steph said. It was a Teresaism meaning "Let's go."

"Ah love mah boots," Deb said, because Teresa loved her insulated boots with the plastic shells. The women, by contrast, hated their own boots. They were too soft to kick good steps, and Deb's soaked up melting snow like a sponge. She thought of them as "slush puppies."

"Teresa," Steph said, "she's . . . heroic." The women thought about this, wondering how they had come to admire a person so thoroughly after knowing her less than twenty-four hours.

"I still don't know why do they do it," Deb said after a while. "I mean, if this is all there is to it." Steph didn't answer. The food had warmed her, and she was sleeping. Deb wondered if she would have accepted an all-expense-paid trip to the Black Hole of Calcutta. At least it would be warm, in the Black Hole. She was sleeping with her icy slush puppies in the bottom of her bag. Everyone had told her she had to sleep with the boots: If you left them out, they'd freeze solid, and you'd never get them on your feet in the morning.

It wasn't fun yet, not as far as Deb was concerned.

They left the base camp carrying light day packs, moving down into a small valley, along a trail that would take them to Mount Jackson, which stood alone, in the middle of the southern Presidential range. The women could see it in the distance. It looked ominous, foreboding.

Everyone was wearing snowshoes, but the writer's rental models had bad bindings, and he was falling behind, adjusting the things every five minutes and cursing steadily.

Eventually, the writer gave up and carried the snowshoes in his hand. He followed the tramped-down trail everyone else made, but every fifty or sixty steps, he fell through the snow into what Teresa called a "spruce trap." Wind had whipped falling snow into a pocket on the lee side of the trees, then new snow had covered the hole. You could tramp right over a spruce trap in snowshoes, but a man on foot, like the writer, would drop waist-deep into the snow. It made Steph feel good, listening to the steady stream of outraged obscenities: The writer wasn't being polite anymore. He was being "natural," and it was as if the curses were a sign of acceptance. She felt so good she laughed aloud, and the writer, pulling himself out of another hole, muttered, "Bitch." Down below, the word was an insult; up here it meant the man respected her enough to curse her out. It made her feel like a legitimate part of an expedition, not a sorority girl on an outing.

They were walking the Appalachian Trail, but the blazes cut into the trees were buried under fresh new snow, and eventually the writer suggested that they forget about trying to find the blazes and "bushwhack" it to the top. It wasn't too difficult: The summit rose stark white against a cobalt-blue sky before them.

As they came out of the valley and began rising, taking a steep slope, Teresa said to plant the spike end of the ice ax into the slope ahead of them. "That way you pull yourself up to it."

On a slope like the expert run on a good ski hill, Deb planted her ax too far uphill, and her feet slid out from under her. She began to slide down the hill, but the writer planted himself and caught her. Deb didn't say anything, but the slide scared her, badly. She didn't know how to stop herself, and the mountain ahead was steeper, covered over in sheets of ice. Steph was talking to her now: a nice calm tone of voice. Deb realized that Steph was trying to talk her up the mountain, that the two of them were helping one another, working through the tough spots together. It was like a kind of telepathy: The two women had never felt closer.

Teresa called a halt. "Too steep for snowshoes now," she said. "We'll leave them here and pick them up on the way back." They kicked steps, moving slowly up the mountain, and on top of a ridge, where the spruce gave way to twisted, wind-tortured dwarf trees two and three feet high, Teresa said, "This is a good spot to practice self-arrests."

It was fun, practicing self-arrests, like children's snow play, but with a serious purpose. It was the only way to stop a long, fast slide down steep snow and ice. Steph tried it first, sitting down on top of a snowy hill, then letting herself go, sliding down the slope. Teresa told her to build up a little speed, then called "Now!" Steph followed instructions perfectly: She turned onto her belly, planted the pick of the ax into the snow, then got her shoulder up over the place where the ax was buried in the snow. She humped up, like a hissing cat, with her toes dug into the snow, and she stopped dead, right there on the steep, icy slope.

When Deb tried it, she saw immediately how easy it was to stop a slide that otherwise might result in injuries, that could, in fact, be fatal. Another trick: a technique. Once you knew the art of self-arrest, steep slopes didn't scare you. As much.

They ate lunch out of the wind, on the lee side of an outcropping of rocks there above the timberline. After everyone finished their cheese and crackers and trail mix, Teresa, who was on the loading dock, asked, "Would, uh, anyone be too bummed if we didn't make the summit?"

"Well," Steph said, "I'd like to go for it."

"Me too," Deb said.

They were thinking almost the same thing: They were thinking that they hadn't come all this way to turn back now, not now when the summit was only an hour away, not now when they knew how to kick steps and stop a slide. Not now.

Teresa and the two guys exchanged looks, as if there was something funny, but they couldn't laugh about it just yet.

"Let's go," Deb said, and Steph added, "We're on the loading dock."

"Absolutely."

They moved up over the loose snow, kicking steps, until they hit a small ice field. There, just below the summit, above the timberline, constant mountain winds had turned the slope into a sheet of sheer ice. The party stopped for a moment, and Teresa brought out her crampons. They fastened to the bottom of the boots she loved: a dozen sharp prongs that bit into the ice and held her stable on the slope. Steph and Deb looked at their instep crampons, which consisted of two little spikes positioned just in front of the bootheel. Anyone could see that the heel was higher than the spikes. It was just as Teresa said: Instep crampons were useless.

"We'll go it without crampons," Teresa said. "Remember, your ice ax is your best friend."

The last slope was steeper, slicker than anything they had been on before, and you had to move slowly, carefully, to prevent a fall. Steph found she wasn't frightened in the least. Her mind was on the summit. Deb kept thinking, Almost there, almost there.

And then they were up over the lip of the slope, on the summit, with the land dropping away on all sides of them, and the wind was howling like a savage symphony up there on the top of the world. Something inside Steph burst wide open, and she whooped, shouting out a wordless cry of joy and triumph. Deb grabbed her, and they hugged one another in that high spot with only the sky above them.

"Hey!" It was the writer calling to them. "Hey, Deb, is it fun yet?"

She saw the three of them standing there: the writer, the photographer, and the guide. Everyone was smiling, and Deb could tell they couldn't help themselves. They felt as good as she did. Deb thought about ski students she'd had: people who finally did everything right and ran the bunny slope all the way without a fall. God, it made her feel good. That's what the writer was feeling, what the guide and photographer felt. Deb knew it, and for just a moment she felt as if she loved them all.

"Yeah," Deb said, laughter bubbling like champagne in her throat, "it's fun."

Steph thought about cotton and crampons, about self-arrests and bushwhacking, about slush puppies and curses and camaraderie—everything she'd learned about cold-weather survival—

and realized that the "fun" Deb talked about left a mark on a person. Reaching a goal not easily achieved: It changed your whole life.

"Better than fun," Steph said thoughtfully.

"Absolutely," Deb said.

This Is a Cave,
This Is the End

▲

It's like, why me?

Burt Grossman, second-year defensive end for the San Diego Chargers, asked the question aloud at a kind of celebration dinner after three days of crawling around in the mud, watching trees fall out of the sky onto people, having bats winging around his head, and hanging from a rope 165 feet above a pit supposedly full of poisonous copperhead snakes. He had climbed and crawled over places with names like Danger Canyon and Death Ledge. He had heard—nobody in San Diego would believe this— he had actually heard a couple of these cave guys, cavers they call themselves, seriously discussing the idea of going back down into the copperhead pit to retrieve part of another guy's face. His face, man.

There were a writer and an editor at the dinner, and they were trying to explain about how they had an idea for an article about fear and whether fear motivates performance on the football field. They wanted a story about "a top-notch defensive" player. They thought defensive guys were supposed to be crazy and fearless. It wasn't true, they said. Nobody in the NFL wanted to back off a cliff and slide down a rope in absolute darkness. Finally, one guy said he would do it, but he canceled at the last minute. It had taken a lot of talking, the editor said, and a lot of the NFL teams didn't get it. "We wanted," he explained, "to take someone who had a reputation for being fearless in one area of sport and "introduce him to another sport."

"Where," the writer added, "there might be an element of fear."

"A sort of worlds-in-collision kind of deal," the editor added.

"Which is more what it turned out to be," the writer said.

Right. When Burt Grossman's people at San Diego approached him about the project, nobody said anything about fear or caves or worlds in collision. Maybe he wasn't listening real hard, but he got the idea that he'd slide down a rope the way they do in the army recruiting ads. Once. Get his face in a magazine. Good promo.

And it wasn't until he was on the plane to Tennessee that he looked at his ticket and saw that they expected him to stay five days. And these guys, these cavers, wanted to take him on a death crawl to the center of the earth.

It was all a horrible mistake.

Happens all the time with Burt. His mouth gets him in trouble. He doesn't even know why, he just started doing it in college. The sportswriters would come around after a game, and everyone was saying the same thing. "We were fortunate to have the momentum. . . ." Burt just started saying what he thought. Still does. A lot of times he ends up putting down other players. "I don't like [Mark] Gastineau, to tell the truth," Grossman told San Diego sportswriters his first day in town. "I don't like [Brian] Bosworth either. Those two go off the handle and criticize everything. Like they say, misery loves company. Look what they got. One got Brigitte Nielsen. The other got . . . what? Seattle."

So now the sportswriters want to talk to Burt after Charger games. He gets quoted a lot. About midseason, some guy sent him a letter. The guy pulled down his pants, sat on a copier, and sent Burt the result. It was a fairly ugly photocopy, with the message "A guy with a big mouth ends up looking like an ass."

So Burt knows there're plenty of people who'd like to see him get his. He's inspired by this knowledge and feels he has to play well to back up his mouth. People are going to watch him on the field, isolate him, because of what he says, and he doesn't want to be, well, embarrassed.

So after he said he'd do this rope stuff, there was no way he could back down. It's not Burt's way.

Burt Grossman arrives in Chattanooga. The writer picks him up at the airport and asks him what frightens him. Burt says he can't honestly say he's afraid of anything. What scares him are movies like *The Exorcist* or *The Guardian*. When he was a kid, he used to be afraid of the dark.

The next morning it's pretty scary right off the bat because they pick him up at the motel and he's got to ride in Trick Howard's truck. People in Tennessee have names like that. Trick. Buddy. Burt grew up in Philadelphia, a Mainline family, fairly well-to-do, went to Pitt, got signed with the Chargers for 8.3 million, and bought a house in swanky La Jolla: He's twenty-three years old and never really hung out with somebody named, like, Goober. He never rode in a truck like Trick's.

It's a Tennessee limousine: a 1969 Chevy three-quarter-ton pickup truck. Trick's got a camper shell on the back that someone gave him. The camper looks as if it's fastened to the bed with Super Glue and Silly Putty. There are stickers on the bumper that read, GUANO HAPPENS. Bat droppings, man. The guy thinks about bat droppings.

To get to these caves, you've got to drive up into the mountains. Trick's truck wobbles on twenty-year-old springs. The roads are twisty, and there are big drop-offs. Suddenly, it becomes *The Exorcist* inside the cab. Seriously. Bees start flying out of the ventilation system on the dash: big yellow jackets.

"Truck's been parked in the woods," Trick explains. He's a little guy, Trick, five-ten, maybe 150 pounds, and he's wearing a black T-shirt that says, I AM BAD CRAZY.

Burt's trapped in a rolling deathtrap driven by a self-described insane person, and he gets stung by bees, twice. The thing isn't a vehicle; it's a horror film careening through the mountains on bad tires. *Friday the 13th* on wheels.

Trick hands Burt a cigarette and says he should chew the tobacco, make a paste, and put it on the stings. As if there's nothing particularly unusual about getting stung by a bee at sixty miles an hour. No way is Burt going to put tobacco spit all over his body.

Trick parks near some rocky cliffs, and there are about twenty people standing around: the writer, a photographer, a whole bunch of cavers and their families, and a couple of other folks out for a Sunday stroll who just stopped by to see what was going on. The cliffs are maybe sixty feet high, and from the top you can see all of downtown Chattanooga and the Tennessee River rolling through the town.

There's a rope tied to a couple of trees, and it hangs over the cliff. The cave dorks help Burt put on a seat harness, which is kind of like a reinforced diaper. There's a long hunk of metal, a rappel rack, connected to the front of the harness. The rack's shaped like a stretched-out horseshoe. The rope goes over one of the bars on the rack, under another, over the next. The bars slide up and down. Get going too fast, and you just slide the bars together. Create more friction. Nothing to it, the cavers say. Nothing can happen.

The main guy training Burt is Buddy Lane, who, it turns out, is vice president of a steel company in Chattanooga. The writer keeps telling Burt what a hero Buddy is: how he was elected president of some caver society, twice. Turns out that when people get lost in caves, Buddy is the one the cops or rangers call. He used to be head of the local search-and-rescue team too. Just last week Buddy had to crawl through a sewer and drag out a worker who was overcome by carbon monoxide.

The writer's telling Burt all this stuff to calm him down, because what you have to do in caves, it turns out, you have to slide down long ropes in the darkness to get where you're going.

The writer says that it's kind of like mountain climbing, except that the point isn't to get to the summit. The point is to go in one entrance and come out the other. That's called making the connection. Sometimes, in caves, the only way to make the connection is to go down a big pit. Some of the cave pits are 450 feet deep, about the same drop you'd take from the top of a forty-story building.

A lot of what the cavers do is exploration. What's down there after the pit? Buddy Lane has discovered literally hundreds of caves, the writer says. Buddy Lane is like this writer's hero: Buddy discovers caves and saves people's lives.

"Buddy's the best," the writer says.

That may be true, but Burt can't think too much about it right now. The cavers seem to want to start working with him right now. They want him to practice on this outdoor cliff in bright sunlight, with everyone watching him. He has to clip the rope into the rack, stand backward, and step off a sixty-foot death cliff. That's real natural.

Burt doesn't even look down. What's the point? If he looked down, he could get scared and call the whole thing off. They'd have his picture in the magazine with a caption that reads, *The Whimpering Coward of San Diego*. Real good promotion there.

Sure enough, the rope holds, and the rack works. Burt's standing in the red and blue wildflowers at the bottom, looking up, and the cavers want him to climb back up on the rope itself. They put little metal gadgets on his feet. The gadgets bite down when he puts pressure on them; they let go when he pulls up. He can, Buddy tells him, walk right up the rope.

And it works, except people have to stop because no one can motor right up the rope without resting. Burt can't help thinking, What if the rope breaks? Every time he stops, two words clang together in his mind: broken . . . rope.

Burt's got a reputation as a weirdo, a big mouth, and he really wouldn't like a whole lot of people to know it, but he's fairly conservative in some ways. Careful. Wears two watches, for instance. Got a 3.85 in economics at Pitt. He hates to think about it, but if something goes wrong in football, he could—the shame of it—fall back on his education. Be a stockbroker.

Burt likes to have it covered. He took his signing bonus last year, put most of it into an annuity, and defers a large part of his salary into the same fund. He should be able to retire at thirty and collect $300,000 a year until he's seventy-five. A lot of his teammates buy eighty-thousand-dollar cars with their money. Burt's still driving the car he had in college. He thinks it's only wise to look to the future, and now, wise guy that he is, he's literally hanging from a thread. The end of his life would sound like this: *twaaaanggg.*

Burt manages to climb the rope a couple of times, and all the cavers are telling him that he's doing fine, that he's ready to try a bigger pit. Not one of the big dark ones, though. The one they want to train him on is a wimp pit, open to the light.

The cavers pack up their gear, and about half the people standing around get into their vehicles and start driving. Burt gets to ride in Trick's truck again, with the bad tires and the bees. An hour later everyone turns at a Baptist church with a sign out front that reads, BELIEVE ON THE LORD JESUS CHRIST AND BE SAVED. The caravan drives up a red dirt road that winds into the hills. There are trees all around, and it's like the jungle or something. The houses are tar-paper shacks. People have pigs and chickens in their yards. Burt tries to imagine what it's like, living in one of these places. You'd get up in the morning, look out your window, and you'd see trees and pigs.

Up near the top of the road there's a dilapidated trailer house with a bunch of empty cardboard drums around and some old timber rotting in the yard. A big sign on a tree at the edge of the forest ringing the house reads, MAD DOG AND CRAZY MAN, KEEP OUT.

The woods are full of really comforting stuff like that.

"Is this where they filmed *Deliverance?*" Burt wants to know. "We gonna see some little kid playing a banjo?"

But the cavers are out of their trucks and walking through the trees up a steep slope. Trick is telling him fun things to know, like: "Sometimes copperheads get washed down into the pit by the waterfall. Watch out for snakes on the bottom."

Oh, now it's Indiana Jones in the snake pit.

"See this?" Trick holds up his right index finger, and it's puffed out and crooked. What happened, Trick says, was that he was at the bottom of the pit and grabbed a copperhead behind the neck with his thumb and forefinger.

"Thought you were faster than a snake, huh?" Burt says.

"I was. But I should have done a three-finger grab. Put the index finger on his head. It's like a big knuckle behind the head, but I felt that knuckle go out of joint, and the head came around, and pow."

"Gee," Burt says, "what else you guys in Tennessee do for fun? Hunt wild boars naked?"

The cavers finally stop at a kind of plateau in all the jungle foliage, and in the middle of the flat area is a strange keyhole-shaped hole in the ground. Burt glances into the pit. They tell him it's 165 feet deep, but you can't see to the bottom because it's dark down there. A big waterfall comes out of a hole in the wall about three quarters of the way down, and it's so loud you have to shout up top. Wouldn't it be all water in the dark at the bottom? Burt doesn't want to think about this at all. He lies down in the grass, and Buddy Lane tells him to watch out for ticks.

"Ticks," Burt says, "what do I care about ticks? I'm going to die in the waterfall."

Burt just lies there, yawning, then Buddy tells him it's time to drop the pit. There are two ropes tied off onto the trees that overhang the pit. One of the cavers, Roger Ling, is already down there, and Buddy Lane will go down with Burt on the second rope. Burt rigs himself, refuses to look down into the pit, backs over a lip of rock, and finds himself dangling in midair. "No pits scare me," Burt howls. He supposes he doesn't sound scared at all. "The only pits that scare me are my own." Ha. The man died with a joke on his lips.

Going down isn't too bad. It's kind of fun. Burt would rappel ten thousand feet if they had a helicopter to come pick him up so he didn't have to climb the rope and think about it breaking all the time. The walls are all heavy, dripping rock, big, looming dark stone, and when the sun breaks through the clouds, these shafts of light slant down into the pit. It's like in a cathedral or something. Except it's spooky.

Halfway down Burt can see that it's really two pits, one a little higher than the other, and the water is falling out of the higher pit into the lower one. Burt can just see the end of his rope on flat rocky ground, right next to where the water from the fall disappears into the ground. Even on the ground, safe, Burt thinks the pit is haunted.

He's thinking, Buddy must have some way to rescue people in a place like this. Maybe they could practice that on me, and I wouldn't have to climb out. The climbing part, man. Awful. And, sure enough, that's when it happened, climbing out.

Sitting right next to Burt at dinner is Buddy Lane. He's eating a hamburger steak. Something soft and easy to chew. Buddy's face is split down the middle, from the bridge of his nose, down one side to his upper and lower lip. There are stitches all over the guy's face, thirty or forty of them, like Frankenstein's monster.

When it happened, Buddy was climbing out, hanging on the rope maybe forty feet from the top of the pit. Burt Grossman was on the other rope, about five feet from Buddy. Suddenly, everyone up top started yelling, "Rock, rock, rock!" But when Burt looked up, it wasn't a rock at all; it was a big tree limb, about the size of a fullback's thigh, and it was coming down the pit, getting bigger real fast, like a 3-D movie. It hit the wall, flipped over, and one end nailed Buddy in the face.

It was Burt's first big pit, and when he glanced over at his instructor, the guy who was supposed to save him if something went wrong, the whole lower half of the guy's face was blood, and his upper lip was . . . gone. Buddy shouted something that sounded like "Clisssshhh."

"I was trying," Buddy explained at dinner, "to say 'climb.' We didn't know what else was coming down, maybe the whole tree was going to come down, and we needed to get out of there. It's just, you can't say *m* and *b* with no upper lip."

"So he's, zoom, up the rope," Burt told the editor. "I'm hanging there thinking, Well, this sure is a lot of fun. I'm dead."

"But you weren't scared," the writer pointed out.

"Oh, no. This seemed real normal to me. Hang from a rope above a haunted pit full of poisonous snakes, and trees fall out of the sky on you. Normal day in Tennessee."

"So what happened after you climbed out of the pit?" the writer asked.

Burt said, "I get to the top, people are talking about, let's go back down into the pit, see if we can find Buddy's lip. And this caver up top, he's a third-year medical student, he says, 'No, Buddy's lip is all here. He just severed some muscles, the other muscles pulled it apart,' and that's why Buddy looked like the damn elephant man. And I was amazed. Really amazed that a guy smart enough to be in medical school, man, he would do something like this."

Burt climbs out of the pit alone. One of the cavers up top has already driven Buddy to the hospital, so Burt gets to ride back to his motel in Trick's truck. Later, at the motel, the writer calls, says that Burt can do what he wants, call the whole thing off.

"Hell no," Burt says. "Show me the Rambo pit. Take me to the bat cave. I want to see Grandpa Munster hanging upside down."

So the next day, the cavers act as if Burt is one of them. Because it's Monday, a workday, there's only four of them now: the writer, the photographer, Trick, and Roger Ling. They all seem real happy that Burt didn't go home when he had the chance. They gear him up with knee pads, elbow pads, leather gloves, and a helmet with a light on it. The place is a commercial cave. You walk through a store where they sell Dr Pepper and Moon Pies right into a big underground room with stone icicles that hang down and ones that stick up out of the floor. Hidden lights—green and red—illuminate the formations. It looks like a room in a porno motel in hell.

Burt gets the idea that they're taking him on a real easy cave walk, but ten minutes later they're out of the lit-up commercial part of the cave, and Burt's crawling on his hands and knees. It's pretty obvious no one goes beyond the motel-room part of the cave. No one but cavers. The light on his helmet is on, and all he can see is the backside of the guy crawling in front of him. Burt feels like a quarterback.

And he has to squeeze through holes and crawl along this ledge that's like the ledge on the outside of building, that narrow, except that it's dark in the cave, and the ledge is muddy, and there's a drop of forty feet to some sharp rocks below. The cavers seem relieved when Burt gets to the end of this narrow crawl.

"That's Death Ledge," Trick says. In the light from Burt's headlamp he can see the words come out of Trick's mouth in little puffs of fog. "Sometimes people freeze up on Death Ledge."

Way past Death Ledge and beyond Danger Canyon, they all stop to rest in a little room. Everyone turns his headlamp off to save batteries. Stick says the cave goes on for miles. There's the big commercial room, then miles of wild cave. Stick says this as if he expects Burt to stand up and shout "Whoopee."

Funny thing though: Burt realizes he isn't afraid of the dark at all. These are pretty much okay guys, and Burt gets the idea that they've decided not to throw him off of one of the forty-story pits because his first experience was such a bummer. They don't come right out and say that, though. In fact, no mention is made of pits at all.

And the deal is, you can sit in the dark with these guys and talk. If anyone got hurt, they'd get him out. It's a kind of team, and Burt understands teams. In the dark you can't see anyone's face, and maybe that makes it easier to talk too.

"Burt, yesterday, before the pit, you were yawning. Does this bore you?" The writer's asking a serious question.

"No," Burt answers. "That's me, I guess. My girlfriend says that too. Says she never knows what I'm thinking. And before a game, I like to lie down on the bench by my locker. And I yawn. I bet I yawn forty times in the hour before the game. My teammates used to get on me about it, but then they saw that it works for me, that I produce." Usually, when people ask Burt about football, he tells them that he gets paid big-time, and that's why he plays. In the dark Burt heard himself actually talking about football. Saying un-Burtlike stuff, like how he loves the game, the mystical part of it.

"I might look big compared to the average guy," Burt says, "but for a defensive end, I'm really small, six-six, two-seventy. And there's guys that can bench a lot more. . . ."

"But you do a four-point-six forty," the writer says.

"There are guys that are quicker."

There was a long silence, and then Burt heard himself getting all transcendental. "There's like a trance you get into. I don't know how to explain it. I don't hear the crowd, and I don't really look at anything in particular. I can see how they're lined up, and I might glance at the quarterback. I might see how my guy's got his feet set. Check his hands, maybe. But you can't plan anything: Every time you plan something out, it doesn't work. So I'm a counterpuncher. They do something; I react. There's no time to think about it. They say I'm a smart player, but what I do isn't really like thinking. It's a flow you get into. A trance."

"What about fear?" the writer asks. Does Burt use fear to psyche himself up for games?

"No. I mean, that's why this is sort of a stupid idea for an article. Football: What's there to be afraid of? It's a sunny afternoon, there're seventy thousand people watching you. Here, in the cave, you've got every fear known to man. Darkness, drowning, falling, freezing to death. I mean, nobody I know would enjoy this. I'm never going into a cave again. Ever."

Next day Burt's wading through waist-deep water in a cold cave with a river running through it, and he's working hard enough that steam is actually rising off the part of his body that isn't under water. The same four guys are trudging along with him, and he's telling them that he wants to go "back to San Diego where people drive actual cars and don't live in houses made out of old beer cans." They're all laughing. Like they don't believe him. Like these cave guys actually think he enjoys this.

They're walking through a round passage with a four-foot-wide shallow river running through it. The water is milky greenish blue, and the passage echoes with curses and laughter. You can see the helmet lights swaying in the dark. It's like those movies where the cops are chasing some serial killer through the sewers.

Burt's thinking aloud. What if you shrunk a guy down to, like, the size of a pinhead? He could rappel down a normal person's throat on a length of sewing thread. Ha. And instead of trees, you could have little pieces of crackers come bombing down him. Cracker bombs.

The cavers are laughing. Trick explains that, after a while, caves tend to make you silly. "Yeah," the writer agrees, "caves sure do snap the thread of linear thought."

And maybe Burt's getting a little used to the caves. The passage, for instance, finally opens up above, and there are these striated, curving walls, all yellow and orange. It's a canyon. Like a little Grand Canyon, only underground, with a milky blue-green river running through it. On one ledge that sticks out overhead there are about fifty bats hanging upside down. With their wings folded, they look like little mice. Burt passes under them, and a couple take off for the entrance. Trick and Roger behind him duck and wave their arms around, just the way anybody else would. These guys have stickers on their trucks—BATS NEED FRIENDS TOO—but they're human beings. Human beings don't like flying rodents in their faces.

And there's a stalactite ahead of him. Burt has learned that stalactites hang "tight" to the ceiling. It's a little thing, two inches long, about as big around as a pencil, and there is a silver drop of water hanging from its tip. "How long does it take to make one of these?" Burt asks.

"Some people say about an inch a century," Roger Ling says.

Burt touches the formation with a big finger, touches it the way you might touch a newborn kitten. "You mean this thing is two hundred years old?"

And they give him the lecture for about the seven-hundredth time: how caves are fragile, and people have to be educated about the beauties and the dangers; they tell him about what a pain it is to have to pull dead people out of the caves on rescue missions. Dead people really gripe the cavers if they died because they didn't educate themselves about the beauties and the dangers. . . .

This lecture goes on and on.

Burt's thinking about the eraser. Yesterday, sitting deep in the wild part of the cave, he felt this strange rock and dug it up. It turned out to be a pencil eraser. He thought he was going where no man had gone before, and he finds an eraser. It was aggravating. Burt understands why the cavers always pick up trash and carry it out of the caves.

"Hey, Trick," Burt calls, "you spray-painting your name on the wall again?"

Which is the last thing cave dorks would do. They treat a cave like a church, and won't even take a leak inside one. World's biggest bladders, man.

And, in a way, it's almost sweet. The cavers want him to like their caves. Burt, natch, is not going to do anything anyone really wants him to do. It's not his way.

Trick and Roger are up ahead, setting up a photo and leaving Burt alone for a moment. There's a pool that is greenish blue in the light, and above it the underground river flows down over a series of rocky stair steps, bubbling up at the narrow spots. Above him there are horizontal ledges coming off both walls: ledges like giant stone platters. Hobbit seats. Stalactites everywhere. And colors. Real subtle, but they stand out after being in the cave awhile: orange and yellow and strange glowing green. It's like an elf garden or something: a real pretty grotto.

Burt motions for the writer. "Hey, look at that."

The writer stares at it for a long time; then he turns around with a big smile on his face. As if he caught Burt.

"Hey. I don't appreciate this," Burt says gruffly. "Just thought I'd show it to someone who might."

And the writer's like, Uh-huh, sure Burt.

Later everyone's sitting in the dark, and no one's saying anything. In a few hours they'll be done, have dinner in a restaurant, and Burt can go home the next morning. He's thinking, Nobody is going to believe this. No one would believe the pit or the underground river. Or Trick, man. The guy's getting paid to help the photographer, and he's going to donate part of the money he's making to the National Speleological Society. Let them use it for education, use it to clean up trash in caves. Trick lives in a converted school bus with his wife. The guy lives in a school bus and wants to throw his money into a hole in the ground. It's not Burt's way, but he kinda admires Trick, Trick's way.

Caves, man. Sit in the dark and let the linear thread snap, think about the things that people love.

Why they love them.

Sit in the dark and think, Why me?

Like maybe there was a reason.

Charioteer

▲

I am standing in a fifty-five-gallon oil drum, on wheels. The oil drum has been split in such a way that the back is open, but the front protects me from the belt down. The wheels are the sort of thing you'd want on a big trail bike. There is about forty dollars' worth of material in the vehicle, which looks like a low-rent version of a Roman chariot. The entire contraption is hooked to two big horses. I am staring at their back ends. We are, it occurs to me, three of a kind.

I have driven five hours, through a blizzard, to stand in this oil drum. The horses are anxious: They don't like being confined in the chute, and they'll run when the gate bursts open.

Imagine this: You are standing behind a Corvette, wearing a pair of roller skates. There is a water-ski rope tied to the back bumper of the car, and you are holding the other end. The driver is revving his engine up to top rpm. There is no telling exactly when he will pop the clutch.

This will give you an idea of what it feels like to stand in a flimsy chariot behind a couple of finely bred cutter horses.

* * *

It was nearly five thousand years ago, in the Diyala region of Sumer, when some Iacocca type improved the performance characteristics of his oxen-driven plow by getting rid of the plow and yoking his team up to a platform on wheels. The new vehicle—the first chariot—was a novel source of fun for a couple of centuries until people began to realize that these chariots would go no faster than an ox could lumber. About 2500 B.C., folks began importing onagers—wild asses—from western India and yoking them up to the new chariots. The history of the chariot from that time onward has been a steady quest for speed. There have been, over the years, quite a few of these wild-ass innovations.

As horses became domesticated, around 2000 B.C., they took the place of the asses. About that time, somebody invented the spoked wheel, which was a lot faster and safer than rounds cut off logs.

In the next thousand or so years the use of chariots spread to China, India, Greece, Rome, and the British Isles. British and Celtic chariots used against the Romans in battle had swords extending from their axles for a fast, nasty run through enemy infantry ranks.

Charioteering, in the ancient world, was a soldier's survival skill, and like many such skills, it became a sport in times of peace. The earliest description of a chariot race for sport can be found in Homer. These races were the most popular event in the ancient Olympic Games, and the chariots actually drew more people to the Roman Public Games than gladiators.

The Roman chariot race held at the Circus Maximus usually pitted four 2-horse teams against one another for a seven-lap race. Since the horses were bred for speed, and the chariots were constructed as lightly as possible, there were a lot of exciting wrecks at the races. Chariots flew into pieces at the slightest contact, and drivers, wrapped in their own reins, were often dragged to death in front of the cheering spectators.

Successful charioteers—the ones who always managed to keep the wheels under them as they ran the Circus—became some of the most well-known and popular men in Rome. In later years, there were four racing organizations—red, green, blue, white—

and since there were few opportunities for commercial endorsements back in the second century A.D., the teams backed and were associated with political and/or religious positions. The later greens, for instance, embraced Monophysitism, and were despised by the blues, who considered them heretics. It was a bad day for Monophysitism as a whole when the blues beat the greens.

There are a lot of theories about the decline of Rome, but I think that when a society comes to believe that Universal Meaning is to be derived from the results of a chariot race, then some important intellectual bulb has burned out. While the blues disputed the greens in some pretty fast theological races, the civilized world entered a dark age, and all its chariots, the fast and the philosophical, were piled up onto the scrap heap of history.

It was well over a thousand years before anyone ever thought to race chariots again, and when it happened, not a soul in miles figured it had anything at all to do with Monophysitism.

There's some controversy about exactly when and where the sport was revived. Some think Wyoming, some Idaho or Nevada. Most of today's racers know of chariot races that took place in the 1920s. As Hart Grover, who sometimes races for the Rexburg Idaho Upper Valley Chariot Racing Club, says, "it probably started when fellows brought their feed teams to town." Rocky Mountain winters can be rough on cattle, and when the snow gets too deep for them to find feed, the rancher is obligated to get hay out into the winter fields any way he can. A feed team usually consists of two big draft horses yoked up to a heavy wagon full of hay.

"Up in Driggs, Idaho," Grover said, "these fellows and their feed teams would meet on the way into town and just naturally fall to racing down Main Street. First organized race I ever saw, the two guys were having an awful lot of trouble getting started, and when they got to the finish line, they both bailed out and went to fighting. I always thought when I was a kid that the finish-line fight was a part of the race."

Cal Murdock, of the Rexburg club, agrees with Grover about

the sport's modern origin. "My dad used to race the big hayracks we brought to town. It got to be a regular thing in the winter carnival in Victor, Idaho. There'd be dogsled races and horse pulls. Carnival stuff: all in good fun. Thing of it is, the hayrack races starting getting a little more serious. Guys started breeding their draft horses down to quarterhorses and thoroughbreds. They'd bring a finer breed, a faster horse, to town. Then they stopped using hayracks and started using sleighs, cutters. Pretty soon guys were making their own sleighs, real light racing cutters, specially built for speed. Well, it generated a lot of interest, and soon enough there were clubs and associations."

Only a few teams run sleighs anymore. Chariot racing is still a winter sport, but conditions vary from bare frozen tracks to packed snow or glare ice, and most racers have found wheeled chariots the best compromise for all conditions.

Unlike the Roman event, modern two-horse chariot teams generally race one-on-one. The approved distance is a quarter of a mile, "because," Cal Murdock explains, "we have to run in some below-zero weather, and the vets say a horse won't freeze its lungs at a quarter of a mile or under."

These days there are chariot-racing clubs in eight western states, where the races are run on most winter weekends.

The first race of the 1988 season was held in Bozeman, Montana, not far from where I live. It was early for the chariots—November—and the track was greasy with a thick, cold, clinging mud. The horses threw big clots of semiliquid goo back onto the drivers, so that men finished the quarter-mile looking like failed mud wrestlers. Each race, the two chariots would come thundering up on the finish line, and you could sense that, with the glop streaming off their faces like something out of a horror film, these guys couldn't see much past the reins in their hands. Just past the finish, the drivers leaned back hard, pulling the horses into a somewhat slower gallop, and outriders—men mounted on fast saddle horses—helped some of the drivers to stop.

The finish line was where you cashed in on your bets, but the races was generally won or lost at the starting gate. It is the starter's job to see that both teams—all four horses—are looking forward and have all their feet on the ground. The gun sounds, the gate slams open, and the horses break, hard. The driver is crouched down in the chariot, his elbows over a front rail built for the purpose. Drivers who don't hook their elbows over the chariot end up lying on their back just this side of the gate. On the first jump after the gun a chariot will actually be airborne for as much as forty feet.

The second move a driver makes is to transfer the reins from both hands to his driving hand. He takes the whip from his mouth with the other hand, and on the second jump, he should be whipping his slowest horse. A team that is mismatched in stride will not only be slow, it will career all over the track. After that, the race is, as Cal Murdock says, not much more "than a controlled runaway."

I was thinking about Cal's words as I stood in the chariot behind two anxious horses. These particular animals were big fellows, old and not necessarily fast anymore, but big and strong and eager. These days, the horses whose back ends I contemplated are used to train younger, faster horses. Trainers yoke up one of these big, savvy old fellows to a promising but perhaps skittish colt they think might make the grade. The older horse will break from the chute when the gate snaps open. The younger horse, must, willy-nilly, floor it for maximum horsepower or be dragged into a humiliating stumble. Horses have their pride.

"You ready?" Therol Brown asked. I had my elbows over the top rail of the chariot, and I said, "Yeah." When the gates popped open, there was a sensation of speed beyond anything I've ever felt in any vehicle, beyond what you feel astride the fastest horse. The ground is right there, whipping by at thirty or forty miles an hour, and the chariot doesn't feel entirely stable. I tried to remember to keep the reins tight so that the horses wouldn't lower their heads and flounder. Still, you can't pull back too hard, otherwise the horses will throw their heads up, slow, and eventually stop. It's a fine line. Therol Brown's advice —"Most important, remember this, don't fall out"—boomed in my brain with biblical force.

It took about twenty-six seconds, all told. After it was over, Therol Brown said, "I was happy to give you a run, but I can't believe you drove five hours through a blizzard for twenty-six seconds. That's just crazy."

I remembered a story Cal Murdock told me: "I was just on a training walk, if you can believe this, trotting around. Well, there's a tongue that goes between the two horses and holds all the weight of the chariot, and it snapped. Dumped me right between the horses, and my arms were in the double trees, and my weight held me there. My head was right between their legs, and they were running scared, just kicking away at my head. I came to in front of the grandstand, bleeding pretty bad. Most of my teeth had been kicked out, and my lower lip was cut off. I was in the hospital I don't know how long, but I lost forty pounds there."

The doctors had to wait for the swelling to go down before they could do any reconstructive surgery, but Cal continued to race. He wore a rubber mask for a while, to keep the dirt from flying into the place where his lower lip had once been. That was the year Cal Murdock won the championship.

I thought about driving five hours through a blizzard to run a couple of horses for twenty-six seconds and decided that when a chariot racer says you're crazy, it's a high compliment.

Survival Skills

▲

"I've been buried alive." The thought began tugging at the edges of my mind, punching little holes in a dream I can't recall. It felt like morning, but the world was black and seamless, dark as death. I was still half-asleep, and it would be, oh, minutes until Panic Central kicked in. I fumbled around in what must have been my own sleeping bag and got a hand free. The black world was solid as rock and bitterly cold to the touch. Fascinating: not only buried alive but packed in ice to boot.

Panic Central attempted to activate the scream-and-gibber mechanism, but it was too early for anything as strenuous as full-bore hysteria. And then it occurred to me, in the midst of a yawn, that I had done this thing to myself. I had just spent my first full night in a snow cave. And survived. Comfortably.

The concepts of survival and comfort were on my mind because my projected three-day trip had turned grim. I had come out to the mountains to do some late-spring ski camping, and had driven to the trailhead confident of good weather. But the jet stream had confounded forecasters: It had unexpectedly looped down over southwestern Montana, bringing cold and snow and wind in such abundance that I felt as if I were being crushed under a fast-moving glacier.

No matter. A man who ventures into the northern Rockies, even as late as April, had better be prepared regardless of the forecast. From the skin out I had worn four layers of chemical clothing, bundled up against what the tiny thermometer hanging from the zipper of my parka had said was an honest 20 below.

I had packed a good mountain tent along with a light, collapsible aluminum shovel. Having set up the tent as a backup, I began digging the cave. Every woodsy survival book you read about this process says it's a piece of cake. This is a lie. Three times I had attempted to build snow caves; three times I had failed.

On my third attempt I discovered that digging through the powder into a sloping drift is a good way to find snow amenable to shaping, and for the first time my cave did not collapse. But I was still both cold and wet. When I mentioned the problem to an acquaintance who had taken a military pilot's survival course in Antarctica, he asked how high I had made my sleeping ledge. "You have to build a ledge?" I asked.

The ledge, I was told, is what keeps a person warm and dry. Cold, dense air sinks to the bottom of the cave, where I had tried to sleep. There had also been an icy puddle there, on the floor of the shelter, because I had cooked dinner, and the camp stove had set the walls to sweating. The ceiling had dripped steadily—it was like living in Seattle—and I evacuated to my backup tent in the dead of night.

This time I had managed to put it all together. Even built a right-angle tunnel into the cave to keep out the wind. Now, my watch said it was 9:00 A.M., but there was no light at the end of the tunnel where the entrance should have been.

I knew, somewhere in the back of my mind, that blowing snow must have drifted over the mouth of the cave, and Panic Central went back on alert. I began to move for the entrance, hit the drift at a crawl that approached warp speed, and came bursting out in an explosion of powder.

The sky was a silvery sheen; the world was white and un-marked, and it hurt my eyes to look at it. Above, at about ten thousand feet, the wind was whipping sheets of powdery snow off cornices that hung cantilevered over the steepest slopes. I was in the lee of the range, sheltered from the high, blasting wind that was pushing the storm east across the valley and into the face of the mountains that rose beyond.

My camp offered an unobstructed view of the valley and the summits to the east. I dug a kind of futuristic snow chair into the slope, lined it with the foam pad that I use under my sleeping bag, and settled back to watch wind and weather in battle with the land. I found myself thinking about the snow cave as fact and the snow cave as fantasy; thinking, in other words, about sur-vival.

My survival fantasies usually involve some unexpected but un-avoidable catastrophe followed by heroic efforts on my part. Equipment is minimal, sometimes nonexistent, and I often have to outwit small, furry animals that become my dinner. In my fantasy everything works. Snow caves don't collapse. Bunnies blunder blindly into my traps. Trout leap into the waiting pan. I am seldom uncomfortable in these waking dreams.

Reality is less pleasant. On one memorable summer trip my brother and I actually wandered into the mountains for a week-end carrying only a bag of gorp, two knives, and a pair of space blankets. We failed to build a fish trap that would trap fish. The lean-to fell over. We froze to death and died, or at least felt as if we had.

What had gone wrong? Hadn't I spent days poring over the woodcraft manuals, imagining various clever scenarios? "Visual-izing," the sports psychologists call it. Mentally rehearsing an ac-tivity, so the theory runs, is a form of preparation. What I discovered, shivering under the space blanket, is the difference between imagination and visualization. In fantasy the snow cave is a solution, cleverly conceived, and it sort of digs itself. In proper visualization you concentrate on the mechanics of excava-tion, a process that is impossible unless you have attempted to dig at least one snow cave before. In other words, visualization without some small experience is mere fantasy.

And it is just this sort of fantasy I see being sold these days on television in the form of what I like to call the Amazing Survival Knife. The thing costs ten bucks, but if you order *now,* you also get: a needle and some thread (shot of a guy sewing up his tent), *and* a hook and line (shot of some fellow landing a three-pound fish at the edge of a lake), *and* a saw *actually capable of cutting down small trees* (shot of two guys using this saw, crosscut fashion, to topple a small tree). All of this gear fits into the hilt of the knife. Order within twenty-four hours and the distributor will add, *absolutely free,* a camouflage sheath for the Amazing Survival Knife.

The commercial did not claim that the knife slices, dices, or makes hundreds and hundreds of julienne fries in just seconds, but it was pretty clear that the distributor was selling survival in the manner that others sell kitchen aids. Clearly, the concept—or more precisely, the fantasy—of self-sufficiency and survival in the wilderness has become a salable item.

The same fantasy accounts for the popularity of James Fenimore Cooper's *Leatherstocking Tales* in the early 1800s; or the blizzard of newspaper stories about Joseph Knowles nearly a century later. In 1913 Knowles, a part-time illustrator, stripped naked in front of a phalanx of reporters and strode boldly into the Maine woods. Two months later he returned, presumably none the worse for wear. "My God is the wilderness," he told the newspapers. "My church is the church of the forest."

We like to think that the rigors of this wild land shaped the national character. We believe that in the ability to survive there is nobility and grace. And for ten bucks you can buy a knife that will ensure your survival. Carry it through the mosquitoes into some woodsy noble church and you're prepared for all eventualities. Or so the commercial seemed to imply.

It is a dangerous dream, I think, the fantasy of the knife. There is an unsupported supposition lurking in the subtext of the sales pitch: that survival is a matter of owning the proper gear. In point of fact, owning such a knife is rather like eating chicken soup to cure a cold: It can't hurt, and maybe it'll help. Just so. Toting the Amazing Survival Knife into the forest won't turn a novice into a competent woodsman, just as owning a fine set of tools doesn't necessarily make a man a good carpenter. We need to practice survival skills, to draw lessons out of early failure.

I had used my cheapest and most sissified piece of high-tech camping gear—a ninety-nine cent butane lighter—to build a small fire, which was now sinking into the snow with a satisfying hiss. The two hours' supply of wood I'd collected from a nearby creek bank was stacked in such a way that I could feed the fire without rising from my wilderness recliner.

In the distance the snow was no longer snow. It was a dirty silver cloud that completely engulfed the eastern mountains, and it lay like a blanket a thousand feet above the valley floor. Directly above, the sky was an impossible cobalt blue, that bright, soaring, clear blue color that comes in the aftermath of a storm.

And now, to the east, the sun—which had been a small silver disk feebly glowing behind the cloud—burst above the snow and weather. It caught the edge of the cloud for a moment so that its full light was momentarily broken and prismatic pinks played across the wall of cloud. Sunrise at noon.

The fact that I had finally succeeded in building a proper snow cave somehow enhanced the view. I had turned a longtime fantasy into reality, building on three successive failures. Nobody ever wants to tell you that you must pay for your fantasy, and that the price is early failure and frustration.

It was still cold—ten below—and there was snow in the air under the blue sky. Tiny diamond crystals, remnants of the night's storm, were drifting about on the wind and catching the sun's light so that, in the valley, above the blanket of cloud, dull pastel rainbows formed. I thought about all those collapsed snow caves, about the Amazing Survival Knife and the failures of fantasy, while the sun and snow made kaleidoscopic patterns in the sky.

The Tomfoolery Factor

▲

When a jackass flies, no one asks how far or how fast. When a jackass flies, people stand amazed. Follow me through on this. One day last October I played my harmonica hanging from a half-mile-long rope anchored at the top of El Capitan. Even though absolutely no one was there to stand amazed, the jackass had sprouted wings. I am absurdly smug about this accomplishment.

The rope had been rigged by a group of rappellers I had once worked with in the southeast, led by a man named Dan Twilley. El Cap is one of the longest overhanging cliffs in the world, and this was the second-longest free-fall rappel ever made on a single rope: 2,650 feet to be exact. The longest was a 3,280-foot drop made in 1980 off Mount Thor on Baffin Island, also led by Twilley.

The rappel was wonderfully terrifying fun. The whole of Yosemite Valley was spread out below me, and as I'd chosen to make my descent just at twilight, I owned half an hour's worth of sunset. Somewhere toward the bottom of the cliff, about three hundred feet above the tops of the trees, I tied off for a few minutes and played some slow and slightly breathless blues.

These blues were not committed on pure impulse. In fact, I had planned it all out ahead of time, had put my harp in a shirt pocket where I could get to it easily, and had even practiced the solo I wanted to play.

It should be understood here that I'm not really any good at the harmonica. People who've heard me often offer such helpful advice as "Shut up with that noise." It's not really my fault, of course. I figure that if I had a nickname, my playing might improve. Hard-blues players all have nicknames: Sonny Boy Williamson, Little Walter, Magic Dick. Some people probably go to hear Norton Buffalo play for his name alone. Buffalo is an incredible harmonica player, no doubt about it. And those who think they can play harp will, after attending a concert by Mr. Buffalo, go home contemplating suicide. I mean, Norton, I admire him—*but has he ever played harp in free-fall rappel?*

I think I can safely say that my harp solo was the very best ever played while hanging from a half-mile-long rope.

This is the sort of attitude my friend Rick Ridgeway calls rank tomfoolery, defined here as the urge to perform essentially civilized acts in uncivilized or extraordinary places. Some people, for instance, have played Frisbee on glaciers, wearing crampons; and a hot campfire topic among climbers has always been the highest-known performance of the sex act. (Ridgeway's estimate of the current record is twenty-six thousand feet.)

Incidentally, I don't count marriages performed in unusual places as tomfoolery. Those who have tied the knot in free-fall while skydiving, for instance, may seem to fit the definition. This is, after all, a civilized act committed in a hostile environment. Marriage, however, is a chancy endeavor. Presumably, the skydiving couple has some experience in free-fall relative work, and reason, history, and experience all conspire to inform them that they will land on their feet. There are no such guarantees about the marriage. It is risk incarnate.

No, tomfoolery doesn't put a person at any *emotional* risk. On the contrary, I think the impulse is an antidote to fear, and some small comfort in a situation where comfort is hard to come by. It is a form of pioneering, a way of making a hostile environment your own. And in my case it may have something to do with incompetence: Those who lack great skill in some human endeavor—say, playing the harmonica—are spiritually buoyed by the fact that perhaps no one else, ever, has committed this particular act under these exact circumstances.

For some reason golf lends itself to the cold comfort of perennial tomfoolery. I suspect this is because it's a game that daily slaps people in the face with their own incompetence. "The game may frustrate me," people seem to say, "but I'm the only person in the world to be frustrated in this precise spot." Yvon Chouinard, for instance, once played a short game at the base of Fitzroy, in Patagonia.

Probably the height of tomfoolery—the highest-known incident —occurred in February of 1971, when Alan Shepard swatted a golf ball. He had a dusty lie, his swing was cramped, bunched up, and he missed the sweet spot. The guy really didn't connect well. No big deal—the point is not that it wasn't done well, but that it was done at all. Shepard played golf on the lunar highlands, in temperatures that stood near 230 degrees Fahrenheit. It was sublime tomfoolery.

True, the force required to drive a golf ball three hundred yards on the earth would translate to a milelong drive on the moon, but a space suit tends to hamper the swing. The longest drive ever recorded anywhere in the universe was an entirely earthbound effort. In 1962 an Australian meteorologist named Nils Lied teed off just outside Mawson Base in Antarctica and drove the ball about a mile and a half across the ice.

Rick Ridgeway is also guilty of some astounding tomfoolery in Antarctica. I'm thinking specifically of the time he went waterskiing just before winter closed down the continent. "We were staying at this Argentine base down there," says Rick, "and those people treated us like kings. Well, we wanted to give them something, but we were traveling light and didn't have anything of material value for them. The only thing we could do was provide a little entertainment."

Ridgeway and his companion, Mike Graber, rigged up a sixteen-foot rubber raft with a twenty-five-horsepower Evinrude and tied a rope to the raft. This left the problem of finding suitable skis. Somehow they'd forgotten their water skis when they'd packed for Antarctica. "We finally decided to try our cross-country sleds," says Rick. "These were fiberglass gadgets, about eight feet long, and instead of runners we had plates of Teflon on the bottom."

Ridgeway piloted the raft, while Graber attempted to ski in between the icebergs. "I don't think he'd ever water-skied before," explains Ridgeway, "and it took quite a while before he got up and we got the sled up on plane." After some private practice Graber and Ridgeway decided they were ready. "We knew the Argentines always ate lunch in front of a big picture window that looked out onto this gorgeous bay. So there they were when we came roaring into view at full throttle. Graber had on a dry suit, but he was wearing a rain jacket and pants over it, so it looked like he was skiing out there in a light jacket and pants. The water temperature was twenty-nine degrees. It wanted to be ice, but the salt content was still a tad too high."

Ridgeway remembers the Argentines coming out of the lunchroom "hooting and hollering, cheering. . . ."

They weren't cheering because Graber had dazzled them with his display of virtuoso waterskiing technique. He wasn't even very good. They were cheering the impulse, the ingenuity, the beautiful absurdity of the act. They were cheering baldfaced incompetence and the pioneering spirit. They were cheering a couple of jackasses in flight.

The Dangerous Sports Club

▲

"You understand why we are holding you?" the British police officer asked.

I was standing before a large desk in a police substation just outside Bristol, England.

In the background several officers were discussing my belt and glasses. I could, perhaps, in a fit of remorse over having watched three guys in tuxedos safely jump off a bridge on elastic "bungee" cords, find myself so filled with remorse that I might hang myself with the belt. Break my glasses and cut my wrists.

"We'll have to put you in a cell with one of the others," an officer said. "Do you have a preference?"

"I don't know any of these guys," I said. "Except Mr. Kirke."

"Mr. Kirke," the officer said. He said it as if he'd heard that name before. He said it as if he knew about all the previous arrests: as if he knew about the giant inflatable melon ball that smashed into a huge pylon and blacked out an entire town; as if he knew about the helium-filled kangaroo that crossed the English Channel at ten thousand feet and had commercial pilots shaking their heads in disbelief. Maybe the officer knew about the grand pianos on skis, or the Kirke-piloted baby carriages careening down hillsides, or the bridge jumps and catapults. Or the giant pink elephants skittering across the surface of Loch Ness. Maybe he knew more than he wanted to know about Kirke and his friends—gentlemen in morning coats and top hats, ladies in formal dresses—thumbing their noses at convention and having entirely too much fun.

"Mr. Kirke," the officer said again. He said it as if the knowledge of this name made him tired.

My cellmate was named Bill, and he was nineteen years old. Bill had not jumped off the bridge, though he was implicated in the jump in that he served champagne to the jumpers and had been wearing a gorilla suit and did help retrieve the elastic cords after the jumpers had lowered themselves on separate climbing ropes and escaped in a boat waiting below. The police had arrived at that time and stared down at the boat, 160 feet below, where the three jumpers and two boat men, all in tuxedos, toasted them with brimming champagne glasses and roared off down the Severn River.

It was this final gesture, I think, that irritated the officers, and comparatively innocent spectators, like myself, were arrested. Bill, as a gorilla, had offered the police some champagne. Now, they had his gorilla suit in the property room—evidence!—and he was in this little cell, five steps long by three wide, and the two of us were sitting on either side of the single cot in the cell. The door was heavy metal, six inches thick, with a single latched window the size of a book in it. The window was shut.

Seven hours later, about four that afternoon, I "helped the police with their inquiries" in the squad room. Officers had diagramed the morning's antics on a blackboard, the way you see TV cops list the clues in a serial-killing case. There was a category called "jumpers," and a description of three men: "first off, blond, 30s." Beside that was the word "boat," followed by more descriptions, and then a section titled "on the bridge," where my name appeared followed by a description, "beard, US."

A courteous officer sat across the table from me. The English officers were so courteous, in fact, that I imagined I was dealing with a very refined form of sarcasm. I glanced out a barred window. David Kirke was sitting on the grass out there, waiting for me, I hoped, and smoking a cigar. He was free as a bird. Kirke had a lot of experience with this sort of thing and had phoned a lawyer in London immediately.

The officer followed my gaze and said, "We released Mr. Kirke without charge." He sounded courteously disappointed about this. "Could you tell me, please, where you met this David Kirke."

"In a pub, north of London, yesterday afternoon."

"And he told you about the Dangerous Sports Club?"

"We discussed it, yes."

Kirke, forty-four, was a burly, pleasantly articulate man with graying hair and protuberant blue eyes full of intelligence and the sort of brilliant innocence inherent only to honest scoundrels. David Kirke, I knew, had once jumped off the Golden Gate Bridge in San Francisco, on bungee cords. That was back in 1979, when I was living there, and I recall the pictures in the papers, along with the rather classic note distributed on site. "We would ask you not to be alarmed. With the possible exception of the jumpers, nobody is subject to danger or inconvenience and there is no reason why one should not proceed about one's business mildly encouraged that it is no longer necessary to get one's feet wet as circumstances force one to jump off a bridge. Bungee jumping (sometimes known as the failure's failure) is merely another attempt to celebrate the strain and tensions of urban life in a suitably dignified manner."

Having disseminated this message, Kirke, smoking a pipe and dressed in a top hat and morning coat, stepped nonchalantly off the 245-foot-high span, plummeted toward certain death, then snapped back to about the 120-foot level and bounced there. He was accompanied by three other men and one woman.

The five jumpers were fined ten dollars apiece for trespassing, and the great columnist for the *San Francisco Chronicle* Herb Caen celebrated the leap in his column. He found front-page pictures of these goofballs hanging off the bridge a fine change from a usual urban front page, fraught, as it is, with death and kidnapping and corruption.

A decade later I ran into David Kirke in the north of England, at an inn near the border of Scotland. Over a light lunch of finely sliced goose breast and horseradish followed by poached salmon in dill sauce—Kirke enjoys fine dining—we talked a bit about how a man comes to make his living inventing and participating in extremely silly but nonetheless life-threatening sports.

As a boy, Kirke explained, he had read Jack Kerouac's work, especially *On the Road,* and found it full of sensible ideas about "mobility and the reasonable pursuit of sensation," all of which seemed to combine nicely with Kerouac's "healthy distrust of bureaucratic authority." Kirke had attended Oxford and studied English. He was especially fond of Proust and Faulkner and went on to lecture at Oxford, though some of his opinions were considered a bit odd. "Freud," Kirke avers, "is best read as a romantic novelist." When such opinions are the stuff of dangerous controversy, some men feel there is not enough dangerous controversy in their lives.

At Oxford in 1976 Kirke teamed with Edward Hulton in an effort to produce a little real danger in his life. They would try out some traditional sports. Supposedly dangerous ones. Life-threatening ones.

With one day's practice they ran the Muattetal, the Olympic whitewater canoeing course in Switzerland. And survived. They raced ice boats. They tried out the Cresta run, a tiny toboggan a man rides on his stomach, like a sled. They climbed the Matterhorn.

"We discovered," Kirke told me over the salmon, "that a lot of sports were invented a hundred years ago and that they have become formalized. They are not nearly so dangerous as practitioners would have us believe. You can learn them rapidly enough using the deep-immersion principle. It becomes an almost philosophical point: Sport today is bedeviled by neosubprofessionals. You cannot just go and learn to scuba-dive anymore. You have to take a forty-hour course over the period of eight weeks and pay someone to tell you things that are available to you in hundreds of books. We found, in Switzerland, that we could save various fees, learn to do things faster, and learn better, because we put our faith in ourselves."

Kirke and Hulton, reacting to the mere whiff of bureaucratic authority in traditional sports, began to invent their own. They built a biplane that should have flown like a hang glider. It stalled and crashed from seventy feet, but Kirke emerged unscathed. "It was the beginning of a delusion," Kirke said, "that my luck would hold in nasty situations."

About that time, Kirke heard about a man named Chris Baker who had one of the new regallo-wing hang gliders that were built to prevent stalls. After a suitable amount of lying about his expertise, Kirke was allowed to fly the glider and—since it was a new sport with no regulation and no bureaucracy—became enamored. The three men—Kirke, Hulton, Baker—expanded on their philosophy at local pubs and lighted on the idea of a club for those who might like to engage in dangerous sports. It could be called, yes, the Dangerous Sports Club. "Precisely," Hulton said. "And our symbol should be a black wheelchair on a sea of blood."

Pub talk.

There was a hang-glider club at Oxford—the Poisonous Butterflies—and the two clubs evolved together to the point that a philosophy jelled: "picnic, drink, run, glide, crash." The colleges of Oxford, many of them founded in the mid-twelfth century, are architecturally magnificent, and Oxford is often called the "city of dreaming spires." By the late seventies, men and women in odd costumes—gorilla suits, for instance—were flying off the dreaming spires, buzzing over garden parties, irritating scowling dons, stampeding the string quartets. Poisonous Butterflies. Dangerous Sports. An arrest here and there.

After an especially formal wedding, the club flew directly to Greece, climbed Mount Olympus, and, still dressed in their wedding finery, launched hang gliders from the summit. (It was David Kirke's fifth flight.) The formal attire felt right. Dangerous stunts should be performed calmly, with dignity and reserve. No gratuitous chest thumping. Formal attire became the club's trademark. People who value decorum and tradition, of course, cringe at the sight. The formalwear tweaks their noses.

"It's a private joke," Kirke said.

Because stunts are performed in the garb of the upper class, the Dangerous Sports Club is thought to be composed entirely of upper-class twits. The press is partially to blame: Sons and daughters of tycoons or members of Parliament get more ink when arrested. Motorcycle mechanics are seldom mentioned. In point of fact the club—which has a shifting membership of perhaps thirty to forty at any one time—encompasses all classes of British society. The only requirements seem to be a certain amount of brain-damaged courage combined with a sense of humor and a flair for the preposterous.

For instance, Chris Baker had always wanted to go to New Guinea and do some vine jumping, that rite of manhood in which young men leap from high towers with springy vines tied to an ankle and are brought up short inches of the forest floor. A quick check with the airlines indicated that the trip was entirely too expensive. What's more, there were probably some rules about jumping. Like maybe you had to be from New Guinea.

Chris wouldn't let go of the idea, however. Perhaps there were similar vines in England. Or . . . or how about a technological solution? And it occurred to David Kirke, who had always loved airplanes, who had built model planes as a child, that the elastic bungee cords used to hold his glider to the roof of a car for transportation were very like the heavy-duty cords used on large aircraft carriers to stop landing supersonic jets. Yes. Surely, such cords could be substituted for jungle vines.

"As far as I know," David Kirke said, "we were the first people to do bungee-cord jumping."

In newspaper articles about the club it is often said that stunts are undertaken with no training and no knowledge of possible outcomes. "Not true," Kirke says. "In point of fact we did computer models for our first jump. One of the people working on it later shared a Nobel Prize, and one is now working on advanced laser technology. The numbers said we wouldn't die."

Rather than build a proper tower for the jump, however, the

boys chose the Clifton Suspension Bridge, the highest bridge in all of England. They jumped. They survived. They were arrested.

The Clifton Suspension Bridge by some quirk of coincidence was precisely as high as the Golden Gate Bridge—245 feet to the water in each case. It seemed only appropriate. . . .

"So you met this fellow in a pub and he said what?" the courteous officer wanted to know.

"He said 'a few of the lads were going to have a go at one of the bridges.' "

"It is time," David Kirke had said soon after I met him, "to let a few of the younger members organize a jump. I suspect they will all be arrested."

We were standing in Kirke's office, a large airplane hangar of a building in an industrial park in the north of England. A section of the hangar had been partitioned off to create an office containing the inevitable fax machine, copier, phone, and computer. A sign on the inside of the door read, YOU'VE HAD YOUR BREAK. IT IS NOT FIVE O'CLOCK. Off in a corner was another small room containing a bed and a pile of books perhaps three feet high. There were books by Graham Greene and Proust; there were biographies and reference books; there were cookbooks and thrillers: It was the helter-skelter collection of a man in love with words. The rest of the place was strewn with coiled bungee cords, more stacks of books, a broken biplane hanging from the ceiling, a huge wooden horse on skis, something that looked like a mummified human being or a cartoon accident victim in bandages—"That's Eric, the club mascot," Kirke explained—and several immense deflated inflatable devices.

Kirke gave me five large scrapbooks full of newspaper clippings about club activities, most of which made the paper due to subsequent arrests. I was sitting out under the biplane, next to Eric, the mummy, perusing the club's dozen years of inspired lunacy. Kirke had provided me with a glass of hundred-year-old sherry and a Havana cigar. "It was," Kirke said, "Oscar Wilde who pointed out that the necessities of life are a luxury; the luxuries are a necessity. This is an epigram to cling to when you live in a tin shack several hundred miles north of London."

The sherry was dry and warm as the Iberian Desert, and the archives were remarkable. Here were men in tuxedos skiing down the green hills of Ireland on skis made of ice. There was a photo of the elegantly garbed gentlemen running with the bulls at the Feast of San Fermin, in Pamplona, Spain, where every year hundreds of young men run through the narrow cobblestone streets chased by at least six killer bulls. Every few years someone is gored to death. To say that Kirke and company ran with the bulls is not entirely accurate: They rolled out ahead of the bulls, on skateboards. Wearing morning coats and top hats.

As far as I could tell, it took two years for club members to squander any money they had, and by 1978 they were looking for sponsors. An independent producer for the BBC signed on to film a DSC (Dangerous Sports Club) gliding expedition off Mount Kilimanjaro. The proper permits were secured, but DSC members were required to climb the nineteen-thousand-foot peak in forty-eight hours. (The trip usually takes six days.) Kirke, a man who has difficulty distinguishing sporting activities from party time, who prides himself on his lack of physical fitness and training, left younger men gasping on the trek. Others suffered from altitude sickness and descended. Not Kirke. The two best hang gliders in the group crashed on takeoff. (No one was hurt.) Kirke launched perfectly. It was his thirteenth flight.

Unfortunately, he flew directly into a cloud, and the BBC got precisely twelve seconds of his backside disappearing into an impenetrable mist. Kirke flew blind, without compass or altimeter, made his way through the cloud, and landed in a coffee plantation twenty-five miles away. There was, of course, no film to defray the costs. Kirke and the club owed over ten thousand dollars in room-service charges alone.

Happily, the producers of the American TV show *That's Incredible!* paid the club eighteen thousand dollars to attempt a bungee-cord jump off the world's highest bridge, the 1,260-foot-high Royal Gorge Bridge spanning the Arkansas River just outside Canon City, Colorado. It was an entirely successful endeavor.

"If there is any terror that unites us," Kirke said of the members of the DSC, "it's the terror of having to take a conventional job." Hereafter, they would attempt to fill the club coffers with money from televised stunts or from advertisers clever enough to hire the club to promote their products.

In the early eighties, for three winters running, club members traveled to St. Moritz, in Switzerland, there to demonstrate, for an international TV audience, alternative skiing techniques. One madman took the ski jump in a lawn chair on skis. Others confined themselves to the slopes. People rode huge wooden horses over the moguls; they piloted biplanes, or stepladders, or bathtubs on skis. Two formally dressed gentlemen rocketed down an expert run at forty miles an hour sitting behind a grand piano.

"It was actually quite a technological challenge, fixing the skis to the grand piano," Kirke said.

"It was a hollowed-out piano, though," I said.

Kirke was offended. "It was a perfectly functional grand piano."

"They didn't actually play. . . ."

"Indeed they did," Kirke said, a bit huffily, I thought. "I believe it was Chopin's *Polonaise in C Minor*. A nobly tragic work, appropriate, I think, and very competently played, given the circumstances." Kirke paused and brightened considerably. "You know," he said, "television footage of our alternative ski devices has been shown all over the world. I have a friend who is a TV producer, and he was doing some documentary work in Africa, I don't know where, say the Kalahari Desert. Swaziland. He had some of these ski tapes and showed them to the people there. Understand, this was in a mud hut, with the electronics running off a gasoline generator, and the audience was composed of people who had never seen snow. And they were rolling on the ground laughing. They loved the spectacular crashes. Now I haven't cleaned up the pollution in our world, or halted the threat of nuclear war, and I would do that if I could, but I can safely say that I have made perhaps half a billion people laugh in my life. There is some small importance to that."

"Did you realize," the police officer asked, "that people could be severely injured, indeed killed, jumping off the bridge like that?"

"I suppose I did."

"And in spite of that, you chose to watch."

"In all honesty," I said, "it made me laugh."

The officer stared at me with courteous disapproval. "It doesn't make me laugh."

The officer's attitude—stiff, proper, stern—brought the beginnings of an involuntary giggle up from the pit of my stomach. I swallowed hard and tried to look remorseful.

"We didn't think about that, did we," the officer asked.

Kirke sometimes actually pulls off an event without getting arrested. He once attempted to fly an ultralight—a kind of hang-gliding device equipped with a propeller and snowmobile engine —across the English Channel. "It was," Kirke said, "a hundred-ten-pound machine, carrying one-hundred-thirteen pounds of fuel and a hundred-sixty-pound navigator." The first attempt was a dismal failure. Kirke crashed into a tree only fourteen miles from takeoff. The second attempt was a success. Kirke flew four and a half hours at two thousand feet, landed in a field, and almost immediately heard the far-off sounds of police sirens, coming closer. A woman in a nearby farmhouse motioned to him: hurry, hurry. Kirke packed up his gear, and the woman guided him to a hidden attic room. "As it happened," Kirke explained to me, "during the Second World War, when France was occupied, this courageous woman had hidden downed British pilots in that very room. She had a certificate of appreciation from the Dutch and British governments." Kirke hid out for a day, savoring the romance of the situation, then escaped.

He wasn't so lucky a few years later when he flew a giant inflatable kangaroo across the channel. The impossible kangaroo hung from several helium-filled balloons, and Kirke piloted the beast from its pouch. "Really," Kirke said, "it was a childhood fantasy: a little boy holding on to some balloons, floating through the air."

Kirke made the crossing at about ten thousand feet and was losing altitude rapidly when he sighted land. The stunt was sponsored by Fosters, the fine Australian beer, and though it hurt him deeply, Kirke was forced to toss out several cases to gain a bit of altitude and avoid some power lines. "I kept a prudent supply," Kirke explained, "but helium balloons are at the complete mercy of the wind, and I could see that I was coming very close to the cross atop a church steeple." It rained cans of Fosters on the churchyard, and Kirke cleared the holy structure by less than a foot. "I truly didn't want to damage a church," Kirke said. "I know they would have been miffed."

Instead, Kirke was merely arrested for not filing a proper flight plan or having a pilot's license. It cost him about eight hundred dollars in all.

Inflatable gadgets occupied his mind for some time. There is the giant inflatable pink elephant he rode across Loch Ness. And the Midori melon ball got a lot of press.

Midori is a Japanese melon liqueur, and Kirke decided to build the largest inflatable melon he could. It stuck him as a distinctive and amusing advertising stunt. The melon ball is sixty-five to seventy feet in diameter. Inside is a gimbal device that keeps the "navigator" upright no matter which way the ball may roll.

It had been thought that, if the winds were right, the massive melon could roll across the Channel from England to France. Kirke's trial run was a disaster. The melon was inflated on a lake north of London. A brisk wind sprang up and seized the melon, which, after all, was about the size of a five-story building. The wind sent the inflatable melon skidding and rolling across the lake. Nothing could stop the giant melon ball. It rolled over a car, causing no damage. It rolled across a roadway, accompanied now by the squeal of tires. "You have to calculate the weight of the air inside the melon ball," Kirke said, "to understand what happened next."

A ball seventy feet in diameter contains about two tons of air. The rogue melon rolled into a cement light post twenty-five feet high and "mashed it." It finally came to rest against an electric pylon, toppled it slightly, and effectively blacked out the town of Telford for some time.

Later Kirke had the melon ball towed between two barges down the Thames, past the houses of Parliament, and everything went swimmingly until a metal towing cable snapped, rebounded against the melon, and punctured it. Kirke felt the enormous thing collapsing around him, cutting off his air. The deflated melon began to sink. Kirke cut his way out with a knife and was —humiliation—rescued by the river police. "Of course," he told the press, "I'm a bit melancholy. Still, this is in the finest British tradition of vessels that sink on their maiden voyage. I'm thinking specifically of the *Titanic*."

"We are not charging you," the polite officer said, in the same tone that a priest might say, "Go and sin no more."

David Kirke and I drove immediately to London, where he had made reservations at a Russian restaurant famous for its quality caviar and vodka. A young woman who works for the British equivalent of MTV was waiting for him in a private booth. I mentioned that my seven hours in jail had provided me with "all the fun of being in the club and none of the risk."

"Just so," Kirke agreed. We discussed his latest adventure, which involved a catapult powered by bungee cords used by twenty-one governments worldwide to deploy drone aircraft. The drones, which go from zero to sixty miles an hour in a second, are used to test weapons systems. Kirke rigged a chair and had himself catapulted over a 650-foot-high cliff in Ireland. He took ten Gs, did not pass out, went from zero to sixty in a second and a half, and managed to deploy his parachute with, oh, dozens of feet to spare.

This stunt was for a Japanese television program, and Kirke was touched that some of the female production assistants had burst into grateful tears when they saw him land safely. Usually, he gets arrested.

We had the lemon-grass vodka delivered in an iced carafe along with great quantities of caviar. Kirke talked about one of the first

DSC events: a party on Rockall, a remote island 220 miles west of Scotland, five days' hard sailing from the mainland. The islet is bounded by walls seventy feet high that are difficult to climb in a tux while hauling a backpack full of champagne and the proper glasses, not to mention caviar with the proper trimmings. Such a party is best ended by a seventy-foot jump into a churning, rocky tidal pool. Kirke had no experience diving, but, as he explains, "I could swim."

In the DSC the idea of sport as a party somehow got confused with the idea of the party as an art form. Kirke had noticed that people attending art-show openings never looked at the art. They drank the wine, ate the cheese, but never looked at the art. Kirke and company sent out invitations to all the movers and shakers in London's art world. It was to be a private viewing of the emerging "Neoclassical School of Futurism." Placed on the wall, inside classical frames, were glasses of spirits, expensive hors d'oeuvres, and full meals prepared by celebrated chefs. "It was," Kirke recalled, "a pleasure watching gallery-going sponge artists stare at all this food and drink. They were afraid to touch it. It was art. It took quite some time for people to realize that the party was the art. And the art was the party. After that it was quite a success: a sixty-broken-glass cocktail party."

We threw down another glass of lemon-grass vodka in the traditional manner. "The police," I said, "don't get it. They said I should ask you what you think you are doing with your life."

Kirke thought it over for a second. He said, "I like to think we in the Dangerous Sports Club hark back to the flamboyant bohemianism of Paris circa 1900, when artists walked lobsters on pink ribbons, and there was a sense that art was something worth dying for." The founder and director of the Dangerous Sports Club signaled for more caviar. "I like to think that what I do closes the gap between parties and life, between living and art, between art and sport."

"Sir?" The waiter was standing at our table.

"More of the beluga," Kirke said, "and perhaps a spot of champagne."

The Howlings

▲

I suppose most people were asleep when it began, but I suspect that many in Juneau were awakened by the continual barking and howling of the dogs. It was a cacophony beyond the usual level of canine complaint, beyond "I'm cold" or "I'm hungry" or "I'm bored" or "there's a real loud motorcycle going by at about fifty miles an hour, and I'd sure as hell chase it down if I had the time." No, these Alaskan dogs were responding to some primeval instinct welling up from below the level of domesticity. In the dark of a moonless night they were howling at an eerie, cold fire sweeping across the sky.

It was one of the more spectacular northern-lights displays anyone in southeast Alaska could remember. The early October weather was fine: a cloudless and balmy 40 degrees at 2:00 A.M. Parents woke their children, and entire families stood out in the middle of residential streets staring up into the living sky. The dark surrounding mountains looked two-dimensional, like cardboard cutouts, and a dim glow played off the highest ridges. Above, the moving curtains of pale green were so vivid that they colored the upturned faces of sleepy kids and wondering adults. If you gave the lights any explanation other than the natural one and added the helpless howling of the dogs as a sound track, this would have been the best scene in an otherwise very bad movie titled *Invasion from Planet X.*

Several days later I was a hundred miles northwest, at the terminus of a long, narrow fjord known as Glacier Bay. Two hundred years ago the bay did not exist. In 1794 explorer Captain George Vancouver observed an ice sheet almost a mile thick and twenty miles wide in what is now the mouth of Glacier Bay. Over the past two centuries the great glacier has been in retreat, and the ocean has followed it to reclaim the deep valleys. The once-monolithic wall of ice has broken into sixteen tidewater glaciers, still grumbling and thundering their way back up into the mountains where they were born. Tides rise and fall as much as twenty feet in Glacier Bay, and these waters eat away at the feet of the dying glaciers. Daily, as the tide ebbs, a new shelf of ice hangs over the sea below. When the weakened ice gives way, blue-green pillars up to two hundred feet high come crashing into the water in an explosion of spray.

I was kayaking Glacier Bay with photographer Paul Dix. We'd spent a few nights on the bare headland across from Riggs Glacier and two more nights near Muir Glacier, on the eastern arm of Glacier Bay. This land that emerged, in the wake of the retreating glaciers, was all bare rock and talus. In a few years a feltlike algal nap will cover the rocks, retaining moisture and stabilizing glacial silt. Next will come moss, then small, flowering plants, followed by an impenetrable morass of alder breaks. These pioneer plants enrich the nitrogen-deficient soil so that, over the years, spruce and hemlock will shade out the alder. Bartlett Cove, at the mouth of Glacier Bay, has a lush, far-north rain forest, and the forest floor is alive with ferns and swampy muskeg.

We were seventy miles from the living land, in the cove that contains McBride Glacier. Dix wanted to take advantage of the fine weather to shoot what we hoped would be some spectacular photographs. John Muir described Glacier Bay as "dim, dreary, and mysterious," but this day the sky was a deep-water blue and the temperature stood at 55 degrees Fahrenheit. The wall of ice glittered in the sun. Dix beached his kayak and climbed a talus slope that rises to the glacier's south edge. We both knew that quicksand often covers the edges of such glaciers and that it was foolish for him to climb alone, without a rope. But Dix is an experienced mountaineer, and he assured me that he could handle it. I could see him, standing on the ice at the edge of McBride Glacier, and I knew that the ice was moving imperceptibly and that he was surrounded by crevasses on all sides.

I could just barely make him out up there, a tiny silhouette with the sun behind it. He waved his arm, a signal for me to paddle my kayak toward the groaning wall of ice. I couldn't move at top speed because the water was littered with chunks of icebergs that had calved off the wall. Some were the size of tugboats, and small rivers had formed on their surface where they caught the sun. I could hear dozens of small torrents. There were other smaller icebergs, floating chunks called bergy bits that clattered against the hull of the boat. The Park Service suggests that kayakers give the glaciers a half-mile's worth of respect. But it was hard to judge distances with only a wall of ice perhaps 150 feet high looming above for perspective.

A block of ice about the size of an eighteen-wheel truck broke loose from the glacier and fell toward the water in the slow motion of massive catastrophes viewed from afar. The pillar of ice, falling on the floating icebergs below, set up a sustained thunder that echoed against the bulk of the glacier and reached my ears almost three seconds after the event. This out-of-synch roar was a measure of distance: Sound moving at eleven hundred feet per second had taken three seconds to reach my ear—thirty-three hundred feet. I was better than a half mile from the wall.

A wave perhaps three feet high formed and rose at the foot of the glacier. It rolled toward the kayak, lifting the largest of the icebergs with it. The water was dirty brown with the melted mud of centuries past. For a time the wave grew in the perspective of proximity, but the blanket of the icebergs on the water weighed it down so that when it hit my kayak, it was only a gentle swell.

Some small specks, sea birds, sailed hard by the glacier's face, diving for the stunned fish and shrimp that had been brought to the surface by the falling ice. I stared at them for a while, paddled in a bit, and calculated that I was floating at the half-mile mark. I felt compelled to paddle in farther. When I could clearly recognize the specks as birds, I stopped again. The icebergs and bergy bits here were newer, fresh from the glacier, and occasionally, in the relative warmth of the sea, they snapped in the way an ice cube pops when dropped into a drink. Closer. The birds—I could make them out now—were arctic terns. The snapping was intense. It was a sound like electricity, out of control.

The wall, it seemed, was a kind of psychological vacuum. I could feel the heat of the sun on my back, the cold of the glacier on my chest, and I began paddling in, fast, dodging the icebergs. Too close: I felt helpless, as if I could not stop. I paddled closer. A chunk of ice roughly the size of a baseball landed on the eighteen-wheeler that had fallen earlier. There was a sharp crack, like a rifle fired at close range, and there was no delay between sound and event. I was moving very fast, but that rifle crack was like a slap in the face—one of those "thanks, I needed that" deals—and I dipped the paddle, holding it hard on my right side to swivel around an iceberg and race back to a sane distance.

At about a half mile I stopped and turned to face the ice again. It sounded as if electricity were crackling on all sides of me. My hands were shaking, and my heart was thudding out of all proportion to the effort expended. All else was silence. Nothing was falling from the wall. It stood blue-green in the shadows, blinding white in the sun. "C'mon," it seemed to be saying, "you wanna try me, c'mon in."

An interior voice, smart and civilized, suggested to me that playing chicken with a glacier is a losing game and no great measure of intelligence to boot. I saw Dix making his way down the talus slope to the beached kayak. We'd had enough. Enough stupidity. I felt both exhilarated and mildly ashamed.

That night we camped at Wolf Point, several miles south of Mc-Bride Glacier. Occasionally, the ice called out to us: a faint booming that rumbled down the wall of rock known as White Thunder

Ridge. The sky was clear, as it had been in Juneau and at Muir Glacier. Once again pale green ghostly lights pulsed across a vast expanse of sky. Somewhere, far off in the thickets below the high point where we were camped, wolves yipped and howled in the darkness. I lay on my back, in my sleeping bag, watching Eskimo TV on the big screen. Traces of red were dancing at the leading edge of the green curtains that swept across the sky. The wolves did not sound much different from the dogs of Juneau.

There was, I recalled then, something wild, wolflike, in the howling of those dogs that one glittering night in Juneau; something that had nothing to do with millennia of domesticity. The same odd, uncivilized impulse, I thought—in my exhilaration and shame—exists in human beings as well: the dumbly atavistic urge to put the body at risk in the face of the simply awesome, to connect with it somehow. It is the way people bark at the northern lights.

Guilty as Charged

▲

The watch had a glow-in-the-dark dial, and it hovered over my face like some odd numerical moon. The timepiece was on my own wrist, which had apparently awakened sometime before my conscious mind. It was 3:25. In the morning. There was a sense of something important being missed. 3:26 . . . 3:27. I was lying on my back, and—judging by the ceiling that seemed to be, well, undulating—this was certainly not my own bedroom. It was, aha, a tent. I was in, yes, a sleeping bag. It was cold out. The air tasted thin. I was late for something. Three-thirty.

I was late, it now occurred to me, for the Grand. We had wanted to be up and cooking breakfast by three. The thought began kicking and shoving, rooting around in my mind, looking for some sensitive nerve, which it finally hit, jerking me into a sitting position. "Dammit," I said.

"Wha . . ." Michael Morgan muttered groggily.

"Sorry, Father," I said. I am not accustomed to waking up with clergymen. Michael is an Episcopal priest, my next-door neighbor, and he was to be my climbing partner for the day's ascent of Wyoming's 13,766-foot Grand Teton. And at 3:34 we were already running half an hour behind schedule.

The tent was pitched in a boulder field at 11,200 feet, just below Tepee Glacier to the east, and to the west, the Lower Saddle, the shoulder of land that joins Grand Teton and Middle Teton. Andy Carson, our guide and the director of Jackson Hole Mountain Guides, was up already, crouched out of the wind in the shelter of an overhang, where he was firing up the stove.

We drank numerous cups of hot coffee, ate several bowls of lumpy oatmeal—carbo-loading for a climb we expected to take a minimum of thirteen hours—then checked over the ropes, carabiners, and harnesses, as well as the gear and food in our summit packs. The wind suddenly died—no doubt due to Father Michael's special connections—and we walked out into the high frozen night.

Actually, our mode of locomotion was more like boulder-hopping than climbing. The slope above us rose to the saddle on a carpet of boulders that ranged in size from beachball to Toyota to two-family duplex. The waning moon was three-quarters full overhead, and most of the rocks rolling underfoot were white or light-colored. We didn't actually need our headlamps. There was something hallucinatory about the moonscape that rose and fell on all sides, something pristine—pure—about the glaciers draped from the summits of half a dozen visible peaks. Spectral spires flanked some of these summits, and it was possible to see all that soaring rock as rampart and remnant of an ancient and alien culture. The night's wind had swept the sky clear of clouds so that bright stars glittered insanely overhead, and the moon's luminescence fell on the glaciers in a way that set them aglow. Summit winds, blowing high above, rumbled down the couloirs in thrumming bass tones, as if played softly on a cathedral organ.

The climb promised to be, as a perceptive critic recently told me, a walk directly into the rarefied realm of mindless adventure, to the heights of self-indulgence, to the summit of athleticism without value. I was guilty as charged, and I had a priest with me to boot.

The Teton Range rises abruptly out of the flat floor of the Snake River Valley, otherwise known as Jackson Hole. These young mountains are a good deal more spectacular than most because they erupt out of the earth in full-blown splendor, without the niggling bother of surrounding foothills. You can see them from good roads in Wyoming, from the north-south interstate in Idaho, from highways in Montana.

Father Michael, who grew up in Butte, Montana, and Lander, Wyoming, had seen and been fascinated by the Tetons since childhood. (In point of fact most American rock climbers eventually make a pilgrimage to the Teton Range: The rock is excellent, the snow and ice moderate. The range is wonderfully accessible, and, given good weather, most properly prepared climbers can leave from the trailhead and reach their chosen summit in two days.)

Although Michael had little experience in technical climbing—and there is no way up any one of the Grand's twenty or so routes without running into some technical pitches—he wanted to climb the mountain. Other peaks were safe: It was only the Grand that beckoned him.

Father Michael had been a runner, but a couple of years ago he laid off the sport, and in the way these things happen, a bout of respiratory illness promptly put him in the hospital for several weeks. "So I hadn't run in a long time," Michael told me, "and I was feeling flabby and ineffectual and thought that if I didn't climb the Grand this year, I might never do it." Michael was in his mid-thirties, a dangerous time to let dreams die.

I agreed to come along on the climb—to horn in on my neighbor's lifelong dream—because of a conversation I had recently with a magazine editor in New York who wanted me to do some "significant" reportage. He said, "Those other things you do, climbing and trekking and all, aren't they really just mindless adventures, self-indulgence? What's the value in them?"

"They pay me," I said.

But it wasn't a very good answer, and the thought of climbing the Grand with Father Michael, a man with a degree in philosophy and a master's in divinity, was attractive. Yessir, I'd get to the bottom of this business about values.

Moving up the Talus above the Lower Saddle, just below the spot where the climbing would get technical, there was a loud crack followed by the thunder of a large rockfall. We crouched under a ledge, though the rocks were clattering down a couloir several hundred yards to our left. Only the day before, a man had been killed in a rock slide on nearby Mount Moran. "He was hit with several refrigerator-sized boulders," a climbing ranger told me. I think we were all a little rattled by the size of this rockfall. That short burst of terror and the perceived proximity of death combined to produce a positively spectacular sunrise.

A little farther on we passed a well-equipped couple on their way down the mountain . . . at eight in the morning; clearly, they had been forced to bivouac. They were climbing several yards apart, in silence, as if they had been arguing.

"Nice morning for a walk," I said.

"Humph," the man replied.

"Gaa," the woman said.

Later, Andy Carson guessed the couple had probably started their ascent at dawn the previous day, rather than 4:00 A.M., as we had. "It's very common to run out of light on the Grand," he said. "I mean, you can just re-create the conversation. They're shivering up there on some ledge, and he says, 'Whose idea was this?' 'It was your damn idea. You wanted to come.' And by now they're half-frozen and the wind's blowing and maybe they've got sleet and the conversation has degenerated into 'I hate you, I hate you, get off my ledge.'" Nothing like a little physical adversity to test the strength of a relationship.

We roped up and did a few technical pitches with Andy leading on good hard rock with plenty of handholds and footholds. The climbing was nothing much more difficult than 5.5—we had spent the previous day warming up on 5.6s and 5.7s—but there were several pitches, one following the other, so that looking back, one felt a pleasant sense of accomplishment. It was a good workout. In places, running water had formed a thin veil of ice over the most obvious holds so that one had to stretch a bit to overextend and muscle the body up a few of the more treacherous sections. I had never quite realized that my climbing style, at such times, is fueled by foul and continuous curses in those places where the fun becomes most intense. It's a good habit to think about with a long, hard fall below you and a priest holding your lifeline above.

We topped out on the second-highest point in the Tetons, a

spire that stands guard to the west of the Grand, a place called the Enclosure. Arranged in a perfect circle at the highest point on the Enclosure were several thin, three-foot-high slabs of rock that stuck up out of the ground, as if reaching for the sky. It was a distinctly man-made arrangement. "The first white men on the Grand found this up here," Andy Carson said. "The Indians did it, but no one knows why or when. There's no history."

I looked down toward the dizzy splendor of Lake Solitude, more than four thousand feet below. There was a vertiginous sense of being large and small all at the same instant. It was that tipsy, timeless feeling of awe a man might translate into a dozen different philosophical constructs. Clearly, the Enclosure was not a blind: There was no game at the summit. This place was a vision quest site, a place where men had come to listen and learn from the spirits. You could hear them up there, calling in the howl of the wind; you could see them in the moving shapes of the clouds. I thought a bit about those damn Indians and their mindless athleticism. Did they draw lessons out of danger, adversity, and personal courage, out of a rockfall sunrise or a bad bivouac? Sure they did.

We reached the summit of the Grand several hours later, and Father Michael said a short prayer, thanking God for delivering us safely to the summit and asking Him to provide us with a safe descent. He asked the Lord to bless those whose physical handicaps prevented them from climbing this mountain, and went on to ask a blessing for those who—for whatever reason—would never climb the Grand. He asked the Lord to let those people experience what he, Father Michael, was feeling in his heart at that moment.

On our descent, we had a hundred-foot rappel with what looked like about two thousand feet of exposure below us. Andy checked the anchor and belayed Father Michael on a second rope. My neighbor—who had rappelled precisely twice in his life —backed up over the lip of the wall without hesitation, putting his faith in the anchor and Andy and the Almighty. Probably not in that order.

"You know," Andy said when Michael was out of earshot, "when I first saw him, I thought he might not make the summit. He didn't seem like a climber, and he wasn't in the best shape at all. But he's got some talent on the rock, and he's determined."

"You see the way he took that rappel?" I asked. "I mean, for a man of God, the guy's got a pair of brass ones."

"And on the summit," Andy said, "that prayer was . . . I don't know, I'm not very religious, but it was . . . ."

"It was not without value," I said.

"Yeah," Andy said. He looked up toward the summit of the Grand. "It was a good prayer."

Author's Notes
and Acknowledgments

▲

"Moonwalk Serenade," which originally appeared in *Rolling Stone,* is a venerable story, a kind of grandfather to the rest. It was written in 1978 and commissioned as an investigation into PCP dealing among lowrider car clubs. During the research I found myself much more interested in lowrider culture than in drug use.

Today the story seems dated in relation to the PCP news peg. Lowrider culture, I'm happy to say, is still alive and vital and very much as portrayed in the article.

An editor named Ron King, presently with the Whittle organization in Knoxville, Tennessee, is responsible for sending me off to climb mountains with sorority girls ("Is It Fun Yet?: A Saga of Sorority Women on Crampons") and to go caving with pro football players ("This Is a Cave; This Is the End"). These are truly twisted stories, and I had a lot of fun with both of them. King also sent me to England to write "The Dangerous Sports Club," a story that cost me seven hours in an English jail. Thanks, Ron, and if there's ever anything I can do for you . . .

The cattle-mutilation story ("A Dismal Lack of Cattle Mutilations") is previously unpublished primarily because it has been rejected by every editor on earth, without exception. Friends and lovers hate it. Casual acquaintances pick fights over it. The story is universally loathed. Its inclusion here is an example of an author exercising ego rather than judgment. The reader is advised to skip right over this one.

"Lechuguilla" is an expanded version of a story that appeared in *National Geographic.*

"Baja by Kayak" is previously unpublished, a story written for this book.

The peculiar amusement institution detailed in the story "Fly Away" is now defunct.

"Antarctic Passages" appeared in *Travel Holiday.*

"Rope Tricks" appeared in the *San Francisco Examiner,* as did "Marquesas Magic."

The story "Chiloé: An Island Out of Time" appeared in *Islands Magazine.*

"Taquile" appeared in *The Discovery Channel Magazine.*

"*Sanghyang* in Bali" appeared in *GEO,* in Germany, and has never before been published in the United States.

Most of the other stories, including the piece on Kuwait, appeared in *Outside* magazine and were assigned by John Rasmus or Mark Bryant, both good friends, both great editors.

And once again, thanks to Barbara Lowenstein: the only agent I've ever had or ever needed.

Thanks also to David Rosenthal, who knows that good things are worth waiting for.

Beverly Sandberg is responsible for keeping my office in order. I'm no help at all. Thanks, Bev.

Gloria Thiede has typed up transcripts for most of my interviews. As far as I know, she seldom makes fun of me behind my back. Thanks, Gloria.

About the Author

TIM CAHILL is the author of four previous books. He lives in Montana and is currently *Outside* magazine's editor-at-large and a contributing editor for *Esquire*.

ABOUT THE TYPE

This book was set in Sabon, a typeface designed by
the well-known German typographer Jan Tschichold (1902–74). Sabon's design is based upon the
original letter forms of Claude Garamond, and was
created specifically to be used for three sources:
foundry type for hand composition, Linotype, and
Monotype. Tschichold named his typeface for the
famous Frankfurt typefounder Jacques Sabon, who
died in 1580.